Hardaway Revisited

Hardaway Revisited

Early Archaic Settlement in the Southeast

I. Randolph Daniel, Jr.

The University of Alabama Press
Tuscaloosa and London

∞

The paper on which this book is printed
meets the minimum requirements of
American National Standard
for Information Science-Permanence of Paper
for Printed Library Materials,
ANSI Z39.48-1984.

Library of Congress Cataloging-in-Publication Data

Daniel, Randy.
Hardaway revisited : early archaic settlement in the
Southeast / I. Randolph Daniel, Jr.
p. cm.
Includes bibliographical references and index.
ISBN 0-8173-0900-4 (acid-free paper)
1. Hardaway Site (N.C.) 2. Paleo-Indians—North Carolina.
3. Paleo-Indians—Southern States. 4. Indians of North America—North
Carolina—Antiquities. 5. Indians of North America—Southern
States—Antiquities. 6. North Carolina—Antiquities. 7. Southern
States—Antiquities. I. Title.
E78.N74D35 1998
975.6'73—dc21 97-10131

British Cataloguing-in-Publication Data Available

For Becky

Contents

Tables

Figures

Acknowledgments

This book represents a revised copy of my dissertation that I submitted to the University of North Carolina at Chapel Hill (UNC) in 1994. While conducting this research, I was fortunate to receive considerable guidance and support, which I wish to acknowledge here. Special thanks are due to the members of my doctoral committee: Steve Davis, Al Goodyear, George Holcomb, Vin Steponaitis, Trawick Ward, and Bruce Winterhalder. As director of the Research Laboratories of Anthropology (RLA) and the chair of my committee, Vin Steponaitis deserves special credit. Vin supported my research in numerous ways, almost on a daily basis. In particular, Vin's sound advice was critical (in both senses of the term) while I wrote (and rewrote) the National Science Foundation grant eventually used to support the quarry and collections survey that were essential to placing the Hardaway site in a regional context. Similarly, his substantive and editorial comments considerably improved an earlier draft of this manuscript. Daily support was also provided in the RLA by Trawick Ward and Steve Davis. Much of the data I have analyzed here was excavated by Trawick during several summers in the 1970s when he was field supervisor of fieldwork at Hardaway. He and I had innumerable conversations during my research as I attempted to understand vicariously the nature of the fieldwork at Hardaway. Likewise, Steve aided my research by answering my many computer questions, by facilitating my cataloging, and eventually by replacing the material in the collections. Steve also provided detailed comments on a draft of this document. (With Steve and Vin, two former editors of *Southeastern Archaeology,* on my committee, I did not want for editorial criticism.)

Al Goodyear's work has had a fundamental influence on my research that predates my return to graduate school. During this project, Al made several trips to the RLA, where we had intense discussions concerning early Holocene archaeology. I was always inspired by the enthusiasm with which he addressed problems of typology, chronology, raw material use, and site formation. Al also identified the *pièces esquillées* I had overlooked in the assemblage. I also appreciate the help of Bruce Winterhalder and the late George Holcomb, who read and commented on this manuscript.

I am especially indebted to the late Bob Butler, whose geological expertise was invaluable to my research, although he was not a formal member of my committee. Bob devoted a considerable amount of time to this project, which included numerous winter days spent surveying the Uwharrie Mountains for rhyolite quarries. I particularly enjoyed these trips, during which time he shared his considerable knowledge of the geology of the Carolina Slate Belt.

Several other colleagues contributed in a variety of ways to the completion of this project. In particular, Joffre Coe, Gary Glover, David Moore, and Billy Oliver provided information concerning their experiences at Hardaway. Thanks are also due to David Anderson, David Meltzer, and several anonymous reviewers who provided critical comments on an early draft of my National Science Foundation proposal. I am also grateful to David Anderson and Larry Kimball for reviewing the manuscript and recommending its publication.

Tommy Charles deserves special thanks for putting me in touch with several collectors from South Carolina. Tommy also graciously allowed me access to his collections survey data. Thanks also go to Jim Michie for allowing me to view the Taylor assemblage. It was largely the result of our conversations concerning the unique variability of stone types in the Taylor collection that got me to thinking about Taylor's implications for Early Archaic settlement. Finally, my understanding of the Early Archaic has benefited from informal discussions with other colleagues including Mark Brooks, Steve Claggett, Joel Gunn, Larry Kimball, Mark Mathis, Alan May, Tom Padgett, Ken Robinson, Ken Sassaman, Ann Tippitt, and Tom Whyte.

The quarry research and subsequent collections survey were made possible by the assistance of several people and institutions. Foremost, financial support was provided by the National Science Foundation (BNS-8921648). Rodney Snedeker and Michael Harmon were particularly helpful in our survey of the Uwharrie National Forest. Similarly, the cooperation of the staff at Morrow Mountain State Park is appreciated. The Office of State Archaeology in Raleigh (especially Steve Claggett) also supported our survey. The survey around Asheboro was facilitated by John Arsenault, John Davis, Mike Murrow, and Bill Terrell. Estella Stansbury provided the office assistance necessary to ensure that the NSF grant was handled properly.

The Aluminum Company of America (ALCOA), Badin Works, deserves particular thanks for allowing the RLA to excavate at Hardaway and its cooperation in the quarry survey conducted during this project. In particular, ALCOA is also thanked for its continued stewardship of the Hardaway site, which on November 5, 1990, was designated as a National Historic Landmark.

I am also indebted to the numerous individuals who allowed me to record their collections or otherwise assisted me in the collections survey: Massey Bick, Blake Boyd, Edsel Davis, Lottie Davis, Robert Dunham, Gabriel Fogel, R. V. "Whitey" Graham, Ernie Hinson, Macon Hunter, J. M. "Buck" Lawrence, Ben Lovell, Jimmy Mabe, Tammy Mabe, William Norton, Phil Perkinson, Leonard Perrit, Mitchell Powell, Doug Rader, Pressley Rankin and the Rankin Museum, David Reddick, David Rich, Reid Ringer, Rob Siewers, Sam Smitherman, Paula Story, Will Thompson, Prentiss Treadway, Bob Weaver, E. Wheeler, and Warner Williams.

Over various semesters many students in the RLA helped in the artifact processing and cataloging, including Jimmy Blanton, James Brown, Karen Courtney, Lauren Cuningham, Walter Davis, Dean Foster, Trevor Gunn, Chip Harris, David Hylton, Jonathon Kendall, Britt McMaster, Stephen Oljeski, Anthony Restar, Anna Shugart, and Brandy Weiss. I also appreciate the efforts of Patrick Livingood in preparing several of the maps illustrated here.

I also wish to acknowledge the financial support provided by the Research Laboratories of Anthropology and the Department of Anthropology during my period of study at UNC. In particular, I also gratefully acknowledge the On-Campus Dissertation Fellowship awarded me during the late summer and fall of 1992 by the Graduate School of The University of North Carolina at Chapel Hill that allowed me the opportunity to finish a draft of my dissertation. Lori Higginbothan read the page proofs.

The transition from dissertation to book was greatly facilitated by the patience and professionalism of Judith Knight, Suzette Griffith, and the staff of The University of Alabama Press. Marcia Brubeck provided the copyediting. The computer skills of Steve Davis and Tom Maher of the Research Laboratories of Anthropology were largely responsible for the artifact photographs.

Finally, I am indebted to my wife, Becky, for her indulgence while I transformed my dissertation into this book, and to Madeline, Megan, and Matthew, whose most welcome (and exhausting) arrival gave me just the excuse(s) I needed to delay its completion.

1

Introduction

During the summer of 1948, test pits placed in two sites along the Yadkin River demonstrated for the first time that stratified alluvial sites of some antiquity existed in the Carolina Piedmont (Coe 1964:8–9). There, at the Lowder's Ferry and Doerschuk sites, Joffre Coe began to make temporal sense of a "hodgepodge of projectile point types" previously known in the Piedmont from surface collections and shallow plow-zone deposits. The stratigraphy at these sites allowed Coe to distinguish a sequence of Archaic complexes that was virtually unknown elsewhere in the Southeast. Although both sites were deeply stratified, the earliest identified component was associated with the Middle Archaic period, which we know today dates to less than 8,000 years ago.

At yet another site, also first tested during the same summer, a relatively undisturbed Early Archaic sequence was found. This was the Hardaway site, located just upstream from Doerschuk and Lowder's Ferry, which, somewhat paradoxically, was neither as deeply stratified nor located in the floodplain of the Yadkin (figure 1.1). Rather, it was on a hilltop high above the river. Nevertheless, the early sequence at Hardaway was eventually linked to Doerschuk and Lowder's Ferry, so that the Archaic sequence of the Carolina Piedmont was completely defined (Coe 1964:figure 117). This sequence was eventually adopted over much of the Southeast.

In recent years increased attention has been focused on the identification of Early Archaic site function and settlement patterns in the Southeast. And yet the exact function of the Hardaway site, which has significant implications for any settlement model in the region, has not figured prominently in any such research. The data necessary to investigate this problem have been available for some years in an extant but unanalyzed collection of material from Hardaway curated by the Research Laboratories of Anthropology at the University of North Carolina at Chapel Hill. This collection forms the basis for a functional interpretation of the Hardaway

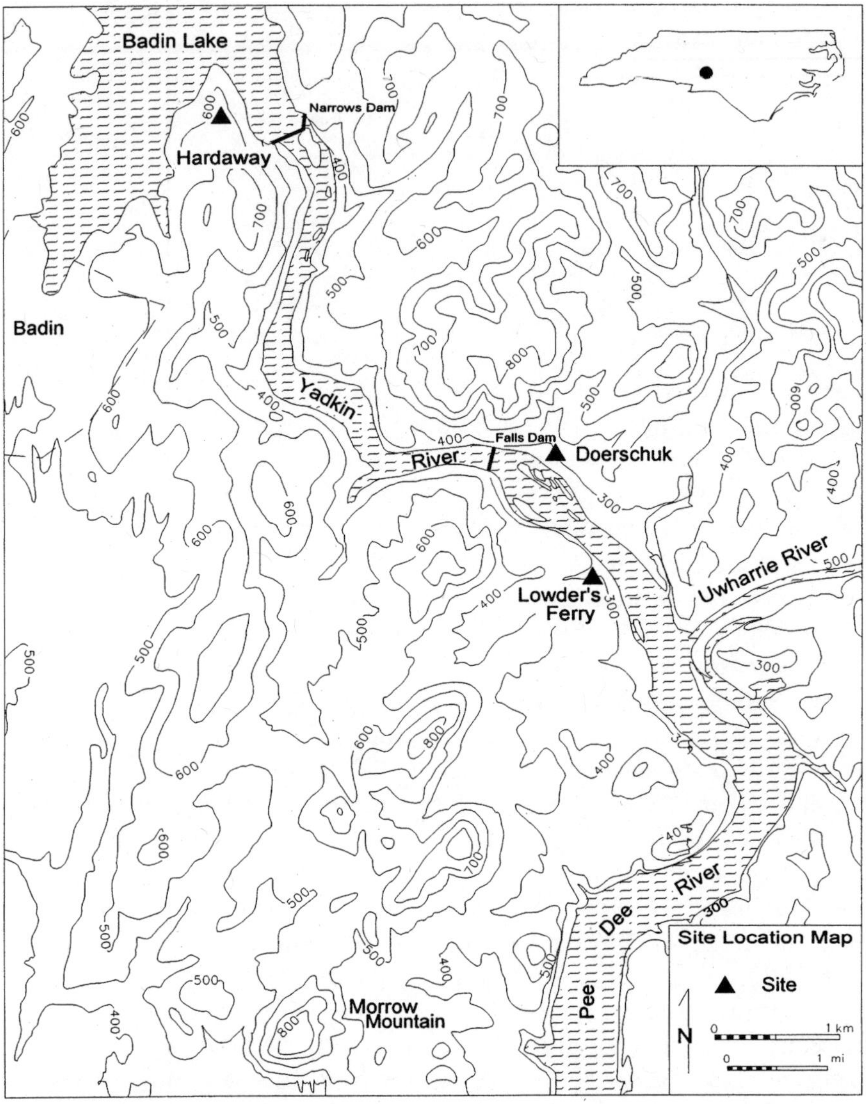

Figure 1.1. Site locations

site, set forth here. This study also includes a stone raw materials study with an extensive survey of projectile point collections.

The raw materials study encompasses a quarry survey designed to identify petrologically the rhyolite sources so abundant around Hardaway and to assess the probability that any of these locations was the source of the rhyolite that is so plentiful in the assemblage itself. In addition, the presence of rhyolite and other raw materials is examined on more than 3,000

Early Archaic points primarily distributed in private collections in North and South Carolina. The collections survey addresses the geographic range of Early Archaic adaptation in the Carolinas and, when combined with the site functional analysis, allows Hardaway to be viewed from a regional perspective. Both the site functional study and the collections survey have implications for current views of Early Archaic settlement in the Southeast. In particular, the results of these analyses suggest a much different view of Early Archaic adaptations than has previously been proposed.

THE EARLY ARCHAIC PERIOD IN THE SOUTHEAST

The Early Archaic period has traditionally been viewed as a time of cultural readaptation from Pleistocene to Holocene environments. By convention the start was set at 10,000 B.P. (e.g., Caldwell 1958; Cleland 1976; Dragoo 1976; Stoltman 1978). More recent palynological data, however, have indicated that climatic amelioration may have begun significantly earlier in the southeastern United States, where early Holocene climatic and vegetational conditions appeared as early as 12,500 B.P. (Delcourt and Delcourt 1985:19; Delcourt and Delcourt 1981:table 3). Similarly, rather than a marked change in cultural adaptions between the preceding Paleo-Indian period and subsequent Early Archaic adaptations, some researchers are now stressing an "adaptive continuity" between Paleo-Indian and Early Archaic groups (Meltzer and Smith 1986). Consequently, the time range for the Early Archaic has been extended to as early as 10,500 B.P. and is believed to have continued until the onset of relatively modern biotic conditions at about 8,000 B.P. (e.g., Anderson and Hanson 1988, Anderson and Sassaman 1996; Goodyear 1982; Smith 1986; Steponaitis 1986).

The Early Archaic in the Southeast is marked by a chronological sequence of distinctive point types. This sequence begins with the lanceolate Dalton forms (ca. 10,500–9,900 B.P.) and continues with the Hardaway Side-Notched and related points, such as Bolen and Taylor (ca. 10,000–9,500 B.P.), followed by Palmer Corner-Notched and Kirk Corner-Notched points (ca. 9,500–8,900 B.P.) and finally a series of bifurcate-base forms, including MacCorkle, St. Albans, Lecroy, and Kanawha (ca. 8,900–8,000 B.P.).

The identification of the above sequence dominated much of Archaic research from the 1950s through the 1970s. As mentioned previously, some of the earliest work in establishing these sequences was done by Coe (1964), who documented a composite sequence built from excavations at the Doerschuk, Hardaway, and Gaston sites located in the North Carolina Piedmont. Subsequent work at St. Albans in West Virginia (Broyles 1971),

Russell Cave in Alabama (Griffin 1974), Thunderbird and related sites in northern Virginia (Gardner 1974, 1977), and several sites in the Little Tennessee River Valley (Chapman 1973, 1975, 1976, 1978) indicated that the above sequence could be generalized over much of the Southeast. Additional work during the past decade has continued to support and refine the sequence for portions of Georgia (Anderson and Schuldenrein 1983, 1985; Tippitt and Marquardt 1984), Florida (Daniel and Wisenbaker 1987), Alabama (Driskell 1996; Goldman-Finn and Driskell 1994), and North Carolina (Claggett and Cable 1982).

As mentioned previously, Archaic research since the 1970s has been concerned with identifying Early Archaic site function and settlement patterns. As part of this research, several settlement models were generated for particular river valleys. The best known examples include the "Dalton settlement hypothesis" for the Mississippi alluvial valley of northeast Arkansas and southeast Missouri (Morse 1971, 1973, 1975a, 1975b, 1977; Price and Krakker 1975; Schiffer 1975a, 1975b), the "Flint Run model" for the Shenandoah Valley of Virginia (Gardner 1977, 1983); the "riverine/interriverine model" for the Carolina Piedmont (Goodyear et al. 1979; House and Ballenger 1976; House and Wogaman 1978); and the "Little Tennessee River model" for eastern Tennessee (Chapman 1975, 1977, 1978).

These models generally included variations of a settlement system characterized by a base camp/extractive location dichotomy of site types (cf. Binford and Binford 1966). That is, Early Archaic settlement included two site types: residential locations and special use sites. The former site type formed the center of economic and social activities for a hunter-gatherer group and was occupied for relatively long periods of time; the latter site type was produced by subgroups of residential sites generally for the purpose of resource procurement and occupied for a shorter period of time. Primarily because of factors relating to preservation, sites were categorized as to type on the basis of the identification of "functional groups" of tools categorized to determine the nature and range of activities conducted at Early Archaic sites. But while efforts were made to test proposed site types by empirically documenting and comparing site assemblages, little headway was made in empirically identifying the geographic ranges that comprised the proposed settlement systems.

Also during the late 1970s and early 1980s a series of very influential theoretical papers on hunter-gatherer settlement were published by Lewis Binford and Albert Goodyear. It is fair to say that these works structured much of the subsequent research on Early Archaic settlement in the Southeast—even into the 1990s—including this study. In particular, at least four papers by Binford (1977, 1979, 1980, 1982) dealt with interpreting archaeological assemblage variability and hunter-gatherer settlement systems. In these works Binford introduced the concepts of *curated* and *expedient* technologies and outlined his middle range theory on *forager* versus *collector* settlement strategies. The terms "curated" and "expedient" refer to opposite ends of a tool use-life continuum (Binford 1977, 1979). Curated tools are made in anticipation of future use; they are carried from place to place, maintained, reused, and sometimes recycled into other tool forms. Expedient tools, in contrast, are made and used in response to an immediate need and are not maintained for future use. The significance of these two concepts lies in the realization that frequencies of any particular tool in an assemblage may not directly reflect the intensity of its use at a site.

Binford (1980) also introduced the terms "forager" and "collector" to describe two ends of a subsistence-settlement continuum analogous to the curated-expedient continuum. Foraging strategies are generally employed in more uniform environments and entail the movement of entire social groups to resource areas. Only rarely are special use sites created by this settlement strategy. Collectors, on the other hand, employ a "logistical" settlement strategy such that resources are routinely moved to consumers by special task groups. This latter settlement strategy is largely a response to regions with incongruent resource distributions or with pronounced seasonal-temperature differences.

Another notion concerning hunter-gatherer settlement introduced at this time was the idea that "exotic" stone in archaeological assemblages might act as a material signature of the geographic mobility of hunter-gatherer groups (Binford 1979). Recent Early Archaic settlement models have relied heavily on this notion as much as on any other of Binford's ideas.

Meanwhile, Goodyear (1979) published a paper in which he argued that the use of cryptocrystalline stone was an adaptive strategy for making both portable and flexible tools in a lifestyle characterized by high mobility. This argument was adduced to explain the predominance of high quality "exotic" stone recovered in Paleo-Indian assemblages; in most cases this stone was recovered hundreds of miles from its geological source. Moreover, following Binford (1979), Goodyear argued that this gathering of raw materials was a by-product of normal group movement through a region and thus reflected distances moved within hunter-gatherer settlement systems. Although this argument was applied specifically to Paleo-Indian groups, its influence on Early Archaic research has clearly been felt over the last decade (e.g., Anderson and Hanson 1988; Sassaman et al. 1988).

Armed with these theoretical frameworks, then, research in the late 1970s and early 1980s—predominantly in Georgia and the Carolinas—

saw further attempts at understanding how the organization of stone tool technologies reflected settlement adaptation (e.g., Anderson and Hanson 1988; Anderson and Schuldenrein 1983; Claggett and Cable 1982; O'Steen 1983). In particular, insights were beginning to be made in the identification of Early Archaic mobility ranges through the location of quarry sources and the subsequent tracking of the archaeological distributions of their raw material.

Much of this work began in South Carolina, where researchers began to identify stone macroscopically in archaeological assemblages with their possible sources. Source locations included the Coastal Plain Allendale chert quarries in South Carolina and the Piedmont Morrow Mountain rhyolite quarry in North Carolina (e.g., House and Ballenger 1976:126–127; House and Wogaman 1978:53–57; Novick 1978). Chert sources in Georgia (Goad 1979) and Tennessee (Kimball 1985) also began to be investigated.

One of first systematic attempts to locate prehistoric quarries along the Coastal Plain and to characterize their stone petrologically, however, was made in Florida (Upchurch et al. 1981). The results of this work were soon applied to the study of the Paleo-Indian period (Daniel and Wisenbaker 1987; Goodyear et al. 1983). Similar research on prehistoric quarries followed in the South Carolina Coastal Plain (Anderson et al. 1982), particularly with the Allendale sources along the Savannah River (Goodyear and Charles 1984; Upchurch 1984). Later syntheses of excavations within the Savannah River Valley (e.g., Anderson and Hanson 1988; Anderson and Schuldenrein 1983) coupled with data on point type and raw material from large-scale surveys of collections in South Carolina and Georgia (Charles 1981, 1983, 1986; Goodyear et al. 1989; Sassaman et al. 1988; Sassaman 1996) appeared to document the extensive movement of this chert across the Coastal Plain and into the Piedmont. In these discussions, archaeologists began to interpret this chert movement as evidence of widespread mobility for Early Archaic groups in the region.

In addition to attempts at mapping the geographic extent of hunter-gatherer ranges, work was performed to determine how settlement was organized (i.e., foragers versus collectors) within particular regions. Claggett and Cable (1982:13), for example, proposed that postglacial warmings in the North Carolina Piedmont resulted in a shift from collector strategies with few residential moves and greater site specialization to a foraging strategy with more frequent moves and less intersite variability. Moreover, Claggett and Cable inferred that this settlement strategy should be reflected in Early Archaic stone tool assemblages recovered at the Haw River site in the eastern Piedmont (Claggett and Cable 1982). Collector technologies, it was reasoned, should exhibit a greater degree of formalized curated tools than forager technologies (cf. Binford 1979, 1980). This postulated trend from curated to expedient technologies was believed to have been identified at Haw River, albeit earlier in the sequence (i.e., between the Hardaway-Dalton and Palmer occupations) than anticipated (Claggett and Cable 1982:761–763).

Following this line of research, Anderson and Schuldenrein (1983) saw a similar pattern in a series of Palmer/Kirk assemblages from ten excavated sites and eighty-eight surface-collected sites in North Carolina, South Carolina, and Georgia that "appear to be characterized by an expedient technology, with a low overall occurrence of formal, curated tools" (Anderson and Schuldenrein 1983:205). In addition, the incidence of projectile point raw material variability was examined from several assemblages as a measure of group mobility. A fairly high occurrence of artifacts made from Coastal Plain chert was seen in Piedmont sites and, it was argued, represented evidence of extensive movement along river drainages (Anderson and Schuldenrein 1983:201–205). Following arguments outlined above, Anderson and Schuldenrein viewed the combination of predominantly "expedient technologies" and long distance movement as "more typical of residentially mobile foraging groups" (Anderson and Schuldenrein 1983:205). In contrast, then, to earlier settlement models that characterized Early Archaic groups as collectors, Anderson and Schuldenrein proposed that these prehistoric hunter-gatherers more likely exhibited settlement characteristics resembling foragers. This view also tended to support the Haw River model.

To summarize, research on Early Archaic settlement largely began during the 1970s with the pioneering Dalton studies of the central Mississippi Valley. Similar studies were also undertaken for Dalton and notched-point complexes about this time in the Shenandoah Valley of Virginia and the Little Tennessee River Valley. This work, with the possible exception of Schiffer's (1975a, 1975b) and Price and Krakker's (1975) characterizations of Dalton adaptations, portrayed Early Archaic settlement as "logistically" focused. By the 1980s, however, the focus of research on Early Archaic settlement had shifted to Georgia and the Carolinas, where models were proposed that emphasized greater residential mobility or "foraging" adaptations (Anderson and Hanson 1985, 1988; Claggett and Cable 1982). More recently, discussions of Early Archaic settlement—some in the form of retrospectives of sorts—have occurred for Virgina (Gardner 1989), North Carolina (Cable 1996), and Tennessee (Carr 1995; Kimball 1996).

Yet the work conducted in the Savannah River Valley, where a new settlement model was developed and subsequently generalized to cover the South Atlantic Slope, that has arguably had the greatest impact on Early Archaic research in the Southeast (Anderson and Hanson 1985, 1988). This model, which subsequently became known as the band-macroband model, is noteworthy because it incorporates aspects of both logistical and forager-based adaptations in a balanced consideration of both the biological and social needs of prehistoric hunter-gatherers. The significance of the band-macroband model for Early Archaic research was highlighted at a 1991 symposium on Paleo-Indian and Early Archaic research in the Southeast that was held on the campus of the University of South Carolina. Virtually every symposium participant who addressed the problem of Early Archaic settlement had been influenced by Anderson and Hanson's work. The following section therefore provides a summary of the model and its implications for the work reported here.

THE BAND-MACROBAND MODEL

Anderson and Hanson (1985, 1988) proposed a model of Early Archaic settlement for the South Atlantic Slope based on analyses of local and regional resource structure, theoretical arguments about the biocultural needs of hunter-gatherer populations, and evidence from the archaeological record. In particular, the model is noteworthy for the balanced treatment it affords both environmental and social variables as they relate to cultural adaptations. It points to four "limiting factors" that provided the basis of Early Archaic adaptations along the South Atlantic Slope: (1) seasonal and spatial variation in resources; (2) mating-network regulation; (3) information exchange; and (4) demographic structure.

Individual bands are proposed to have occupied each of the eight large drainage systems along the South Atlantic Slope while forming part of a larger macroband unit necessary to maintain viable mating networks. The regional (macroband) territory included watersheds that extended from the Ocmulgee drainage in Georgia to the Neuse drainage in North Carolina. Seasonal movement occurred along drainages between the Piedmont and Coastal Plain with logistical base camps located in the upper Coastal Plain during the winter, while foraging camps were occupied in both physiographic zones during the remaining part of the year. Furthermore, some cross-drainage movement occasionally took place at Fall Line "aggregation loci" that functioned to facilitate information exchange and maintain mating networks.

This model was tested by examining artifact assemblages from seven Early Archaic components located in the Savannah River basin (Anderson and Hanson 1988:272–280). Following a trend in assemblage analysis noted earlier, curated-to-expedient tool ratios were constructed and compared among the seven assemblages as a measure of site use and group mobility. An independent measure of site use was also provided by a cluster analysis of the seven assemblages, which supported the results of the curated-to-expedient tool indexes. That is, sites were divided into four clusters represented by a series of short- versus long-term base camps and specialized extractive sites.

A second aspect of Anderson and Hanson's model was concerned with mobility. Using data collected by Charles's extensive South Carolina collections survey, stone types identified for Early Archaic points from along the Savannah River were used as a measure of group mobility (1981, 1983, 1986). Four categories of raw materials were identified (Coastal Plain chert, quartz, Slate Belt metavolcanic stone, and Ridge and Valley chert) that have mutually exclusive natural distributions within the Coastal Plain, Piedmont, and Mountain regions. The sample of points was dominated by chert from the Coastal Plain and by quartz presumably from the Piedmont. Frequency distributions for these two types of raw material indicated a gradual reduction in the percentage of the use of the respective raw materials along the drainage as a function of the distance from their geological source areas (Anderson and Hanson 1988:280–281). These distributions were presented as evidence for group mobility along the length of the Savannah River drainage.

In sum, while their formulation remains speculative, Anderson and Hanson have presented the most comprehensive settlement model to date incorporating biological, social, and ecological elements in its construction. Yet while the Savannah River sites have provided a partial test for their model, the identification of site types and settlement ranges as they relate to Early Archaic adaptation remains to be demonstrated in other areas of the South Atlantic Slope.

THE BAND-MACROBAND MODEL AND THE PRESENT BOOK

The Hardaway site has significant implications for any settlement model in the region. As mentioned previously, Coe's analysis of the Hardaway site focused on tool typology and cultural chronology, with less emphasis on site function and settlement adaptation. Until now, the exact nature of the activities carried out at Hardaway were unclear. Moreover, with the exception of a preliminary attempt to examine settlement mobility by comparing tool ratios among assemblages from several dozen Early Archaic sites in the Southeast (Anderson and Schuldenrein 1983), an evaluation of any settlement model that included the Hardaway site could not be done.

Questions concerning site function and settlement adaptation are addressed here by: (1) a functional study of the Hardaway site and (2) a collections survey of the raw material distribution of Early Archaic points in the Carolina Piedmont and Coastal Plain.

The problem of site function is examined through a technological and morphological analysis of the tool assemblage coupled with an intrasite spatial analysis. Next, an artifact raw materials distribution study is used to address the geographic range of Early Archaic cultural systems. Since the scale of hunter-gatherer adaptations is that of a region and not a site, the raw material survey permits Hardaway to be placed in a regional context. This phase of the study involved a collections survey to record data on point type and raw material similar to that reported by Anderson and Hanson (1988:figure 8). Essentially, this collections survey addressed the problem of band adaptation by tracing the movement of stone raw material—primarily in the form of rhyolite—both within and across the Yadkin–Pee Dee drainage.

Finally, this discussion brings us to another important aspect of the present research: the quarry survey and stone raw materials study. The metavolcanic stone types mentioned in this book were identified on the basis of a raw materials study designed to record systematically the numerous metavolcanic quarries known to be located in the Uwharrie Mountains in the vicinity of the Hardaway site and to characterize them petrologically. This portion of my research was a joint effort with J. Robert Butler of the Department of Geology at the University of North Carolina at Chapel Hill. The work has been reported elsewhere (Daniel and Butler 1991, 1996) but is summarized in Chapter 3 and provides an important baseline for future researchers interested in the identification of metavolcanic stone types recovered in archaeological sites in the Carolinas.

This book presents the results of my analysis and interpretations. Chapter 2 describes the history of excavations at Hardaway and discusses the stratigraphy and the sample of units analyzed in this study. Chapter 3 describes the stone raw materials found in the Hardaway assemblage and discusses their possible sources. Chapter 4 provides a detailed morphological and technological examination of the Hardaway assemblage and offers some speculations concerning tool functions. Chapter 5 discusses the organization of the assemblage at Hardaway with respect to blank production and tool use life. Together, these two chapters provide the basis for inferences about site function and about the organization of an Early Archaic technology with respect to settlement adaptation. Chapter 6 presents the results of the spatial analysis of the stone remains, providing further evidence concerning site function. The results of the collections survey are used in Chapter 7 to address the question of the geographic range of adaptation of the former inhabitants of the Hardaway site. Finally, Chapter 8 evaluates the Anderson-Hanson (1988) model in light of the results presented in the previous six chapters. The implications of these results take the form of an alternative model of Early Archaic settlement along the South Atlantic Slope.

2

Excavations at Hardaway

This chapter presents the history of excavations at Hardaway, a review of the site's stratigraphy, and a discussion of the features and units selected for analysis. Because I was not present during the fieldwork, I had to familiarize myself with the excavations through the field notes, maps, and photographs on file at the Research Laboratories of Anthropology. In addition, I had many conversations with several participants in the actual excavations, including Joffre Coe, David Moore, and Trawick Ward. These discussions greatly helped me understand the nature of the fieldwork at Hardaway. Therefore, in describing the excavations, I occasionally cite these conversations as well as information taken from field notes.

HISTORY OF EXCAVATIONS

The Hardaway site was brought to Coe's attention by Herbert M. Doerschuk, a local collector who was familiar with a number of archaeological sites in the Uwharrie area. Coe first visited Hardaway in 1937. During the summer of 1948, following eleven years of intermittent surface collecting, a single 5 ft^2 (1.5 m^2) test unit was excavated in the apparent center of the site.

Subsequently, a second square was excavated in early 1951 just south of the first unit. Both units revealed a thick midden densely packed with stone debris below a plow zone. Below the midden lay a second thin humic soil zone just above the clay subsoil. In addition, a poorly preserved burial was found just below the plow zone during the 1948 excavations (Coe 1964:60).

> The number of specimens recovered from the two squares was astounding. Over 1,500 artifacts of various types were collected and catalogued. It was noted that most of the pottery occurred in the

> upper part of the midden and in the plowed soil, and that most of the projectile point types, previously observed at the Doerschuk Site, were also found in the upper levels. An attempt to show a meaningful relationship between these and the new types that were being found at this site, unfortunately, was unsuccessful on the basis of their segregation by artificial six inch levels. All types seemed to occur at all levels, and if the work had stopped at this point it might have been assumed that this was another "homogeneous" site. [Coe 1964:60]

Work did not stop at Hardaway, of course, but several years went by before it resumed. Actually, the work at Hardaway was part of a larger research effort by the Research Laboratories of Anthropology to identify stratified sites in the alluvial floodplains of the Carolina Piedmont (Coe 1964:9–13). At that time the Archaic sequence of the area was virtually unknown, and it was hoped that this work would help identify potential Archaic complexes. Coe (1964:8) realized that such identification would not be possible on the basis of surface collections or the excavation of relatively shallow plow-zone deposits. Consequently, during the late 1940s, excavations were conducted at two other sites, Doerschuk and Lowder's Ferry, just downstream from Hardaway (Coe 1964:14–55). Here deep excavations isolated stratigraphic deposits that, when combined with the work at Hardaway, would eventually permit the early cultural sequence of the Carolina Piedmont to be identified.

The 1955–1959 Excavations

Because of the success at Doerschuk and Lowder's Ferry, and in recognition of the potential at Hardaway, the Carolina Aluminum Company in 1954 (now Aluminum Company of America) granted a lease so that more extensive excavations could be conducted at the latter site. Work began in earnest the following year (figure 2.1). From 1955 to 1957, twenty-three squares totaling 575 ft^2 (53 m^2) were excavated (Coe 1964:60).

A large amount of cultural material was again recovered. Of particular interest was the range of projectile point types. Many of these types—from Caraway Triangular to Stanly Stemmed—had been identified previously at Doerschuk and Lowder's Ferry, but several other new point types were found at Hardaway. The excavation in arbitrary levels, however, thwarted attempts to recognize any point type occurring earlier than the Middle Archaic. "It was still impossible under those working conditions to do more than remove the soil by the same method of arbitrary levels,

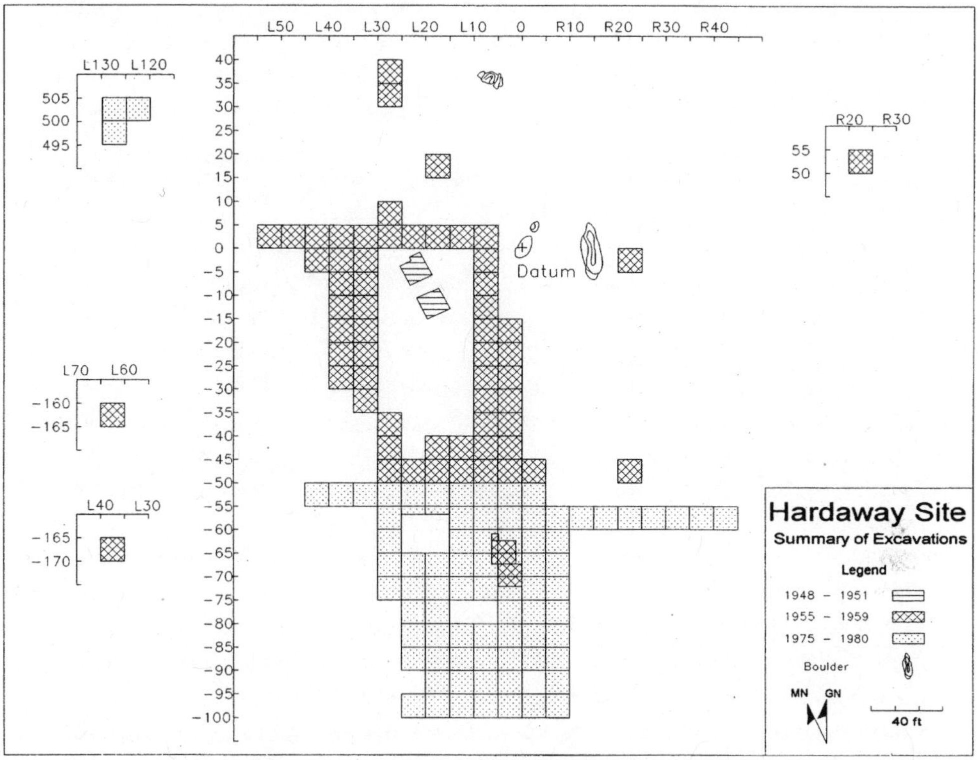

Figure 2.1. Summary of excavations at the Hardaway site

which, in general, continued to produce the same arbitrary results. . . . Thus, in light of the information that had been gained from the site by the fall of 1957, it was concluded that any further excavation by arbitrary levels and in single isolated units was a waste of time and a destruction of potential data" (Coe 1964:60).

The following two seasons of excavations, primarily in the summers of 1958 and 1959, saw the excavation methods modified, so that earlier point types from the Kirk through the Hardaway complexes were more clearly defined. Coe summarized the summer of 1958 as follows. "In July, 1958, a camp was set up on the site and the area was intensively excavated for a period of six weeks. This time, however, a different and more satisfactory method of excavation was employed. A section of the former excavation from 0L35 to –20L35 was cleared, and the exposed north-south profile (fig. 49) was examined as a unit for the purpose of gaining a better understanding of the nature of those deposits (fig. 50). Zones I through IV were defined more precisely and a keener awareness of the ever-present intrusions was developed. The excavations during this period were controlled by the natural zones and every observed intrusion was separated from the zone area. Furthermore, every concentration of rocks or stone chips was cleaned and examined as a unit, and many of these turned out to be well defined hearths that could be identified with a specific culture group" (Coe 1964:61).

A similar methodology was followed in 1959. During the last two summers further trench excavations connected the two earlier trenches and formed the rough borders of a rectangle around the presumed heart of the site. In addition, three isolated squares were dug to the east of the main trenches, resulting in the excavation of thirty-six additional units. During the 1950s excavations Coe was assisted by several students and interested amateurs, including Philip Baldwin, James Bullit, Lewis Binford, Ed Gaines, Walter Gaines, Archie Leak, David Phelps, Jewell South, and Stanly South.

Following the 1959 season, the Research Laboratories of Anthropology ceased work at the site for over fifteen years. Much of the work described above was reported by Coe in his 1964 benchmark work *Formative Cultures of the Carolina Piedmont.* To say that the work at Hardaway stopped, however, is not entirely accurate, since much time and effort was spent intermittently monitoring the site and chasing away pothunters (reports on file, Research Laboratories of Anthropology). Prior to Coe's publication there had been some potting at the site, but after the publication of *Formative Cultures,* the vandalism increased enormously.

Nevertheless, in 1975 Coe felt that although the site had been severely damaged, the lower Palmer and Hardaway zones might still be intact. Thus a final phase of work was carried out at the site between 1975 and 1980 (figure 2.1). The objectives of this fieldwork were to define site limits, to obtain subsistence data, and to identify potential intrasite-site activity areas. It was also hoped that this work would result in the recovery of carbon samples for the absolute dating of the early components at Hardaway (Ward 1983:63).

The 1975–1980 Excavations

Field methods during the 1970s basically followed the plan that had proved successful during the 1958 and 1959 seasons. Some modifications to the excavation procedures, however, were necessary because of the new objectives and the amount of site destruction.

As before, trench excavation proceeded by flat shovel skimming in 5 ft

(1.5 m) squares, with all soil being screened through 0.5 in (1.3 cm) mesh using hand sifters. Because of widespread potting, the initial step was to remove the disturbed backfill and isolate undisturbed soil. The intact deposits were subsequently troweled in order to identify features and possible intrusions, which were documented and removed separately. Intact soil zones were recorded in black-and-white and color photographs and were mapped to scale prior to excavation. Wherever possible each zone was arbitrarily divided into top and bottom during excavation. Since the transition between Zones 3 and 4 was often vague, it was sometimes difficult to assign a context to material recovered from the interface of the two zones. Therefore, it was thought that material from the top of Zone 3 or the bottom of Zone 4 could be regarded as more representative of each zone. Excavation continued into undisturbed clay (Zone 4), usually no more than 0.3–0.4 ft (9–12 cm), at which point artifacts generally ceased to be recovered.

Each recognizable tool was three-dimensionally plotted within the undisturbed zones. The remaining cultural material was bagged and labeled according to square and zone provenance. Horizontal and vertical control were maintained by referring to the site grid and using a transit and stadia rod. Standardized soil samples were also taken for each zone.

When a trench was finished, a continuous profile was cleaned, photographed, and drawn. Additional field notes were recorded on standardized daily reports, profile elevations, and feature forms. In addition, the field supervisor wrote weekly summary reports.

The excavations began in the summer of 1975 and, with the exception of the summer of 1978, continued for each summer thereafter until 1980 (Ward, field notes, 1975, 1976, 1977, 1979, 1980). Trawick Ward was the field supervisor for each field season. Field crew personnel varied each summer but consisted of four to five people, including Ted Bradstreet, Ralph Bunn, Dan Clement, Neil Davis, Gary Glover, Mike Johnson, David Moore, Bill Oliver, Sam Pratt, Dan Simpkins, Lee Tippit, Kit Wesler, and Jack Wilson. When the five seasons of work had been completed, a large block immediately south of the 1950s work had been excavated. A few isolated units were also dug away from the knoll north and south of the main excavations (figures 2.1–2.2).

The main excavation area, near the southern edge of the knoll, initially appeared to have suffered less looting than other parts of the site. Unfortunately, potting activity in this area was worse than anticipated. Virtually all of Zone 2 had been disturbed in this area, and only discontinuous pockets of intact Zone 3 were encountered. Even Zone 4 had not escaped damage. Yet in spite of the potting activity, extraordinary numbers of artifacts

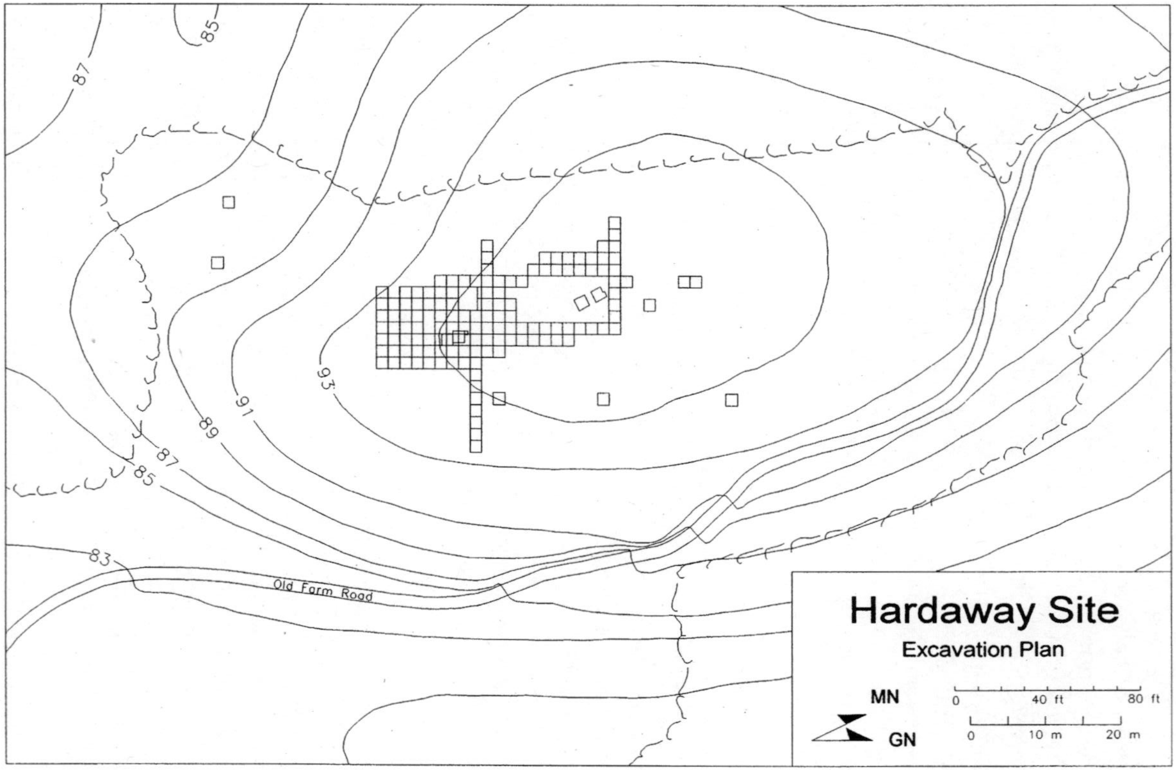

Figure 2.2. Excavation plan and topographic map of the Hardaway site. Adapted from Coe 1964:figure 48.

were still present in both the disturbed and the undisturbed soil. "Getting massive amount of material today, we filled up 5 banana boxes with 29 bags of material . . . from one 5′ × 5′ unit we will get 8–9 banana boxes" (Ward, field notes, June 9, 1975). In addition, several features were uncovered during the excavations. Most of these were small shallow basins that are discussed later in this chapter.

Although a summary of this second phase of fieldwork was subsequently written by Ward (1983), until now no detailed analysis of any of the data has been attempted. Similarly, with the exception of a master's thesis describing about 500 unifacial tools recovered during the 1955–1957 excavations (Hall 1983), and a pilot study for the present research (Daniel 1986), no detailed analyses have been undertaken on the artifact assemblage recovered from Hardaway.

STRATIGRAPHY AND SITE FORMATION

Four natural soil zones were distinguished at Hardaway (figure 2.3). Zone 1 was an 8–10 in (20–25 cm) deep plow zone that contained a mix of cultural material from the Middle Archaic to Historic periods, all of which had been stratigraphically identified at Doerschuk and Lowder's Ferry. Underlying the plow zone was what was described as the Kirk midden, which was over a foot thick in the deepest part of the site. Coe (1964:57) notes that about 40 percent of the midden was stone debris, with the remaining 60 percent being soil. This zone was associated with the Kirk complex, a related series of three point types, identified as Kirk Corner-Notched, Kirk Stemmed, and Kirk Serrated. Coe (1964:70) indicates that the Kirk-Corner Notched forms were associated primarily with the lower part of the midden, while the stemmed varieties were associated with the upper portion.

Underlying the midden was a humic zone (Zone 3) no more than 5–6 in (13–15 cm) thick, resting upon a red clay soil called Zone 4. This clay was a residual soil predominately formed from the underlying greenstone bedrock. The top portion of Zone 3 was associated with the Palmer component, while the bottom portion of Zone 3 and the top of Zone 4 were associated with the Hardaway component (Coe 1964:figure 49).

While Coe (1964:9) attributed his initial success in finding the deep deposits at Lowder's Ferry and Doerschuk to luck, his subsequent analyses of the sites' stratigraphy and his hypothesis for predicting the location of other alluvial sites along Piedmont floodplains was a geoarchaeological study ahead of its time. Yet the Hardaway site, located high on a hilltop, was formed differently, since it was "not stratified in the same sense as those found in the alluvial plain" (Coe 1964:13). By this statement Coe

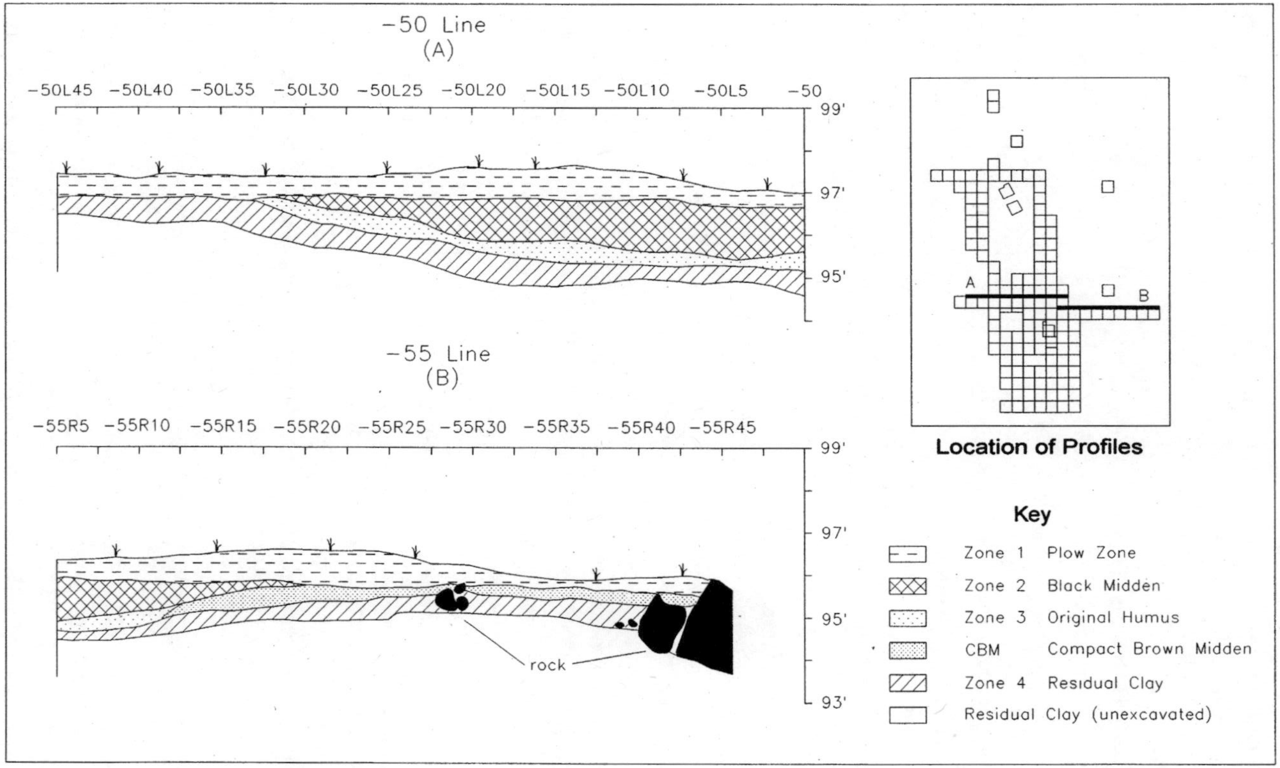

Figure 2.3. Hardaway site profiles

meant that Doerschuk, Gaston, and Lowder's Ferry had been created by floodplain deposits that contained a "series of occupational levels separated one from the other by sterile flood deposits of sand and silt" (Coe 1964:16). No such depositional history was noted for the Hardaway sequence. Rather, site formation was portrayed as having involved cultural activities and natural erosion of varying intensity.

> There was not enough activity at this site during the Hardaway or, perhaps, an even earlier period for soil or debris to accumulate through human use. Instead, erosion continued and the hearths and other signs of their scattered camps remained exposed on the surface. During the succeeding Palmer period, there was sufficient debris brought in to reverse the normal rate of erosion and actually to build up the soil over part of the site to a depth of five to six inches. Yet this build up took place over such a long period of time, and the general activity around the camps created such disturbances, that there never existed any sharp demarcation between the two periods. It was not until the Kirk period that any substantial accumulations of debris took place, and even this must be considered in terms of many generations and not as a single catastrophic avalanche. [Coe 1964:60]

To a certain extent, then, Hardaway was an exception to Coe's expectation that stratified sites would be found primarily in floodplains. Although Coe defined the stratigraphy and its correlation with the archaeological sequence, the depositional origins of the soil zones at Hardaway are still not clearly understood. For this reason a closer look at the site stratigraphy is addressed here.

The soil descriptions and profile data from the 1970s excavations provide additional information that can be used to update our understanding of the Hardaway site stratigraphy. The following interpretations reflect my review of field notes and color slides of site profiles and a cursory examination of soil samples from the Hardaway site. My interpretations have furthermore benefited from discussions with Coe and Ward concerning their field observations at Hardaway and with Albert Goodyear concerning late Pleistocene and early Holocene depositional systems in the Southeast (see Goodyear, in press).

Coe (personal communication 1991) has stated that rather than being completely rounded, the hilltop upon which the site rested was at one time basin shaped. In fact, the slope of the Zone 4 clay subsoil in the north-south profile depicted by Coe (1964:figure 49) hints at this shape. This phenomenon is more fully illustrated in the profile drawing in figure 2.3; note that Zone 4 exhibits a basin-shaped profile across the top of the southern toe of the knoll, with the thickest deposits of Zones 2 and 3 being in the basin bottom located in the center of the block excavations. Furthermore, Zones 2 and 3 thin out along the edges of the hilltop as Zone 4 begins to level off (figure 2.3).

In addition, Zone 3 also exhibited a slight color change along both the eastern and western edges of the excavations. The typical Zone 3 soil was a purplish to reddish brown loamy clay that changed to a brown loamy soil described as a "light brown midden" along the southernmost 15 to 20 ft of profiles (Ward, field notes, June 19, 1976). At this point the excavations were nearing the edges of the knoll top, and digging ceased: "We are definitely off the main portion of the site and the material is thinning out and producing a different stratigraphy" (Ward, field notes, August 7, 1975).

A somewhat similar stratigraphic change was noted along the eastern edge of the excavations (figure 2.3). Here Zone 3 was described as a "compact brown midden" (CBM), the nature of which was a source of much consternation to the crew; although it had an undisturbed feel during excavation, the top portion contained nails and coal (Moore, field notes, 1977). Zone 3 did resemble the CBM, but the latter stratum was darker brown and more compact in texture than Zone 3, and it contained many limonite and hematite inclusions. Furthermore, the CBM tended to become thinner and even less like Zone 3 as the trench extended further east.

At one point the excavators thought that they might have encountered a layer of fill associated with work done on the site by the Hardaway Construction Company. Because of its compact feel during excavation, however, the presence of numerous artifacts, and the fact that the nails and coal occurred only in the top portion of the zone (perhaps pressed into an otherwise undisturbed zone by heavy machinery), the excavators concluded that it was an undisturbed zone. In fact, the excavators considered the CBM more like Zone 3 in artifact composition than the light brown midden along the western portion of the site. This view was reinforced by the recovery of at least two Hardaway and several Palmer/Kirk points in the CBM. The presence of modern cultural material was accounted for by natural migration downward in the soil matrix. Unfortunately, potting in the area of the trench had destroyed any horizontal transition that might have existed between Zone 3 and the CBM (Moore, July 18–July 29, 1977).

While the eastern, southern, and western extent of the four-zone sequence was documented by the 1970s work, the northern limits of this stratigraphy are less well known. Some evidence suggests that it extends less than 50 ft (15 m) north of the 1950s work. A profile in *Formative*

Cultures, for example, suggests that the stratigraphy is rapidly thinning at unit 35L25 (Coe 1964:figure 49). An examination of the profile of the only other unit excavated just north of the main block excavations (50R25) indicates that the stratigraphy had completely changed to a plow zone over subsoil (Phelps, field notes, August 8, 1958).

In view of the observations noted above, I suggest that the soil strata seen on top of the knoll at Hardaway are pedogenically modified soil horizons that formed after a "filling in" of a large depression in the residual clay. I want to emphasize, however, that the following discussion is speculative, and confirmation must await specific pedologic analyses.

Zone 2 ("midden"). Underlying the plow zone and characterized by a high density of stone debris, soil zone 2 was described as a loose brown loam (Ward 1975). This was probably some sort of A-horizon, possibly a leached-out humus soil.

Zone 3 ("original humus"). Zone 3 appeared as a reddish-brown to purplish loamy clay (Ward 1975) that was probably some form of B-horizon. The reddish brown color suggests a humus-enriched soil from Zone 2 with some accumulation of iron. The zones referred to as "light brown midden" and "compact brown midden" may represent differentially modified B-horizons related to Zone 3. This point is discussed further below.

Zone 4 ("residual clay"). The underlying top of the red clay (Zone 4) also appears to have been some type of argillic or weathered B-horizon. This zone eventually graded into the C-horizon clay and bedrock.

Even if the above interpretations are reasonably accurate, the exact nature of site formation on the hilltop still remains to be explained. One implication of the previous discussion, however, is that natural forces may have played a larger role in site formation than was originally thought. That is, the sloping sides of the Zone 4 clay could have promoted the deposition of material in the bottom of the basin. This process, in turn, would have aided stratification.

Such a process may also partly account for the occurrence of the light brown midden and compact brown midden soil zones. If Zone 3 represents a B-horizon, as suggested above, then the two zones described as a light brown midden and compact brown midden may represent differentially altered B-horizons, perhaps related to their association with a thinner overlying soil deposit outside the basin.

It should also be mentioned that the excavators regarded these two zones as associated with a somewhat different Zone 4 clay than that present inside the basin. In view of this observation, the more weathered B-horizon (top of Zone 4) may not have existed outside the depression. In fact, at the edges of the excavations, only relatively shallow deposits of plowed soil overlying clay subsoil remained, and in some cases bedrock was encountered very near the ground surface. At that point only A- and C-horizons appear to have been present.

In summary, the stratigraphy exhibited at the Hardaway site may have resulted from the filling in of a large depression on the hilltop. This deposit, pedogenically modified, subsequently produced the soil zones observed during the excavations. The origin of the depression is unknown. Perhaps the hilltop formed in this way, or maybe it was created by a major erosional episode. In any event, it began to "fill in" sometime between 9,500 and 10,500 years ago. Evidence of filling includes the presence of Hardaway and Palmer deposits that were eventually modified into B-horizon soils. A much different depositional event took place later and caused a massive accumulation of stone debris. Sometime after the Middle to Late Archaic, the deposition stabilized, resulting more or less in the modern landform.

The exact nature of the mechanism of deposition within the depression remains obscure. Given that stratification is more apparent within the depression than elsewhere on the hill, I have proposed a larger role for natural processes in site formation than was originally perceived. Processes such as colluviation and/or soil creep, for example, seem to be indicated here.

The significance of the Hardaway site for southeastern archaeology cannot be overemphasized (see Smith 1986; Steponaitis 1986). Yet despite its importance in establishing an Early Archaic projectile point chronology, the depositional history of the Hardaway site remains something of an enigma. The Hardaway site proved critical in forming the projectile point sequence for the Carolina Piedmont, but it is often overlooked that Hardaway was not a floodplain site with well-defined alluvial deposits like the Doerschuk and Gaston sites—or most other early Holocene sites in the Southeast (e.g., Chapman 1977, Claggett and Cable 1982, Tippitt and Marquardt 1984)—although the difference was certainly clear to Coe (1964:63).

Rather Hardaway's location on a ridgetop and its formation there have been taken largely for granted or ignored while its point chronology was adopted. Clearly, the reason has been that subsequent work has focused on floodplain sites—where sites have been excavated that tend to support the sequence—so that understanding of formation processes on ridgetop sites like Hardaway has been largely moot.

An understanding of site formation at Hardaway, however, is important for two reasons. First, the study of site formation can partly address the important question of site function at Hardaway by helping us understand both the cultural and the natural forces affecting the density of material at the site. If this density results from high rates of refuse disposal, then Hardaway represents an intensity of occupation virtually unknown in the Piedmont. On the other hand, if the density of material reflects erosion or site deflation, then the density of material may result more from natural processes than from cultural ones.

Second, an understanding of site formation may have implications for identifying other stratified upland site locations. In this connection the recent work of Goodyear (in press) concerning the geoarchaeological understanding of late Pleistocene and early Holocene depositional systems in the Southeast is significant. In his synthesis, Goodyear (in press) has noted a pattern in the depositional contexts of certain stratified early sites in the Southeast that relates to the geological recognition of the Pleistocene-Holocene boundary. In the floodplains of the Piedmont, this boundary is marked by alluvial sands overlying a weathered and sometimes eroded clay stratum. On the basis of previous geological, palynological, and climatic work, Goodyear relates the clay stratum to widespread erosional events by flooding that took place sometime during the late Pleistocene. The overlying sands are the result of subsequent floodplain buildup at the onset of the Holocene. The Pleistocene-Holocene contacts at these sites are usually modified B-horizon soil zones. If the interpretations of the soil zones presented earlier are accurate, it is interesting to note that a similar contact may exist at Hardaway. The implications for recognition of a Pleistocene-Holocene stratigraphic boundary in nonalluvial Piedmont sites are still debatable; however, the possibilities are suggestive enough to warrant additional investigation.

In sum, while floodplains obviously exhibit the greatest potential for the presence of buried early sites in the Piedmont, the Hardaway site stands as a reminder that stratified nonalluvial sites may also exist. Although a clear picture of the depositional history of the Hardaway site remains to be created, it appears to share a common trait with floodplain sites regarding a B horizon stratigraphic marker. Further research involving soil scientists and geologists is therefore essential to clarify the nature of site formation at Hardaway and to identify other locations elsewhere in the Piedmont.

CULTURAL STRATIGRAPHY

Whatever the site formation processes at Hardaway, the present analysis provides an opportunity to examine projectile point distribution by natural soil zone. (The excavation units used in this study are discussed in the following section.) As Coe (1964:57) reported, the excavation levels correlated only roughly with the natural soil zones, and his interpretations of

Table 2.1. Frequency Distribution of Points by Zone from Selected Units at the Hardaway Site

Type/ Subtype	Zone 2	Zone 3	CBM	Zone 4
Unidentified	213	86	11	23
Small Triangular	-	1	2	1
Yadkin Triangular	6	1	-	-
Unidentified stemmed	11	-	5	5
Savannah River Stemmed	8	2	-	-
Morrow Mountain Stemmed	33	5	-	2
Kirk Stemmed and Serrated	26	8	-	-
Stanly Stemmed	47	18	-	2
Bifurcate	1	-	-	-
Kirk Corner-Notched				
Unground excurvate base	2	2	-	-
Unground straight base	23	7	-	3
Ground excurvate base	1	7	1	1
Ground straight base	15	7	-	2
Palmer Corner-Notched	4	10	1	9
Corner-Notched indeterminate	2	6	2	-
Side-Notched indeterminate	1	2	-	1
Taylor Side-Notched	-	1	-	-
Hardaway Side-Notched	1	4	-	3
Hardaway Side-Notched preform	2	1	1	1
Small Dalton	-	6	-	1
Hardaway-Dalton	3	6	1	15
Hardaway-Dalton preform	2	8	-	10

the stratigraphy were based upon his field observations of the excavation by natural zones in 1958 and 1959 and the data analyzed by arbitrary levels from the 1955–1957 seasons.

Table 2.1 lists the distribution of points analyzed by zone in this study. Of particular interest, however, is a subset of this data listed in table 2.2. This table includes those points from the 1970s excavation that were excavated by level designations (i.e., top or bottom) within each zone. Al-

Table 2.2. Frequency Distribution of Points by Zone and Level from Selected Units at the Hardaway Site

Zone	Level	Small Triangular	Yadkin Triangular	Savannah River Stemmed	Morrow Mountain Stemmed	Stanly Stemmed	Kirk Corner-Notched	Palmer Corner Notched	Small Dalton	Hardaway Side-Notched	Hardaway Dalton	Total
II	bottom	-	2	-	1	1	6	1	-	-	2	13
III	top	-	-	-	3	-	1	5	3	1	1	14
III	bottom	1	-	1	1	-	2	3	2	4[a]	2[b]	16
IV	top	1	-	-	-	-	-	4	-	1	2[c]	8
IV	bottom	-	-	-	-	-	-	-	-	1	-	1

[a]Count includes one Taylor Side-Notched. Preform count = 1.

[b]Preform count = 4.

[c]Preform count = 1.

though frequencies are not high, the results do lend further support to the stratigraphic sequence of points to which the arbitrary level data alluded (Coe 1964:table 7). Furthermore, the data in table 2.2 also provide empirical support for the correlation of point types with particular levels *within* each soil zone depicted by Coe (1964:figure 49) as well as Coe's (1964:64–70) comments concerning the association of points with soil zones.

While all varieties of Kirk points were present in Zone 2 (the Kirk midden), for example, Coe (1964:70) indicates that Kirk Corner-Notched points were primarily associated with the lower portion of the zone. This statement is supported by table 2.2, where the Kirk Corner-Notched point is the most common type at the bottom of Zone 2 (46 percent, n = 6). Similarly, Palmer Corner-Notched points predominate at the top of Zone 3 (36 percent, n = 5), followed by approximately equal frequencies of Hardaway Side-Notched points and preforms (31 percent, n = 5, including one Taylor-like Side-Notched point), and Hardaway-Dalton points and preforms (37.5 percent, n = 6) points at the bottom of Zone 3. The sequence tends to break down, however, in Zone 4, where approximately equal frequencies of both Hardaway points and Palmer points were recovered at the top of Zone 4. Finally, only a single identifiable point—a Hardaway Side-Notched point—was recovered from the bottom of Zone 4.

These data, then, make clear, as I observed earlier, that Hardaway was not as clearly stratified as Doerschuk or Gaston or several other alluvial sites subsequently excavated in the Southeast and mentioned in Chapter 1. About eighty potsherds were recovered from Zones 3 and 4 among the units analyzed here despite assiduous attempts to identify and separate disturbed contexts during the excavations. Given Hardaway's location on a hilltop and the potential for disturbance on heavily reoccupied sites, however, the presence of the potsherds should come as no surprise. In fact, despite the mixing of cultural materials, we might say that Hardaway was very well stratified.

Nevertheless, I have resisted the notion that individual complexes could be separated by zone within the Early Archaic. Rather, in the following analyses I have combined Zone 3 (including the CBM) and Zone 4 as representative of a single Early Archaic component—albeit one representing numerous intermittent occupations over several hundred to perhaps a thousand years or more (table 2.3). While in doing so I undoubtedly obscure potential variability during this time, I consider the merging of the two zones less problematic than an attempt to justify the identification, for example, of a Hardaway-Dalton versus a Palmer Corner-Notched complex would be.

Table 2.3. Frequency Distribution of Stone Tools (Excluding Points) by Zone from Selected Units at the Hardaway Site

Type	CBM	Zone 3	Zone 4	Total
Biface I	4	112	35	151
Biface II	23	296	74	393
Biface III	5	109	42	156
Indeterminate biface	4	108	57	169
End scraper Ia	3	81	47	131
End scraper Ib	-	28	12	40
End scraper IIa	7	49	26	82
End scraper IIb	-	28	16	44
End scraper III	-	4	4	8
End scraper IV	-	10	15	25
End scraper V	2	49	28	79
Side scraper I	-	11	9	20
Side scraper IIa	6	146	60	212
Side scraper IIb	1	14	8	23
Side scraper III	3	78	34	115
Side scraper IV	-	12	9	21
Pointed scraper	-	7	2	9
Oval Scraper	-	5	-	5
Miscellaneous scraper	-	13	3	16
Indeterminate scraper	4	125	83	212
Perforator/drill/graver	2	16	9	27
Denticulate	-	2	-	2
Hafted spokeshave	-	2	-	2
Waller knife	1	-	-	1
Core/scraper	-	2	4	6
Chopper	1	6	3	10
Adze	-	2	-	2
Hammerstone	3	38	10	51
Hammerstone/abrader	-	2	-	2
Hammerstone/anvil	-	12	4	16
Grindingstone/anvil	-	4	7	11
Anvil	-	1	-	1
Core	9	54	18	81
Pièces esquillées	-	-	3	3
Engraved stone	-	5	1	6
Indeterminate ground stone	-	1	-	1
Other worked stone	-	3	2	5
Unmodified cobble/stone	1	35	1	37
Total	79	1,470	626	2,175

FEATURES

A total of sixty-five features and five burials were recorded during the excavations at Hardaway. None of the burials was associated with the Early Archaic component. Moreover, within the squares examined here, only eight features appear to have been associated with the early component. I have divided the features into four categories: pits, rock concentrations, postholes, and natural or modern disturbances (i.e., tree falls, root disturbances, rodent burrows, and potholes).

The most numerous cultural features identified at Hardaway were pits—usually in the form of shallow basins, circular to oval in shape, with gently sloping sides. Of the thirty-four features identified during the 1958 and 1959 excavations, at least twenty-five were basin-shaped pits, seventeen of which were interpreted to have been hearths (Coe 1964:61). They were generally 1–3 ft (0.3–0.9 m) in diameter and usually less than 1 ft (0.3 m) deep. Pit fill included artifacts, animal bone fragments, and charcoal, and some were at least partially lined with rocks (Coe 1964:61,83). The vast majority of these pits had their origins in the Zone 2 midden (Coe 1964:figure 52), and many contained Middle to Late Archaic points in their fill (Phelps, field notes, 1958, 1959).

The remaining pits were distinguished from shallow basins by straighter sides and bottoms that were rounded to flat. Except for the absence of rocks, their contents were similar in nature to the shallow-basin hearths. These features also originated in Zone 2, and they were interpreted as refuse-filled pits (Phelps, field notes, 1958, 1959). Field notes for the 1958 and 1959 excavations also indicate that an additional ten pits were not assigned feature numbers. These were mostly of the nonbasin variety.

Ten of the features excavated during the 1970s were also pits, mostly of the shallow-basin type, but they were not identified as hearths (Moore, field notes, 1977; Ward, field notes, 1975, 1976). Rather, they appear to have been refuse filled, containing artifacts, animal bone fragments, and charcoal. It should also be noted that, according to field records, the texture and color of Zone 3 soil tended to obscure features, so that their identification was difficult. Moreover, during excavations in the 1970s, unlike the 1950s, it was not possible to trace the level of origin of the pits identified during the 1970s work because of the pothunting in the upper zones.

The remaining cultural feature categories include rock concentrations and postholes. Six rock concentrations were uncovered during the 1958 and 1959 excavations, and four were interpreted as hearths. Two additional concentrations were uncovered in 1975. The nature of this feature category is discussed in more detail below. Postholes, on the other hand, were not usually assigned feature numbers. Generally they were plotted and numbered sequentially within individual excavation squares. While approximately twenty-five postholes were identified in this fashion, four others were not identified as such until after they were excavated and had been assigned feature numbers. Their distribution showed no obvious patterning.

Natural or modern disturbances constitute the final feature category. The vast majority of these disturbances were identified prior to excavation and were removed separately from the surrounding zone without being assigned a feature number. Sixteen such disturbances were not identified, however, until after excavation was complete and a feature number had been assigned.

After carefully examining feature records and artifacts, I selected a group of eight features that may be assigned tentatively to an Early Archaic association (table 2.4). The remaining features were eliminated either because their stratigraphic origin and/or associated diagnostic artifacts postdated the Early Archaic (as was the case with most of the 1950s features) or because their stratigraphic origin was questionable and they lacked associated diagnostic artifacts (as was the case with most of the 1970s features). The discussion below involves two categories of features: pits and rock concentrations.

Pits

Feature 8. This feature was a shallow, basin-shaped pit identified as a hearth (figure 2.4). It was somewhat circular in shape and measured 0.24 × 0.75 ft (0.27 × 0.23 m) in size and 2.9 ft (0.9 m) in depth. Four rocks are depicted that cover most of the surface of this pit. Profile drawings indicate that the top of the pit was located near the bottom of Zone 3, while the bottom intruded into the top of Zone 4. Material recovered from the pit fill included one biface fragment, one core fragment, stone debitage, and charcoal. No diagnostic artifacts were associated with this pit, and it was assigned an Early Archaic date on the basis of its stratigraphic origin.

Feature 21. This feature was also a basin-shaped pit interpreted as a hearth (figure 2.5). It was one of the largest basin-shaped hearths recorded at Hardaway and was somewhat irregularly shaped, measuring 4.3 × 2.9 ft (1.3 × 0.9 m) in plan view and approximately 1.47 ft (0.45 m) deep. The top of the feature was noted at the interface of Zones 3 and 4; the bottom of the feature extended well into the red clay. At the bottom of the feature and just to the west of its center, a smaller pit 0.72 ft (0.22 m) in diameter extended 0.49 ft (0.15 m) below the floor of the feature. It was covered by a large rock. Unfortunately, no further information was noted about the relationship of this smaller pit to the rest of the feature,

Table 2.4. Distribution of Lithic Artifacts from Selected Features at the Hardaway Site

	Feature							
Type	8	10	20	21	35	37	40	41
Palmer Corner-Notched	-	-	-	2	-	-	-	-
Kirk Corner-Notched	-	-	-	-	-	-	2	-
Side-Notched indeterminate	-	-	-	-	-	-	1	-
Indeterminate point	-	-	-	1	-	-	5	-
Biface I	-	-	-	-	-	-	5	-
Biface II	-	-	-	4	-	-	8	-
Biface III	1	-	-	1	-	-	7	1
Indeterminate biface	-	-	-	-	-	-	3	1
End scraper Ia	-	-	1	2	-	-	2	-
End scraper Ib	-	-	-	-	-	-	-	1
End scraper IIa	-	-	-	3	-	-	2	-
End scraper III	-	-	-	1	-	-	-	-
Side scraper IIa	-	-	-	2	1	-	4	2
Side scraper IIb	-	-	-	-	-	-	1	-
Side scraper III	-	-	-	1	-	-	6	1
Side scraper IV	-	-	-	2	-	-	-	-
Miscellaneous scraper	-	-	1	-	-	-	-	-
Indeterminate scraper	-	-	2	7	-	-	1	2
Graver	-	-	-	-	-	-	1	-
Chopper	-	-	-	1	-	-	1	-
Core	1	-	-	1	-	-	1	-
Pièces esquillées	-	-	-	1	-	-	-	-
Hammerstone	-	-	-	1	-	-	1	-
Hammerstone/anvil	-	-	-	-	-	-	-	1
Grindingstone/anvil	-	-	-	-	-	-	1	-
Other worked stone	-	-	-	1	-	-	-	-
Unmodified cobble/stone	-	-	-	-	-	-	4	-
Flake	60	-	157	241	83	15	2,692	197
Total	62	-	161	272	84	15	2,748	206

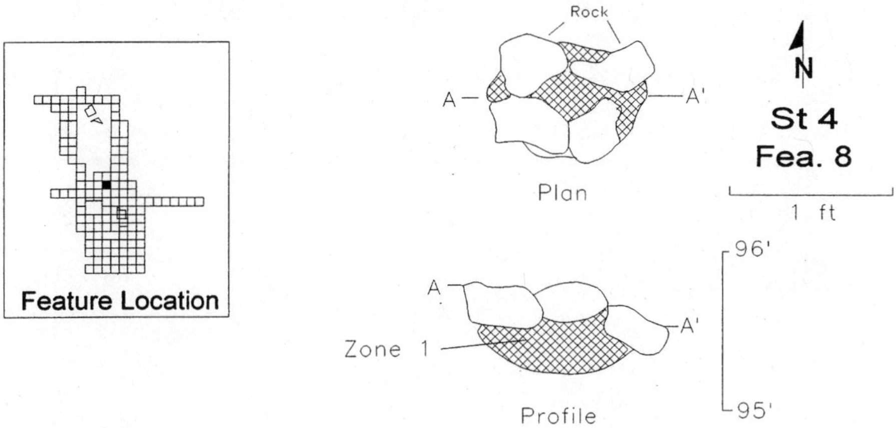

Figure 2.4. Feature 8

nor was there any mention of the feature's fill beyond noting that it contained artifacts and charcoal.

Artifacts diagnostic of the Early Archaic period include two Palmer Corner-Notched points (which could not be located for analysis), and two Type I end scrapers (table 2.4). While field notes identified this feature as

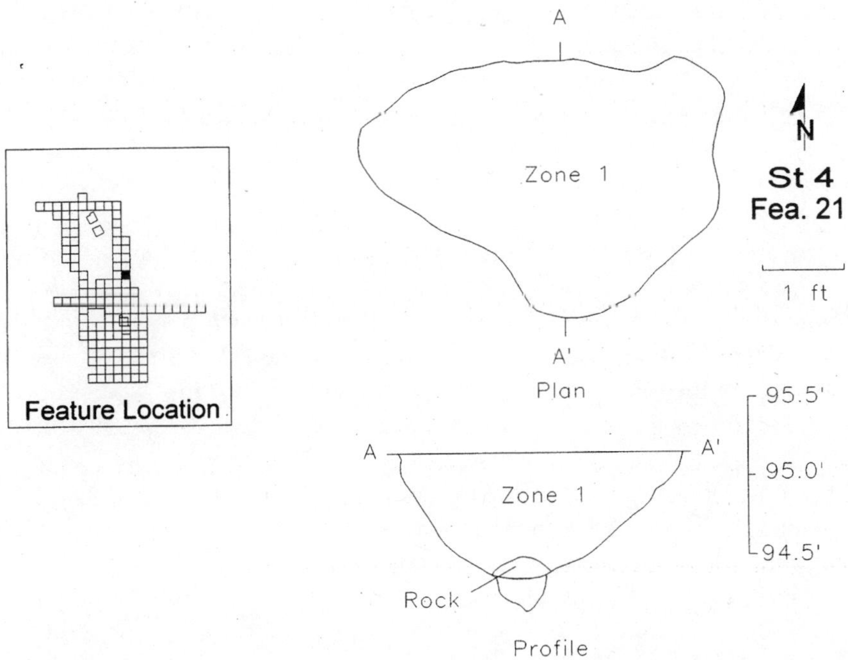

Figure 2.5. Feature 21

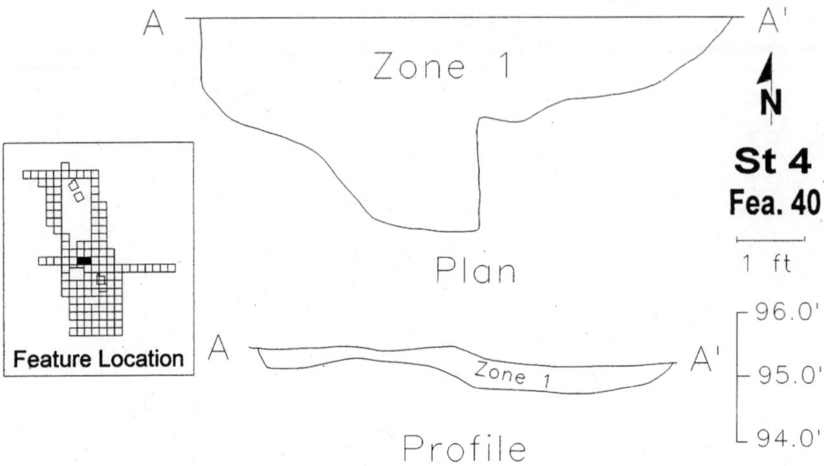

Figure 2.6. Feature 40

a hearth, in size and shape it more closely resembles features interpreted as roasting pits identified on late prehistoric sites in the Carolina Piedmont (Ward and Davis 1993:38).

Feature 40. Feature 40 was observed at the top of Zone 3 as a somewhat basin-shaped pit that was difficult to define (figure 2.6). It was 0.39 ft (0.12 m) in depth and about 8.2 × 3.3 ft (2.5 × 1 m) in extent, but Ward (field notes, 1976) suggested that this may have been a filled-in natural depression rather than a purposely dug pit and that part of the feature may have been cut away by an adjacent trench during the 1958 excavations.

Artifacts abundant in the feature fill included over 2,000 flakes and numerous stone tools (table 2.4). This latter group includes primarily bifaces, end scrapers, and side scrapers. Animal bone fragments and charcoal were also recovered. The only temporally diagnostic artifacts recovered were two Kirk Corner-Notched points, but two Type I end scrapers were also located in the feature fill. In addition, one unidentified side-notched point and one chipped-stone adze were also present in the fill. While the observed origin of the pit in Zone 3, the projectile points, and the Type I end scrapers all indicate an Early Archaic association, this temporal assignment should be regarded as only tentative, since its stratigraphic origin may have been obscured by the disturbed Zone 2 that overlaid it. In this regard it is noteworthy that one potsherd was also recovered in the feature, but it was located adjacent to a large root disturbance.

Feature 41. Feature 41 was observed as a vague mottled brown stain at the top of Zone 3 (figure 2.7). Ward (field notes, 1976) noted that this

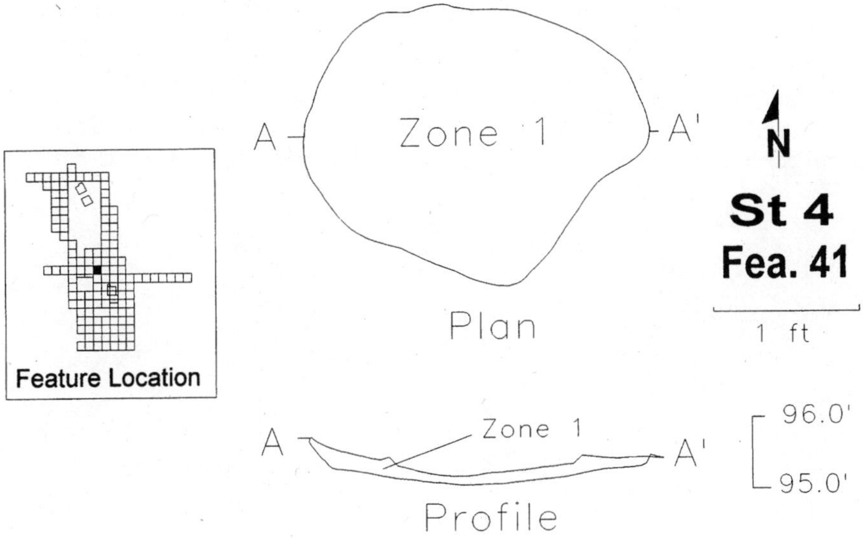

Figure 2.7. Feature 41

feature resembled a lens deposit more than a pit. Thus, like Feature 40, it may have represented a filled-in depression. It was roughly oval in shape, approximately 2.4 × 1.8 ft (0.73 × 0.57 m) in size and only 1 ft (0.3 m) in depth. It contained animal bone fragments, flakes, and several stone tools. One of the latter was a Type I end scraper, whose presence would suggest, although not conclusively, an Early Archaic temporal association. No temporally diagnostic points were recovered from the fill.

Rock Concentrations

Feature 10. Information about Feature 10 is sketchy, but it was recorded as a single rock about 1.2 × 0.7 ft (0.38 × 0.22 m) in size partially embedded in the top of Zone 4 (figure 2.8). No associated artifacts were recorded with the feature, but charcoal was noted around and under the rock, and it was interpreted as a hearth. Its temporal assignment was based on its stratigraphic context.

Feature 20. Feature 20, a concentration of rocks and artifacts, was identified as a hearth associated with the Palmer component, and it is pictured in *Formative Cultures* (Coe 1964:figure 51). It was defined by a loose concentration of approximately fourteen rocks at the interface of Zones 3 and 4, and covered an area about 0.9 × 0.9 ft (0.3 × 0.3 m) in size (figure 2.9). Artifacts associated with the feature included stone debitage, animal bone

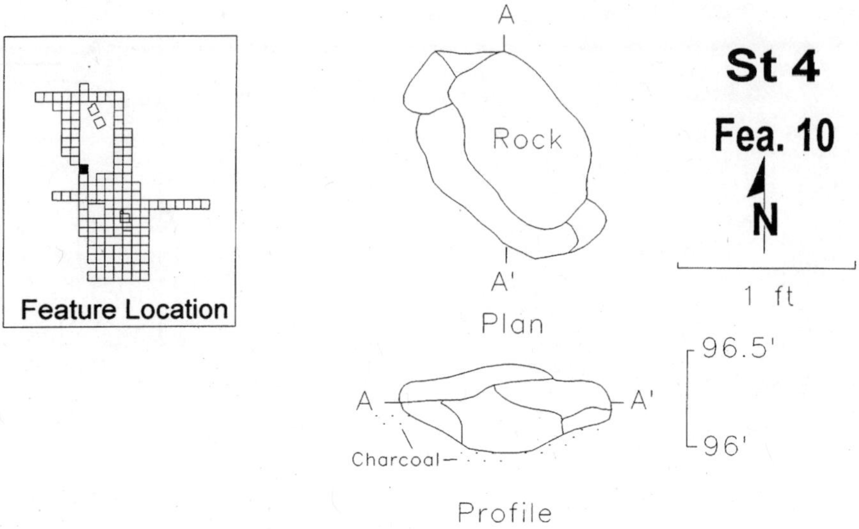

Figure 2.8. Feature 10

fragments, charcoal, and four scrapers including a Type I end scraper. It was placed with the Palmer component on the basis of its stratigraphic association as well as its end scraper association.

Feature 35. Feature 35 was defined primarily by a loose concentration of about ten small to medium-sized rocks in Zone 4 that covered an area about 4.9 × 3.9 ft (1.5 × 1.2 m) in size (figure 2.10). One side scraper and several flakes were the only artifacts associated with the feature, although charcoal and animal bone fragments were also noted. While it was initially

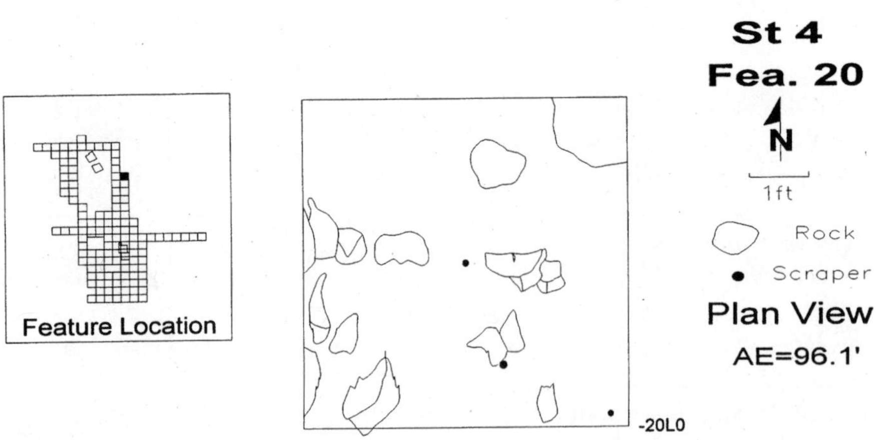

Figure 2.9. Feature 20

Figure 2.10. Feature 35

thought to have been a hearth, this feature upon excavation appeared more like an accumulation of naturally occurring rock (Ward, personal communication 1992).

Feature 37. Like Feature 35, Feature 37 was defined by a loose concentration of rocks (figure 2.11). Approximately twenty small rocks were clustered in an area about 2.6 × 1.6 ft (0.8 × 0.5 m) located in Zone 4. The only artifacts directly associated with the feature were a few flakes, although a hammerstone was noted 2 ft to the southeast of the rock cluster. Like Feature 35, too, this feature appears to have been a natural concentration of rock rather than a hearth (Ward, personal communication 1992).

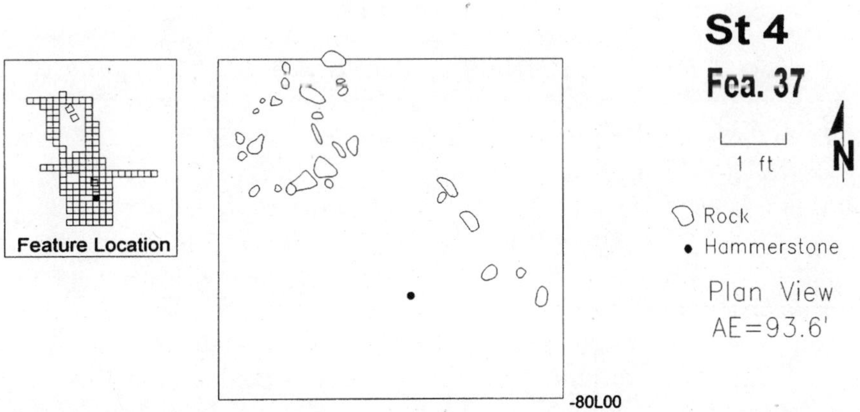

Figure 2.11. Feature 37

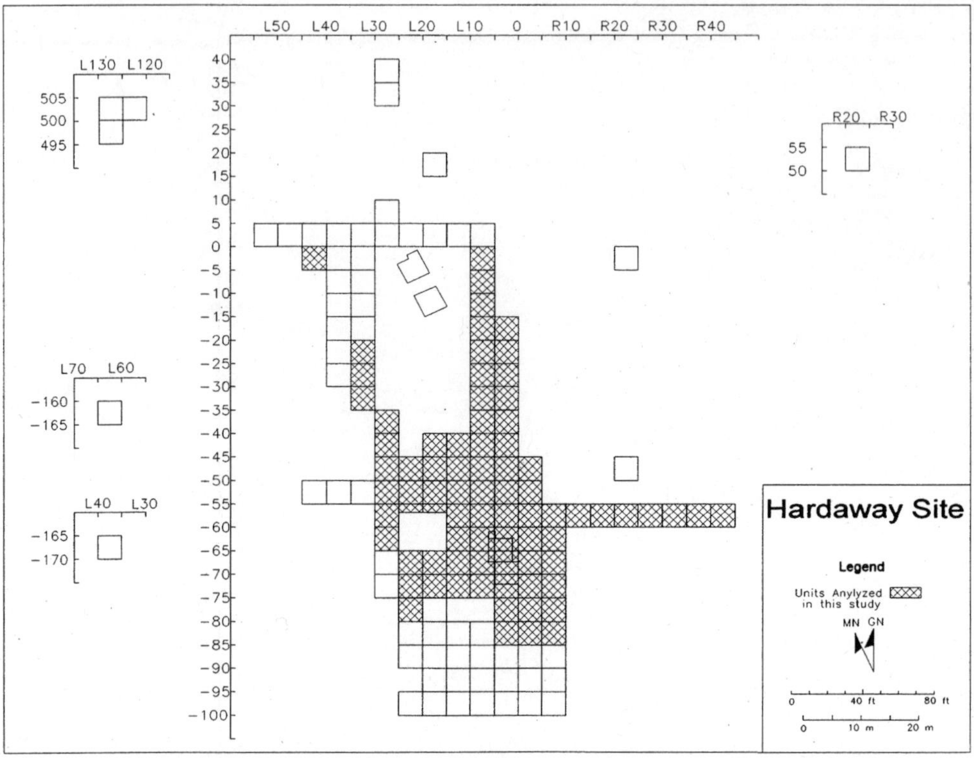

Figure 2.12. Units analyzed in this study

Feature Discussion

Among the four pit features, at least two (Features 40 and 41) may simply be natural depressions that collected artifacts. Whether the artifacts deposited in these features were the result of natural or cultural processes cannot be determined. The remaining two features include one large and one small basin-shaped pit. Unfortunately, information concerning the excavation of these two features (Features 21 and 8) is scanty, but they were both identified as hearths.

Similarly, at least four other features were uncovered in the lower zones in the form of a loose concentration of rocks, artifacts, bone fragments, and charcoal. While two of these features were identified as hearths, two other similar features were interpreted as naturally occurring rock accumulations that were fortuitously associated with cultural material. In the absence of any other information concerning the two concentrations interpreted as hearths, and given that rock, charcoal, and bone fragments occurred throughout Zones 3 and 4 along with artifacts, the interpretation of Features 10 and 20 as Early Archaic hearths might be questioned.

UNITS OF ANALYSIS

A total of eighty units covering 1920 ft^2 (178 m^2) were chosen for analysis (figure 2.12). Of these, twenty-nine units were from the 1958–1959 seasons (RLA accession no. 1010), and fifty-one units were from the 1975–1980 excavations (RLA accession no. 2312). These unit counts include two squares from the 1950s work that were reexcavated during the 1970s. An emphasis was placed on analyzing stone artifacts from contiguous units containing some amount of undisturbed Zone 3 (or CBM) and Zone 4—the Early Archaic component. All plow-zone and Zone 2 artifacts from these units were excluded from analysis, as was any material identified from disturbed context. The one exception to this exclusion was the group of points from Zone 2 that were used to report on the stratigraphy discussed earlier in the chapter. The next chapter describes the results of the analysis of all artifacts from the Early Archaic component.

3

Stone Raw Materials

This chapter briefly describes the stone types found in the Hardaway assemblage; possible source locations of these raw materials are also noted. Broadly speaking, the raw materials identified here can be divided into four stone types: metavolcanic and metasedimentary stone, chert, and quartz. The chert and quartz categories reflect current archaeologically recognized raw material types, but the metavolcanic and metasedimentary stone types defined here are somewhat new (cf. House and Wogaman 1978:51–57; Novick 1978).

Of particular interest is the metavolcanic stone commonly called rhyolite. Rhyolite dominates the Hardaway assemblage (Chapter 4) and outcrops near the site in the southern Uwharrie Mountains. A quarry survey was performed in the Uwharries as a part of this project. Approximately twenty-seven quarries were located and were sampled for petrologic analysis (Daniel and Butler 1991, 1996). In sum, our survey work has located and petrologically characterized approximately twenty-seven quarries in or adjacent to the Uwharrie Mountains. Pinpointed among these sites was the location of the dark gray, aphyric, and often flow-banded rhyolite so abundant in the Hardaway assemblage. In addition, the sources of three porphyritic rhyolite types present in the assemblage were also located. These rhyolite sources near Hardaway appear to be microscopically, if not macroscopically, distinct from a series of additional stone sources at the northern end of the Uwharries, which for the most part can be classified as rhyolitic tuffs. A significant percentage of the tools from Hardaway appear to have been made from tuffs, but whether they came from these sources is unclear. In any event, it appears that Morrow Mountain was the most intensively exploited source in the region during the Early Archaic.

This work provided the basis for the identification of the metavolcanic and metasedimentary stone types summarized below. A brief discussion of the geologic setting of the Uwharrie Mountains precedes the raw material descriptions.

GEOLOGIC BACKGROUND

The Carolina Slate Belt consists of metavolcanic and metasedimentary rocks extending approximately 600 km from Virginia to Georgia; it has a maximum width of about 140 km in central North Carolina (Butler and Secor 1991:66). The rocks were formed as a result of the eruptions of a chain of volcanic islands surrounded by shallow seas during the Precambrian period. The lava, ash, and sediment deposited by these eruptions were later metamorphosed, folded, and faulted, so that they were exposed to the erosion that eventually formed the present land surface of the Uwharrie Mountains.

Although the Uwharries are called mountains, they are actually inselbergs, being the erosional remnants of an ancient and higher Miocene peneplain (Kesel 1974). By the start of the Pliocene epoch, streams flowing east across the Piedmont from the newly formed Continental Divide had altered the nearly level surface of the peneplain and had exposed the more resistant rock as elevations. Thus, while the rocks comprising the Uwharries are several hundred million years old, the erosion that created them is actually relatively young, geologically speaking.

Topography

Today, the Uwharries consist of a loosely defined, narrow chain of mountains approximately 46 km long between Badin and Asheboro in Stanly, Montgomery, and Randolph Counties. As identified on U.S. Geologic Survey (USGS) topographic maps, the northern end of this chain borders the eastern edge of the Uwharrie River and a major tributary, Caraway Creek, near Asheboro in Randolph County. The mountain range then crosses the Uwharrie River and, bordering the river's western edge in Montgomery County, eventually terminates near Badin in Stanly County at the river's confluence with the Yadkin. The Uwharries tend to range from 150 m to 300 m in elevation and have hilly peaks, narrow ridge crests, and steep slopes. They account for significant portions of both Uwharrie National Forest and Morrow Mountain State Park (figure 3.1).

Geology

The Albemarle-Asheboro area forms one of the best known geologic regions of the Carolina Slate Belt (e.g., Butler 1986; Butler and Secor 1991,

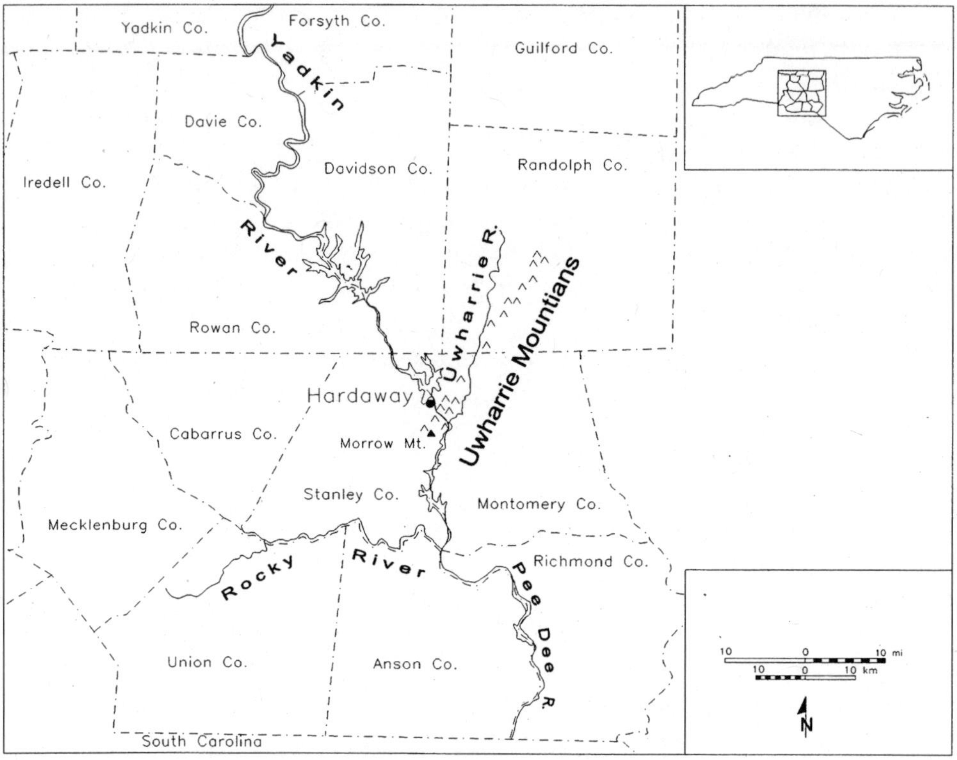

Figure 3.1. Location of the Uwharrie Mountains

Conley 1962; Harris and Glover 1988; Milton 1984; Seiders 1981). Three geologic formations compose the Uwharries: the Uwharrie, Tillery, and Cid formations (Butler and Secor 1991:figure 4-5).

The exact age and geologic relationship of some of these formations have been the subject of recent debate (J. Robert Butler, personal communication 1992), but they can be generally described as follows. The Uwharrie formation, which is the oldest of the three, represents the northern half of the Uwharries. It is a complex arrangement of felsic metavolcanic rocks with lesser amounts of mafic tuffs and layered beds of reworked volcanic debris (Butler and Secor 1991:67–69).

The Tillery and Cid formations roughly divide the southern half of the mountain chain. The Tillery consists of laminated to thinly bedded metamudstone and argillite. The Cid formation (at the southern most end of the chain) is also predominantly a metasedimentary sequence, although it does contain locally abundant metavolcanic rocks (Butler and Secor

1991:67–69).While volcanic units constitute only a minor portion of both the Tillery and Cid formations, one such unit is of particular archaeological significance. This unit is Morrow Mountain rhyolite, which is present at a contact between the Tillery and Cid formations to the south and west of Hardaway (Conley 1962:plate 1). Although the rhyolite unit has been assigned tentatively to the upper Tillery formation, its exact status with respect to either the Tillery or the Cid formation is still unresolved (Harris and Glover 1988; Milton 1984). Be that as it may, it forms the erosionally resistant mountaintops around Hardaway, which were extensively mined prehistorically for raw material.

It should be noted that the term "Morrow Mountain rhyolite" describes a lithologic unit covering several mountains around Hardaway and is not restricted to Morrow Mountain itself (Conley 1962:plate 1). Specifically, it refers to a series of mixed lava flows originating from several vents that produced an almost sheetlike deposit in the area. The relatively rapid cooling of this lava and the low-grade metamorphism of the region has produced the rhyolite's good-to-excellent conchoidal fracture (Butler 1986; Conley 1962:15). It could more accurately be called metarhyolite, but the term "rhyolite" is retained here for the sake of simplicity.

The Hardaway site itself lies on Badin greenstone, a significant lithologic unit within the lower Cid formation, which is adjacent to and occasionally in contact with the Morrow Mountain rhyolite unit (Conley 1962:plate 1). Like the rhyolite, this greenstone unit forms the erosionally resistant tops of other mountains in the vicinity. The final lithologic unit of importance in the area is argillite, which is part of the Tillery formation. Argillite underlies both the greenstone and rhyolite and forms the stream valleys for the Uwharrie and Pee Dee Rivers (Conley 1962).

STONE TYPES

Four broad classes of stone types were identified in the Hardaway assemblage: metavolcanic stone, metasedimentary stone, chert, and quartz.

Metavolcanic Stone

The Carolina Piedmont contains a wide variety of metamorphosed igneous rock. Among those types identified in the Hardaway assemblage are rhyolitic flows, rhyolitic tuffs, and greenstone. Although rhyolitic breccia was not seen in the Hardaway assemblage, it was present in the collections survey. The most important of these raw materials, however, were certain rhyolitic flows and tuffs derived from quarries located in the Uwharrie

Mountains (Daniel and Butler 1991, 1996). Approximately twenty quarries in the southern Uwharries around Hardaway were sampled for petrologic analysis. Collectively, the rhyolite from these quarries is called Uwharrie rhyolite.

Rhyolite is a very fine-grained igneous rock that is composed mainly of quartz and feldspar, with minor amounts of accessory minerals such as biotite, hornblende, and iron oxides. Rhyolites are formed in a volcanic environment, either at or near the surface of the earth. Rhyolite is commonly porphyritic; that is, it has larger crystals (phenocrysts) in an aphanitic groundmass. "Aphanitic" denotes a grain size in which the crystals are too small to be seen with an unaided eye. In the Uwharrie Mountains, the phenocrysts in rhyolite are typically quartz and/or feldspar, 1 to 3 mm long, in a dark groundmass that is microcrystalline or cryptocrystalline. Aphyric rhyolite, which lacks phenocrysts and is entirely aphanitic, is rare in the Uwharrie Mountains.

Uwharrie rhyolite can be subdivided into distinct types based on color, grain size, and the presence or abundance of special features such as phenocrysts, flow banding, and spherulites. In general, this rhyolite exhibits a fine-grained texture that exhibits a gray to grayish black color in fresh specimens. Upon weathering it develops a white chalky outer coating that in some cases reveals a distinct flow banding. The nature and relative abundance of phenocrysts (or the absence of phenocrysts in the aphyric variety), are particularly useful in subdividing the rhyolite, as phenocrysts are present or absent in restricted areas within the rhyolite unit around Hardaway, usually including one or two mountaintops.

Aphyric Rhyolite. This rock is a rhyolitic flow that is distinguished by its dark gray color and homogeneous fine-grained texture. Its most distinctive characteristic, however, is flow banding, which is most pronounced on weathered specimens. This rhyolite is almost certainly the "flow banded rhyolite" previously described by Novick (1978:427). Flow lines are generally very thin (i.e., only a few millimeters) and alternate in a pattern of light and dark gray. In some fresh rhyolite, however, flow lines are relatively inconspicuous (figures 3.2–3.3). Similarly, some extremely weathered specimens also lack discernible flow banding; these specimens exhibit an extremely chalky grayish white exterior. Although this rhyolite has a very homogeneous appearance, some specimens exhibit small spherulites (measuring ca. 1 mm in diameter) that appear as tiny patches of radiating fibers. These spherulites may occur in the absence of flow banding.

Aphyric rhyolite dominates the Hardaway assemblage (see Chapter 4) as well as the collections survey (see Chapter 7) and was probably obtained almost exclusively from Morrow Mountain, which is located just 8 km

Figure 3.2. Aphyric rhyolite from Morrow Mountain: (a-b) geological specimens from Morrow Mountain; (c-e) artifacts from Morrow Mountain

south of Hardaway (Daniel and Butler 1996). Morrow Mountain (31St18) is clearly the most spectacular quarry identified in the Piedmont and appears to have been the most intensively exploited quarry in the region during the Early Archaic. It was first recorded in the Research Laboratories of Anthropology site files in 1958, although it had apparently been known as an archaeological site much earlier. Today Morrow Mountain is the

Figure 3.3. Aphyric rhyolite artifacts in the Hardaway assemblage: (a-b) Hardaway-Dalton points; (c-d) bifaces

main feature of the state park bearing its name. Quarry debris is present virtually everywhere on the mountain. In fact, rhyolite flakes and chunks are so dense that they literally pave most of the summit and slopes.

Although Morrow Mountain has been known for decades, it has received little systematic archaeological investigation. Recent investigations included a reconnaissance survey of about 162 ha of park ground, along with some surface collecting and limited excavations on Morrow Mountain (Hargrove 1989). This work indicated that the quarry encompassed the summit and slopes of the mountain as well as about 600 meters of the narrow ridge extending north of the mountain (Hargrove 1989:18).

Porphyritic Rhyolite. Three types of porphyritic rhyolites are recognized on the basis of the presence of certain phenocrysts: (1) plagioclase porphyritic, (2) quartz porphyritic, and (3) plagioclase-quartz porphyritic. These phenocrysts are disseminated in a fine-grained to sugary textured groundmass that is light to dark gray in color. Flowbanding is less pronounced, if it is present at all, among this group. Quarries of this rhyolite group are abundant within a radius of a few kilometers around Hardaway on both sides of the Yadkin River and can be associated with specific mountains (Daniel and Butler 1996).

With respect to previously existing raw material categories, the term "felsic tuff" (Novick 1978) used by many South Carolina archaeologists corresponds to the plagioclase porphyritic rhyolite mentioned above. Similarly, the category "porphyritic rhyolite" corresponds to the plagioclase-quartz porphyritic rhyolite described here (see Novick 1978:427–428 for descriptions of "felsic tuff" and "porphyritic rhyolite"). I made these determinations on the basis of conversations with several South Carolina archaeologists and after examining the raw material type collection at the South Carolina Institute of Archaeology and Anthropology.

Rhyolitic Tuff. The term "tuff" refers to an alternative form of volcanic deposition. Volcanic eruptions can expel material as magma, as in the case of rhyolitic flows mentioned above, or as ash and dust, as in the case of rhyolitic tuffs. The tuffs seen in this study, both in artifacts and at quarries, are variable in color and texture. This variability includes various shades of green to light gray and both fine and somewhat coarse-grained stone. The heterogeneous nature of these tuffs suggest they came from several source locations. Some examples resemble rhyolitic tuff sources identified in the northern Uwharries near Asheboro (Daniel and Butler 1996); others do not. Nevertheless, these other sources probably lie within in the Carolina Slate Belt.

Rhyolitic Breccia. Although no examples of this raw material were noted in the Hardaway assemblage, a few breccia points were noted in the collections survey (Chapter 7). Breccia is a coarse-grained rock composed of angular, broken rock fragments that are relatively large (i.e., a few millimeters in diameter) and are cemented together in a finer-grained matrix.

No volcanic breccia quarries were observed in Uwharries, although outcrops of this stone were observed during the survey. One such quarry, however, was located in Chatham County about 74 km northeast of Hardaway (Daniel and Butler 1996).

Greenstone. As mentioned previously, greenstone is another significant lithologic unit around Hardaway (Conley 1962). It is a dark green, compact rock that is somewhat coarse grained. Greenstone is found in the Hardaway assemblage primarily in the form of hammerstones and anvils (Chapter 4). Its virtual absence in the flaked-stone assemblage is probably explained by its hard, dense nature and relatively poor fracture qualities in comparison with the rhyolite.

Metasedimentary Stone

In contrast to the quantities of metavolcanic rock noted in the Hardaway assemblage, relatively minor frequencies of only two types of metasedimentary stone were observed: argillite and a green metasiltstone.

Argillite. Argillite is another major lithologic unit around the Hardaway site, underlying both the greenstone and rhyolite (Conley 1962). It is a metamorphosed sedimentary rock composed of alternating silt and clay layers. Fresh argillite is light to dark green in color; it also appears in various shades of gray. The major characteristic of this rock is its thin graded bedding, generally less than 15 mm in thickness (Conley 1962.5). This bedding all but precludes a predictable conchoidal fracture in most specimens. Moreover, the poor flaking quality and soft nature of argillite make it a less desirable stone for knapping than rhyolite. Although numerous argillite outcrops were observed during the quarry survey, none were identified as having been quarried prehistorically. Nevertheless, the argillite in the Hardaway assemblage was probably obtained locally.

Green Metasiltstone. Green metasiltstone is a very siliceous-looking green material that actually resembles a green chert. It has apparently been described elsewhere as a welded vitric tuff (e.g., Novick 1978:428). Petrologic analysis, however, identifies this substance as a metasiltstone closely related to the argillite sequence (Daniel and Butler 1996). Unlike argillite, green metasiltstone is of particular interest because of its apparent high flaking quality. Indeed, even fluted points, commonly known for being manufactured from high quality cryptocrystalline raw materials (e.g., Goodyear 1979), have been found made from this stone in North Carolina (e.g., Tippitt and Daniel 1987:figure 9.8a). Moreover, it is likely that this is the same stone identified as "green silicified slate" in Perkinson's (1971, 1973) survey of fluted points for North Carolina. Unfortunately, the source of this stone has not yet been located. The petrologic similarity of this metasiltstone to argillite would suggest a source relatively close to Hardaway, however. I discuss this possibility at greater length in Chapter 4.

Chert

The category of chert includes all cryptocrystalline rock identified archaeologically as Coastal Plain chert and Ridge and Valley chert. Other cryptocrystalline rock, such as chalcedony and jasper, is also included.

Coastal Plain Chert. The primary type of Coastal Plain chert identified in both the Hardaway assemblage and the collections survey appears to be "Allendale chert." This chert is named for its source in western Allendale County, South Carolina, which represents the greatest source of cryptocrystalline stone raw material known within the state. There, in the vicinity of the Savannah River, several quarries have been mapped, tested (Goodyear and Charles 1984), and examined petrologically by a geologist (Upchurch 1984). The few examples in the Hardaway assemblage are dark yellow or brown, typical of the earth colors that characterize Allendale chert (Goodyear and Charles 1984:5). Some examples also display a glossy pink to dark red tint that is presumably the result of heat treating (Anderson 1979). An additional characteristic of Allendale chert is the presence of tiny fossils in its groundmass.

Ridge and Valley Chert. These cherts are very fine grained and lustrous and are generally dark blue to bluish gray in color. The few examples seen in the Hardaway assemblage (Chapter 4) and collections survey (Chapter 7) appear to be a variety of chert referred to as "Knox chert" that occur in nodular and tabular forms along the lower Little Tennessee River and its tributaries in East Tennessee (Kimball 1982, 1985).

Jasper. Several varieties of jasper were identified in the Hardaway assemblage and collections survey. Generally this stone ranges from a dark brown to fairly homogeneous honey-colored material. Some specimens also display a waxy gloss.

Known jasper sources are rare in the North Carolina Piedmont. One such source is recorded in Stokes County (SK38, Research Laboratories of Anthropology site file) about 120 km north of Hardaway, but it has not been determined to be the source of any of the specimens examined during this project. That being said, it should also be noted that what archaeologists call jasper in North Carolina sometimes strikingly resembles a honey-colored chert that I have observed from the Allendale quarries mentioned above (see also Goodyear and Charles 1984:115).

Chalcedony. Two varieties of what I have labeled chalcedony were identified in the Hardaway assemblage. One variety is a very fine-grained and glossy semitranslucent reddish orange color, while the other is a fine-grained tan color. The sources of these materials is unknown.

Other Chert. This category accounts for several varieties of cherts that do not fit in any of the above categories. One specimen is a lustrous light gray to grayish green finely banded material that exhibits sporadic dark speckles. Another example is a homogeneous grayish green lustrous stone that appears to be faintly banded. A final specimen is a translucent bluish green, somewhat grainy stone. Although it appears chertlike in quality, it may actually be a variety of quartz from Virginia (Larry Kimball, personal communication 1992). The sources of these cherts are unknown.

Quartz

This category includes the ubiquitous white vein quartz that was used prehistorically as well as the less commonly used quartz crystal and orthoquartzite.

Quartz. Most quartz occurs in milky white or translucent veins ranging from a few centimeters to several meters in thickness throughout the Piedmont; it also occurs in cobble form in the gravels of major Piedmont rivers (House and Wogaman 1978:53; Novick 1978:433). Although quartz outcrops are quite numerous across the Piedmont, the stone's flaking quality appears to have been quite variable. Most archaeological specimens appear crudely flaked, suggesting a relatively poor conchoidal fracture. Other quartz artifacts, however, are quite well made. This latter group appears to have been flaked from a more "glassy" textured quartz.

Quartz Crystal. Quartz also occurs in a colorless, transparent or nearly transparent variety. Moreover, this quartz usually comes in hexagonal crystals of varying size that can be found throughout the Piedmont. Some of the larger specimens, with their glassy texture and absence of impurities, would have made excellent flaking material. A few examples of some small bipolarly flaked crystals from the Hardaway assemblage are discussed in Chapter 4.

Orthoquartzite. Orthoquartzites are composed of quartz sand grains cemented by silica (Novick 1978:433; Upchurch 1984). Although no examples of this raw material are present in the Hardaway assemblage, a few orthoquartzite points were observed in the collections survey (Chapter 7). Orthoquartzite sources are known from the lower Santee River area

(Charles 1981:15; Anderson et al. 1982:120–122) and Savannah River Valley (Goodyear and Charles 1984:116). Although no outcrops of this material are known from the North Carolina Coastal Plain, orthoquartzite has been found in underground corings in Halifax County (Wise et al. 1981).

4

Artifacts

The artifacts recovered from Hardaway were limited almost entirely to stone tools and flaking debris. Excluding points that postdate the Early Archaic period, the first portion of this chapter presents a detailed morphological analysis of over 2,000 tools from the selected units described in the previous chapter and also makes some tentative inferences about tool function. These tools include those artifacts classified as tools on the catalog sheets as well tools and tool fragments I identified during my inspection of the debitage collection. The second portion of the chapter deals with the flake analysis. Ultimately, this chapter provides a framework for interpreting the organization of the stone tool technology at Hardaway as discussed in Chapter 5.

My discussion closely follows Coe's (1964) stone tool classification for two reasons. First, it provides a consistency with the previous work at Hardaway as well as at other Archaic sites, where the classification has been generally employed. Second, in the case of the unifacial tool types, Coe's typology is implicitly based on blank type and modification, which, as the following discussion indicates, is well suited for this analysis.

ANALYTICAL METHODS

Both metric and nonmetric attributes, recorded for each tool type, are described in Appendix A. With regard to statistical procedures, I emphasized the methods of exploratory data analysis (EDA) in looking for significant patterning (Tukey 1977; Velleman and Hoaglin 1981) among metric data. EDA stresses the visual display of data rather than summary statistics. It also has the advantage of not relying on the statistical assumption of normality, an assumption often not warranted with archaeological data. Similarly, EDA relies on the "resistant" measures that are not overly influenced by extreme values. The more resistant measures include the median and the hinge spread, which are depicted in the form of box plots and are commonly used in EDA, since they visually summarize a distribution of values for a particular variable. As the name implies, the data are illustrated in a boxlike graph, with the median indicated as a horizontal line within the box. The edges of the box constitute the upper and lower hinges, which are median values for the upper and lower halves of the data. The difference between the two hinges represents the hinge spread and thus identifies the range covered by the middle half of the data.

The remainder of the graph includes a solid line called a whisker that runs out from each hinge. The whiskers show the range of values that fall within 1.5 hinge spreads. Some data batches include outlier values, which are marked by an asterisk and are termed "outside," and extreme values, which are termed "far outside" and are labeled with a zero. Velleman and Hoaglin (1981:66–69) describe the determination of these in detail.

In addition, although EDA places less emphasis on tests of statistical significance, McGill and others (1978) implemented confidence intervals around the medians of several groups in a graph called a notched box plot. The box is notched, so that it forms an interval around the median, and returns to full width at the upper and lower boundaries of the confidence interval. If the intervals around the medians of two different data batches do not overlap, then the two population medians are different at a 95 percent confidence level. This form of box plot is useful for making simultaneous comparisons between groups and is used extensively in this analysis.

BIFACES

Bifaces are defined by the presence of a flaking pattern intended to cover both faces of the artifact in order to reduce its thickness and sometimes to produce a sinuous working edge. The bifacial series of artifacts from Hardaway includes all points, other bifaces, and adzes.

Points

The majority of identifiable Early Archaic points in the assemblage were classified as belonging to the Hardaway, Palmer, or Kirk complexes (Coe 1964). A few point types, however, could not be assigned to the above categories. Nevertheless, they do resemble Early Archaic point types recovered elsewhere in the Southeast and were classified accordingly.

Hardaway-Dalton Points. The Hardaway-Dalton can be described as a somewhat lanceolate shaped, relatively thin biface with a deeply concave-eared base (Coe 1964:64) (figure 4.1). The Hardaway-Daltons, of course, are technologically similar to the Dalton forms more commonly known

Figure 4.1. Hardaway-Dalton points

from Missouri and Arkansas (Goodyear 1974, 1982; Morse 1971; Morse and Morse 1983).

A total of twenty-five Hardaway-Daltons were recovered in the excavation units examined here. Unfortunately, only sixteen of these could be located for analysis. Of those, six were complete. The remaining ten artifacts included four ear fragments and six specimens that were missing tips and/or ears; a classic example of an impact fracture is present on one of the broken specimens (figure 4.1b).

Two distinctive characteristics of the Hardaway-Dalton include its deep, ground basal concavity and eared base. Basal thinning is also common with flutelike flake scars originating from the basal concavity. Two basal forms are present in Hardaway-Dalton points: one form displays incurvate lateral edges with outflaring ears (e.g., figure 4.1f,g), while the other exhibits more straight-sided lateral edges with ears that point downward (e.g., figure 4.1c,d). The ears on both forms are usually rounded but are occasionally pointed. Coe (1964:64) described the incurvate lateral-edged specimens as having "broad, shallow and roughly parallel" side notches. This characteristic, however, is not to be confused with the distinct, small, U-shaped side notches of the Hardaway Side-Notched discussed below. The significance of this variation in basal forms is unknown, but given that the Hardaway Side-Notched point also possesses small outflaring ears, it is tempting to speculate that the distinction may be a temporal one. There may also be a geographic component to this basal distinction, since the outflaring-eared form is rare throughout South Carolina, being common only in the north-central part of the state (Goodyear et al. 1989). In North Carolina, on the other hand, the outflaring-eared base may be more common.

Blade edges of the Hardaway-Dalton are usually straight, resulting in a triangular shape; however, some blades are convex or excurvate in form (figure 4.1f; Claggett and Cable 1982:plate 3). Blade resharpening often results in a distinct break between base and blade, so that the point has a shouldered appearance. Two additional characteristics of Hardaway-Dalton blade edges are serrations and, to a much lesser extent, beveling. Blade edges, which are lightly serrated with only slight beveling, if any, contrast with Arkansas forms, which are noted for their distinctive alternate beveling (Goodyear 1974).

Hardaway Side-Notched Points. The Hardaway Side-Notched point is the last of the three types that Coe (1964:120) described as comprising the Hardaway complex. It is a relatively small, thin point identified by its small U-shaped side notches and recurved base, which give it its "horned appearance" (Coe 1964:67). These points typically have triangular blades (figure 4.2).

The assemblage includes a total of eight Hardaway Side-Notched points: two complete specimens, five with missing tips, and one basal fragment. On average, Hardaway Side-Notched points are smaller than Hardaway-Dalton points, although some individual specimens can approach the width of Hardaway-Daltons (e.g., figure 4.2e).

Coe (1964:81) originally suggested that the Hardaway Side-Notched type was geographically limited to the North Carolina Piedmont. Subsequent work in the Southeast suggests that this statement is largely correct. Using data gathered by Tommy Charles (1981, 1983, 1986) in a statewide collections survey of South Carolina, Sassaman (1996) has shown that the distribution of Hardaway Side-Notched points is fairly restricted to the northern (i.e., Piedmont) part of the state. It is also noteworthy that Sassaman (1996) observed that over half of these points are made from rhyolite and thus reflects the distribution's proximity to the Uwharrie Mountains. In contrast, the side-notched Taylor point predominates in the

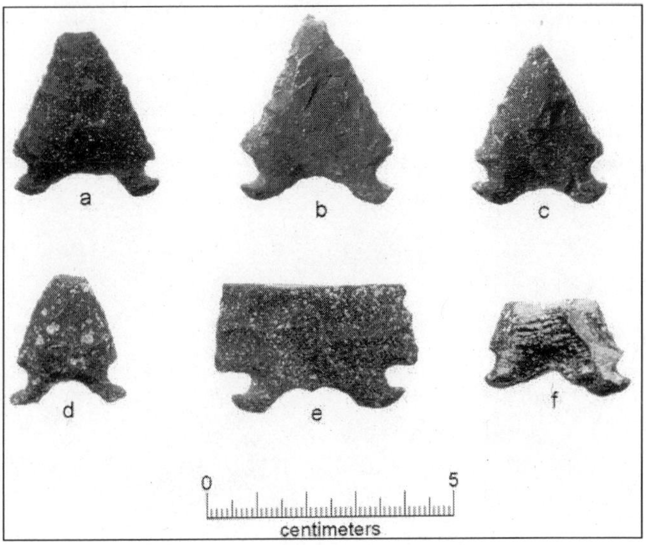

Figure 4.2. Hardaway Side-Notched points

southern half of the state, so that these two points appear to be roughly coeval.

Other Side-Notched Points. A total of six other side-notched points identified in the assemblage do not fit any previously defined cultural-historical category for North Carolina. One of these artifacts somewhat resembles the just mentioned Taylor point (figure 4.3a). It is defined on the basis of its small U-shaped side notches, slight basal concavity, and square basal edges (Michie 1966:123–124). Blade edges are usually beveled, but the specimen here lacks this feature. Moreover, its tip is missing as a result of an impact fracture.

Taylor points are restricted to the southern half of South Carolina, confined to the Coastal Plain and Fall Line areas (Sassaman 1996). The Taylor-like specimen is highly weathered and made from some metavolcanic stone, probably a rhyolitic tuff that may not have its source in the Uwharrie Mountains. This combination of point style and raw material suggests an origin outside the North Carolina Piedmont.

The remaining five side-notched points are also not commonly found in North Carolina. Three specimens (figure 4.3b–d) somewhat resemble the unbeveled Bolen point from Florida (Bullen 1975). The artifact in figure 4.3e was originally classified as a drill and was described as a reworked Palmer (Coe 1964:figure 62c). The notches on this specimen, however, appear to be side notches rather than corner notches. Unlike Palmer points, this specimen also appears to have an eared base; however,

Figure 4.3. Other side-notched points

this feature may have been the result of a break along the base rather than having been intentionally manufactured.

Small Dalton Points. A final group of seven points that also do not fit any previously established cultural-historical types from North Carolina, have been identified in the assemblage as small Daltons, for the lack of a better label (figure 4.4). Several of these specimens were recognized during the 1970s excavations and were casually described as "Hardapalmer" points, since they exhibit technological affinities with both Hardaway and Palmer points.

Two of these points (figure 4.4a,b) actually resemble small Dalton points (Morse and Morse 1983:figure 5.2a). They exhibit a slight to moderately concave-eared base with the appearance of rudimentary side or corner notching. Blade shapes are triangular with marked serrations.

Four other points (figure 4.4c–f) are morphologically similar to the previous two but have somewhat more distinct notching. In fact, the specimen in figure 4.4d could almost be labeled a Hardaway Side-Notched. In any event, some of the these points bear a resemblance to the San Patrice points defined by Webb (1946) and Webb, Shiner, and Roberts (1971) for East Texas and Louisiana. In particular, they bear some affinity to the St. Johns variety of San Patrice (Ensor 1985:figure 2, f–i). Recently Ensor

Figure 4.4. Small Dalton points

(1986) has summarized San Patrice as a Dalton manifestation along the central and western Gulf Coastal Plain and has argued for its chronological placement as a Gulf Coastal expression of the Dalton horizon.

A final broken rudimentary point (not illustrated) is interesting because the blade tip has been resharpened into a spurlike tip. Given their morphology, all these points probably represent a late Dalton manifestation perhaps contemporaneous with or slightly postdating Hardaway Side-Notched points.

Palmer and Kirk Corner-Notched Points. Two somewhat similar corner-notched projectile point types with triangular blades stratigraphically follow the Hardaway Side-Notched point at Hardaway: Palmer Corner-Notched and Kirk Corner-Notched.

Palmer points are identified on the basis of their small size, small U-shaped corner notches, and a heavily ground and usually straight base (Coe 1964:67). Blade shapes are roughly triangular with straight to slightly excurvate blade margins that are commonly serrated and sometimes alternately beveled. Kirk Corner-Notched points (Coe 1964:69–70) are morphologically similar to Palmer points only larger. The blade is triangular in shape, with serrated and sometimes beveled edges. Bases are straight to slightly excurvate but for Coe (1964:70) are distinguished from Palmer points by the absence of basal grinding.

A total of twenty-four Palmer Corner-Notched points (figure 4.5) were

Figure 4.5. Palmer Corner-Notched points

identified in the assemblage, two of which are missing. Of the remaining twenty-two, fifteen are whole, and seven exhibit a broken base, a barb, a tip, or some combination of these. Sixteen of the bases were ground along the entire base; fourteen were distinctly ground, and the other two were lightly ground. One base is unground but perhaps as a result of basal resharpening. The remaining five bases displayed at least partial basal grinding.

A total of seventy-two Kirk Corner-Notched points were identified in the assemblage (figure 4.6). Forty-nine of these are whole, while the remaining twenty-three are broken. I have not strictly adhered to the attribute of basal grinding as a defining characteristic between Palmer and Kirk Corner-Notched points. Rather, I have relied more on overall size and shape as well as certain basal characteristics discussed in more detail below. Following Chapman (1977), I have sorted Kirk points on the basis of the presence/absence of basal grinding and basal shape (i.e., straight or excurvate). With regard to the attribute of basal grinding, approximately half (48.6 percent) of the total sample exhibited at least partial basal grinding.

Coe's (1964) emphasis on size and basal grinding—particularly the latter—has been problematical for other researchers in the Southeast who have tried to separate corner-notched points on the basis of these two attributes. At the St. Albans site in West Virginia, for example, Broyles

Figure 4.6. Kirk Corner-Notched points

(1971:63) identified a small Kirk Corner-Notched point metrically similar to a Palmer point but lacking basal grinding. Even the Charleston Corner-Notched point, which was found stratigraphically earlier than the small Kirk Corner-Notched, exhibited bases that were "smooth but not heavily ground" (Broyles 1971:57). Chapman (1977), working in the Little Tennessee River Valley, has similarly found a relatively broad range of variability in early corner-notched points, which he called the Kirk Corner-Notched cluster. This cluster was stratigraphically separated into Upper and Lower Kirk. While basal grinding was present on points in the Lower Kirk cluster, it was not exclusively associated with these forms (Chapman 1977:53). In fact, two categories of points (categories 31 and 33) from the Upper Kirk cluster displayed basal grinding and were described by Chapman (1977:47–48) as similar to Palmer points.

Similar problems in distinguishing Palmer and Kirk points on the basis of basal grinding have been reported in North Carolina. At the Haw River site (Claggett and Cable 1982), approximately 100 km east of Hardaway, alluvial deposits provided remarkably clear stratigraphic separation among several components containing notched points. Overlying a Hardaway-Dalton zone were three corner-notched occupational zones. Within the

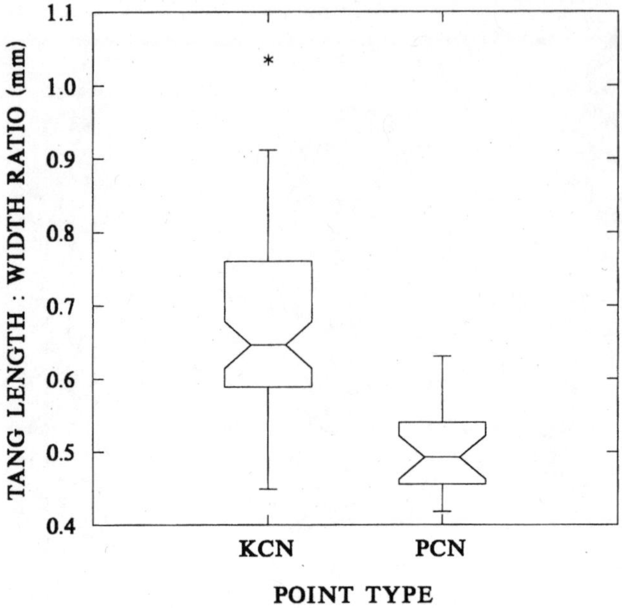

Figure 4.7. Tang length:width ratios box plots for Kirk Corner-Notched (KCN) and Palmer Corner-Notched points (PCN)

lowest of these were several small, basally ground corner-notched points consistent with Coe's Palmer definition (Cable 1982:329). The two overlying zones, however, included examples of larger corner-notched points metrically similar to Kirk points but still exhibiting some degree of basal grinding (Cable 1982:381–382). Thus while the evidence generally supported Coe's observation of the increasing size of corner-notched points through time, it also demonstrated that the attribute of basal grinding did not change as consistently. Given this variability in the presence of basal grinding, Cable (1982:381–382) viewed the differences between Palmer and Kirk points as continuous rather than discrete and even argued for the elimination of the term Kirk Corner-Notched.

All of this emphasis on size and basal grinding does not include the complicating effects that tool use and maintenance can add to typological distinctions. While noting many of the cases described above, Goodyear and others (1979:102) emphasized that corner-notched bases were also subject to alteration during their use life through haft attrition or reflaking altogether (see also Flenniken and Raymond [1986] for a similar discussion concerning notched points). This tendency may be reflected in certain specimens from Hardaway that display a particular pattern of partial basal grinding. In this case, grinding is pronounced on the ears but is absent in the center of the base. The absence may result from haft attrition or intentional reflaking for better binding.

Despite the apparent problems, some researchers have continued to favor the Palmer/Kirk typological labels, particularly in North Carolina (e.g., Davis and Daniel 1990; Oliver 1985; Ward 1983) and South Carolina (e.g., Anderson and Schuldenrein 1983; Goodyear et al. 1979; Hanson and Sassaman 1984; Sassaman 1996), although there is some variation in how size or basal grinding are emphasized as defining attributes. While the present study monitored size and basal grinding, it found another sorting criterion based upon the ratio of tang length to tang width more useful. This characteristic has long been used by University of North Carolina (UNC) archaeologists to help discriminate Palmer points from Kirk points. Generally speaking, Palmer points have a tang that is approximately half as long as it is wide. Consequently, Palmer points have a "stubbier" appearance than Kirk points.

Tang lengths and widths on all measurable corner-notched points recorded in this study indicate that the median tang length:width ratio (0.49) of Palmer points ($n = 20$) is significantly smaller than the same ratio (0.65) for Kirk points ($n = 71$) (figure 4.7). As a further illustration of this characteristic, a scatter plot of tang width versus width for Palmer and Kirk points is shown in figure 4.8. While there is some overlap in the plotted distribution, Palmer points tend to cluster in the lower left of the distribution, while Kirk points cluster in the upper right corner.

Indeterminate Corner-Notched Points. This category includes ten corner-notched points, most of which are broken, that could not confidently be assigned to either a Palmer type or a Kirk type. On the basis of size, however, most of these might be classified as Kirk Corner-Notched.

Two complete points are worth noting. One is extremely resharpened, with its blade extending just a few millimeters above its base. The other point does not morphologically resemble any known cultural-historical type but probably postdates the Archaic period. It is small, made on a flake with slight corner notching, and has a concave base.

Indeterminate Points. This category includes 125 specimens most of which are fragments (e.g., point tips) that could not be assigned to any point type. This total includes 64 unidentified points that were cataloged from the 1950s excavations but could not be located in the collections.

Other Bifaces

A total of 925 other bifaces are present in the assemblage. I have divided this category into four groups: I, II, III, and Indeterminate. Biface manu-

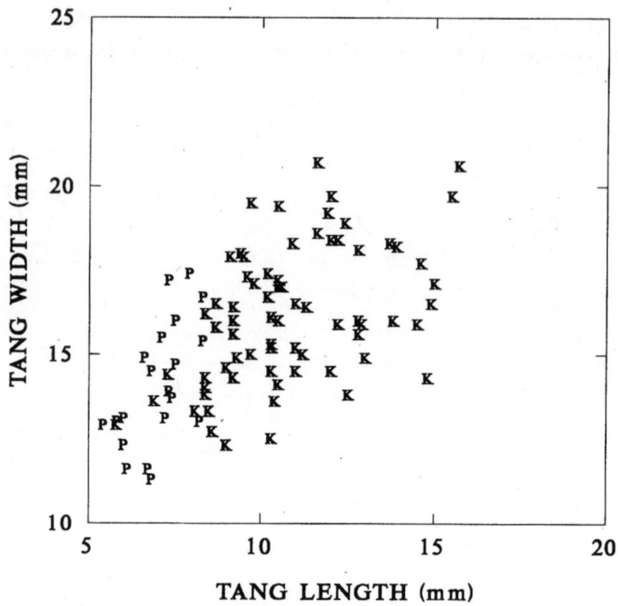

Figure 4.8. Scatterplot of tang length versus tang width for Kirk Corner-Notched (K) and Palmer Corner-Notched points (P)

facture was clearly undertaken at Hardaway (Coe 1964:70), and the following typology attempts to measure this reduction sequence. Coe (1964:50) called these bifaces "quarry blades"; they represent unfinished points, bifacial cores, or tools such as knives. Type II and III bifaces, in particular, may include some of the latter group.

The goal of a lithic reduction sequence is to thin and shape the tool into a finished form. The relative degree of thinness indicates the stage of the continuum at which the product lies. Here the ratio of artifact thickness to width is used as a rough measure of biface completeness. Later reduction stages are relatively thinner than earlier ones, a tendency clear in the Hardaway biface data (figure 4.9).

Type I Bifaces. Most of these bifaces might be termed blanks (Crabtree 1972:42; Muto 1971) in the sense that it is not possible to determine the finished form of the tool (figure 4.10a–c). They are roughly oval to irregular in plan view with a highly irregular flake scar pattern; sometimes it covers both surfaces, but often it is restricted to the margins of both faces, so that a markedly sinuous edge often results. Type I bifaces (n = 132) have the greatest median thickness:width ratio (0.48) of all the bifaces.

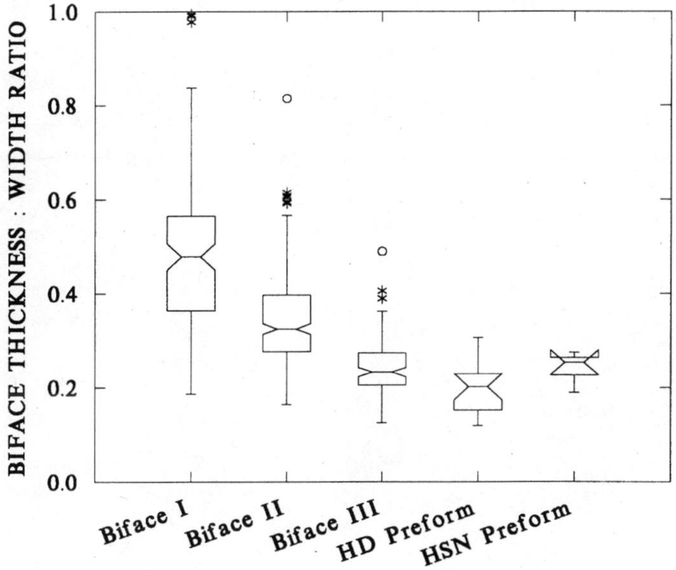

Figure 4.9. Biface thickness:width ratio box plots

Many of these bifaces exhibit deep expanding flake scars on their surface. Multiple hinge and step fractures are also common. Most of these specimens appear to have been reduced originally from large thick flake blanks, while some appear to be made on larger blocky chunks. Many of these bifaces may never have been intended for further reduction into preforms; rather, they more closely resemble bifacial cores. Fifty-six percent (n = 88) of this group were discarded whole. The remaining broken specimens (n = 68) exhibit numerous hinge and step fractures along with some lateral snaps.

Type II Bifaces. Type II bifaces (n = 251) are relatively thinner (thickness:width ratio = 0.33) and more symmetrical than Type I bifaces (figure 4.10d–f). They are oval in plan view and have somewhat symmetrical margins, with a rounded to slightly pointed tip and a rounded base. The tool edges are less sinuous than on Type I bifaces. The flake scar pattern is somewhat irregular and covers almost the entire surface of both tool faces. Moreover, many of the opposing flake scars are in contact and are relatively shallow and less prominent than are Type I biface scars, although some deep scars do occur. Finally, a distinct biconvex cross section is present. Only about 30 percent (n = 122) of these bifaces were discarded whole. Lateral snaps, followed by hinge and step fractures, account for the vast majority of the remaining production failures (n = 283). While many

Figure 4.10. Type I and Type II bifaces: (a-c) Type I bifaces; (d-f) Type II bifaces

of these bifaces were likely intended to become points, at least nine examples appear to be bifacial adze preforms. These preforms are described below in the adze discussion.

Type III Bifaces. Type III bifaces (n = 113) are well-shaped thin specimens (thickness:width ratio = 0.23) with a symmetrical outline and edges that are straight to slightly sinuous (figure 4.11). They exhibit a slightly pointed tip and a rounded to squarish base. Flake scars are closely spaced and cover both faces. Approximately 25.6 percent (n = 49) of this group are whole. Lateral snaps again account for the vast majority of the broken specimens (n = 142).

Included in the Type III bifaces are a group of bifaces that I have labeled preforms (cf. Goodyear 1974:24) for both Hardaway-Dalton (n = 20) and Hardaway Side Notched (n = 5) points (figure 4.11:e–h). These preforms are similar to what Coe (1964:64) described as the Hardaway Blade, which he believes predates the Hardaway-Dalton and is coeval with the fluted point tradition (Coe, personal communication 1986). Coe (1964:64) based his interpretation on artifact morphology and its stratigraphic context, placing emphasis on the relative high frequencies of this type that were recovered from the clay in Level IV.

In contrast, Goodyear (1974:24) has viewed the morphological description of the Hardaway blade as representing a preform for the Hardaway-Dalton. Support for this interpretation is seen in a comparison of dimen-

Figure 4.11. Type III bifaces and preforms: (a-d) Type III bifaces; (e-h) preforms

sions between the two artifact forms in this analysis. A comparison of maximum length, width, and thickness between the preform stage (Hardaway Blade) and the completed Hardaway-Dalton shows that the dimensions of the former are generally larger than those of the latter (figure 4.12). This evidence is consistent with the reduction continuum interpretation, but it is not conclusive, given the emphasis that Coe placed on the earlier stratigraphic context of the Hardaway Blade.

Nevertheless, given the site formation discussion in Chapter 2, the stratigraphic evidence for the earlier context of the Hardaway Blade is not convincing. At best the stratigraphic argument is somewhat equivocal, since almost as many Hardaway-Daltons were found in Level IV as Hardaway Blades (Coe 1964:table 7) albeit perhaps not buried in the clay. Moreover, when the frequency distributions of both types are examined by *zone,* slightly greater frequencies of Hardaway-Daltons are found to have been reported from Zone 4 than preforms (Hardaway Blades) (table 2.1). In short, since Hardaway points were manufactured at the site, their preforms must exist, and it seems more parsimonious to interpret the Hardaway Blade as a preform rather than as a separate point type.

Indeterminate Bifaces. This is a residual category for broken bifaces (n = 173) too fragmentary to be placed confidently in any of the previous categories.

Bifacial Adzes. Chipped-stone adzes were not reported in the original site

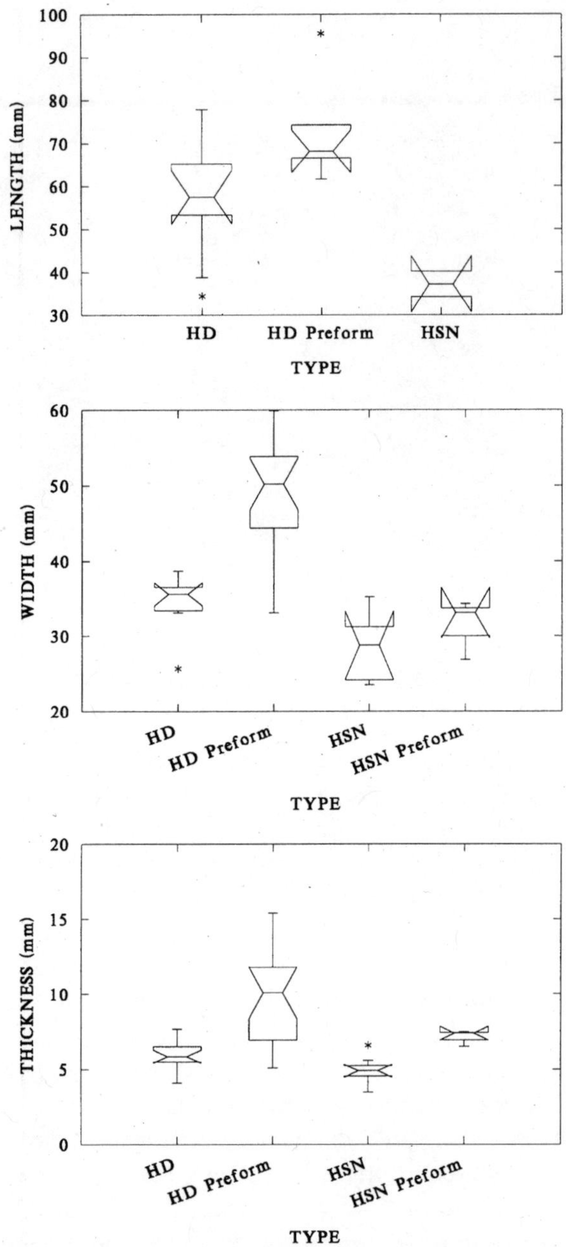

Figure 4.12. Box plots comparing dimensions of length (top), width (middle), and thickness (bottom) for Hardaway-Dalton points (HD), Hardaway-Dalton preforms (HD Preform), Hardaway Side-Notched points (HSN), and Hardaway Side-Notched preforms (HSN Preform)

Figure 4.13. Bifacial adzes and preforms: (a) adze; (b) adze bit; (c-e) adze preforms

report but are clearly present at Hardaway. One complete specimen and one adze bit were identified in the assemblage, along with several preforms mentioned earlier (figure 4.13). These artifacts resemble the Dalton adze described from Arkansas, which was interpreted as a hafted, heavy-duty woodworking tool (Gaertner 1994; Goodyear 1974; Morse 1971; Morse and Goodyear 1973). The complete adze is somewhat oval in outline and bifacially worked (figure 4.13a). The bit is convex in shape and is located at the maximum width of the tool, which tapers down to a rounded butt; the lateral edges are heavily ground. The bits on both the whole and broken specimen (figure 4.13b) display the customary beveled working edge that characterizes the adze (Semenov 1964:126). Portions of both bits are smoothed or extremely ground on both faces. Most of this grinding appears to be from manufacture, although portions of the surface appear slightly polished perhaps as a result of use. In addition, some scratches or striations can be seen on the ground surfaces and are oriented so that they are both parallel and perpendicular to the bit. It is unclear whether these striations resulted from use or from manufacture by grinding. The maximum extent of this grinding on the obverse bit face of the complete specimen is over 35 mm, and at least 20 mm in extent on the bit fragment. Also noteworthy is that the complete specimen appears to have been rendered unusable by a flake scar that gouged approximately one-third of the bit edge.

As noted above, several of the Type II Bifaces described above have been identified as adze preforms (figure 4.13c–e). These preforms tend to have oval shapes in plan view with one end, presumably the butt, being slightly narrower than the other. To finish these specimens into adzes it would be necessary only to manufacture the bit and to grind the lateral and basal edges heavily.

Given their primary association with Dalton remains in Arkansas, these adzes may date as early as the Hardaway-Dalton component, but a few instances of adzes recovered from Early Archaic contexts have been reported outside Arkansas. Both a chipped adze and a polished adze were reported from Kirk strata at the G. S. Lewis site along the Savannah River (Anderson and Hanson 1988:275, figure 6). Similarly, chipped and ground "celts" have also been reported from Kirk and Bifurcate strata at Bacon Farm and Rose Island in the Little Tennessee River Valley (Chapman 1975:16, 1978:68). These adzes may thus not be exclusively a part of a Hardaway-Dalton tool kit.

UNIFACES

Unifacial tools are defined by the presence of intentional flake removal from one surface along one or more margins of an artifact edge. In most cases this retouch is presumed to shape the working edge or bit, although in some cases this mode of retouch is also intended to shape the tool to facilitate hafting. The unifacial series of artifacts from Hardaway primarily includes several types of end scrapers and side scrapers.

End Scrapers

End Scrapers are defined by the presence of steep, regular unifacial retouch that forms a relatively narrow convex bit or working edge. This bit is usually located transversely to the long axis of the tool. A total of 425 end scrapers present in the assemblage have been divided among seven types that include five end scraper types based upon Coe's typology and two additional types defined herein. The various types are defined on the basis of bit size and overall tool shape, which presumably relate to the presence or absence of hafting modifications.

Type I End Scrapers. The Type I End Scraper is a distinctly shaped uni-

Figure 4.14. Type I end scrapers: (a-d) Type Ia end scrapers; (e-i) Type Ib end scrapers

facial tool that has long been associated with both the Paleo-Indian and Early Archaic periods. Coe (1964:73–76) defined two related types at Hardaway on the basis of their small size and triangular to droplike morphologies. Type Ia end scrapers (*n* = 136) exhibit a triangular to trapezoidal shape in plan view with well-executed retouch along their lateral and distal edges (figure 4.14a–d). In cross section, these end scrapers are most often flat trapezoidal (30.1 percent) or offset triangular (17.6 percent) in shape (table 4.1). Type Ib end scrapers (*n* = 41) are similar in form to Type Ia end scrapers except that the former display extensive retouch across their dorsal surface, which gives "the whole upper surface a smooth rounded contour" (Coe 1964:75). Consequently, this latter type exhibits a highly formalized droplike form in plan view and predominately plano-convex (58.3 percent) cross sections (figure 4.14e–i).

Bits on both end scrapers are very well made and display relatively steep continuous unifacial retouch. Median bit widths are moderate among all end scrapers in the assemblage (figure 4.15), and with their relatively shallow bit depth they exhibit only slightly convex-shaped bits. Type I end scrapers are the smallest end scrapers in the assemblage (figure 4.16). This small size probably results from their manufacture on small flake blanks that have undergone extensive modification. Such modification has traditionally been interpreted as the result of hafting, and the specimens from

Table 4.1. Cross-Section Tabulation of End Scrapers

Type	Triangular		Offset Triangular		Flat Trapezoidal		Convex Trapezoidal		Concave Trapezoidal		Plano-Convex		Other		Indeterminate		Total	
	n	%	*n*	%	*n*	%	*n*	%	*n*	%	*n*	%	*n*	%	*n*	%	*n*	%
Ia	15	11.0	24	17.6	41	30.1	8	5.9	6	4.4	10	7.4	13	9.6	19	14.0	136	100
Ib	2	4.9	3	7.3	10	24.4	1	2.4	-	-	24	58.3	1	2.4	-	-	41	100
IIa	13	14.9	15	17.2	25	28.7	6	6.9	1	1.2	3	3.4	6	6.9	18	20.7	87	100
IIb	11	25.0	6	13.6	13	29.5	4	9.1	3	6.8	3	6.8	3	6.8	1	2.3	44	100
III	-	-	-	-	3	33.3	-	-	1	11.1	4	44.4	-	-	1	11.1	9	100
IV	-	-	2	8.0	6	24.0	3	12.0	1	4.0	1	4.0	11	44.0	1	4.0	25	100
V	9	11.4	12	15.2	11	13.9	5	6.3	5	6.3	8	10.1	22	27.8	7	8.9	79	100

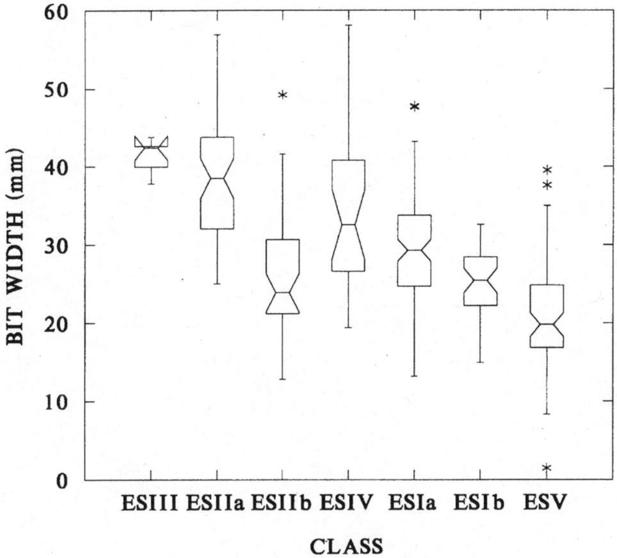

Figure 4.15. Box plots comparing end scraper bit widths

Hardaway appear consistent with this interpretation. Their small size and regularized form, the presence of retouched and tapered lateral edges and thinned proximal elements, and the occurrence of lateral notches all qualify as characteristics of once-hafted tools (Keeley 1982).

The presence of lateral edge retouch was designed to taper and reduce the width of the blank to facilitate hafting (table 4.2). In all cases this retouch was applied to the dorsal surface of the tool. Similarly, additional retouch was sometimes focused on the proximal end of the specimen in order to thin that tool segment to facilitate hafting (table 4.3). This thinning was accomplished by removing several small flakes from the dorsal or ventral faces of the tool or from both faces. While some of the flaking observed on the dorsal surface near the striking platform may have been fortuitous (i.e., the result of the manufacture of the flake blank itself), most did not appear to be. Likewise, the location of flake scars on the ventral surface of end scrapers is clear evidence of deliberate attempts to thin the bulb of percussion. Additional evidence for hafting on Type I end scrapers can be found in the form of small U-shaped notches present on the lateral edges of a small percentage of specimens (table 4.4). Coe (1964:76) called these features haft notches. These notches form small indentations along the tool's lateral edges manufactured from small multiple flake scars that appear to have originated from the ventral surface of the tool.

The variety of modifications to the proximal ends of these end scrapers

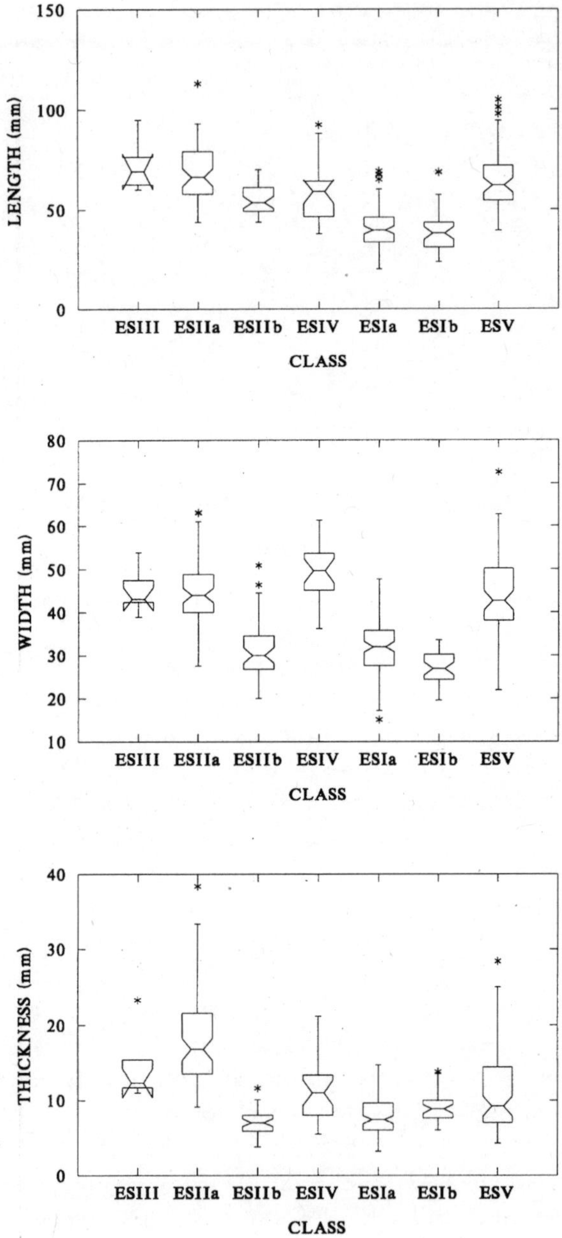

Figure 4.16. Box plots comparing end scraper dimensions of length (top), width (middle), and thickness (bottom)

Table 4.2. Location of Lateral Retouch on End Scrapers

	Right Lateral		Left Lateral		Bilateral		Absent		Indeterminate		Total	
Type	*n*	%	*n*	%	*n*	%	*n*	%	*n*	%	*n*	%
Ia	12	8.8	13	9.6	77	56.6	26	19.1	8	5.9	136	100
Ib	-	-	1	2.4	40	97.6	-	-	-	-	41	100
IIa	12	13.8	5	5.7	41	47.1	12	13.8	17	19.5	87	100
IIb	4	9.1	10	22.7	23	52.3	4	9.1	3	6.8	44	100
III	-	-	-	-	7	77.8	1	11.1	1	11.1	9	100
IV	2	8.0	3	12.0	5	20.0	13	52.0	2	8.0	25	100
V	11	13.9	14	17.7	44	55.7	2	2.5	8	10.1	79	100

Table 4.3. Proximal Thinning Location on End Scrapers

	Dorsal		Ventral		Dorsal and Ventral		Absent		Indeterminate		Total	
Type	*n*	%	*n*	%	*n*	%	*n*	%	*n*	%	*n*	%
Ia	72	52.9	1	.7	10	7.4	28	20.6	25	18.4	136	100
Ib	22	53.7	1	2.4	13	31.7	4	9.8	1	2.4	41	100
IIa	34	39.1	1	1.1	12	13.8	18	20.7	22	25.3	87	100
IIb	26	59.1	3	6.8	1	2.3	7	15.9	7	15.9	44	100
III	2	22.2	-	-	4	44.4	1	11.1	2	22.2	9	100
IV	2	8.0	4	16.0	-	-	17	68.0	2	8.0	25	100
V	1	1.3	-	-	-	-	69	87.3	9	11.4	79	100

Table 4.4. Lateral Notch Location on End Scrapers

	Right Lateral		Left Lateral		Bilateral		Absent		Indeterminate		Total	
Type	*n*	%	*n*	%	*n*	%	*n*	%	*n*	%	*n*	%
Ia	3	2.2	1	0.7	2	1.5	103	75.7	27	19.9	136	100
Ib	1	2.4	3	7.3	4	9.8	32	78.0	1	2.4	41	100
IIa	-	-	-	-	-	-	65	74.7	22	25.3	87	100
IIb	1	2.3	1	2.3	-	-	38	86.4	4	9.1	44	100
III	-	-	-	-	-	-	7	77.8	2	22.2	9	100
IV	-	-	-	-	-	-	23	92.0	2	8.0	25	100
V	-	-	-	-	-	-	73	92.4	6	7.6	79	100

indicate that more than one mode of hafting was employed to secure these tools (cf. Keeley 1982:799). With reference to hafting, Morse (1973:27) has suggested that the extensive lateral retouch on Dalton end scrapers in Arkansas would permit easy insertion into a hollowed-out antler handle. The presence of lateral retouch and proximal thinning on the majority of

Type I end scrapers from Hardaway is consistent with hafting in this manner. The small widths of these scrapers is also consistent with small diameter hafts made of bone or antler. The presence of haft notches, on the other hand, would certainly imply that at least a small number of the end scrapers from Hardaway were secured by wrapping. No obvious traces of a mastic were observed on the Type I end scrapers; of course, this absence may relate to preservation factors.

Certain distinctive breakage patterns are also suggestive of hafting. Broken specimens occur in the forms of both proximal and bit tool ends that exhibit lateral snaps at the presumed hafting point. The same breakage pattern has been observed at the Brand site, where Goodyear (1974:44) considered it unlikely that these small tools could have been used forcefully enough without hafts to snap them in this manner.

Finally, an additional accessory often noted on end scrapers is the "graver spur," which occurs in low frequencies on both Type Ia and Ib end scrapers (table 4.5). It is worth noting that this feature is virtually absent on the other end scraper forms in the assemblage. Graver spurs are flaked on the left or right side of the specimen at the juncture of the tool bit and lateral edge. An isolated example of a bilateral occurrence of a graver spur is present on a Type Ib end scraper. Spurs appear triangular in plan view and could have been used for moderately robust graving activities.

Type II End Scrapers. Type II end scrapers were defined by Coe (1964:76) as being made on flakes about twice as long as their width and with retouch restricted primarily to the bit edge. Two related types were identified, differing primarily in blank size: Type IIa end scrapers were made on "large, thick irregular flake[s] that [were] casually shaped at one end," while Type IIb end scrapers were manufactured from "thin, narrow, prismatic flake[s]" (Coe 1964:76) (figure 4.17).

It should be noted that I have included a number of specimens as Type II end scrapers that exhibit lateral edge retouch, which, given a strict read-

Table 4.5. Spur Location on End Scrapers

	Right Lateral		Left Lateral		Bilateral		Absent		Indeterminate		Total	
Type	*n*	%	*n*	%	*n*	%	*n*	%	*n*	%	*n*	%
Ia	7	5.1	3	2.2	-	-	103	75.7	23	16.9	136	100
Ib	1	2.4	2	4.9	1	2.4	36	87.8	1	2.4	41	100
IIa	1	1.1	1	1.1	-	-	66	75.8	19	21.8	87	100
IIb	1	2.3	-	-	1	2.3	36	81.8	6	13.6	44	100
III	-	-	-	-	-	-	7	58.3	2	16.7	9	100
IV	-	-	-	-	-	-	25	100.0	-	-	25	100
V	-	-	-	-	-	-	79	100.0	-	-	79	100

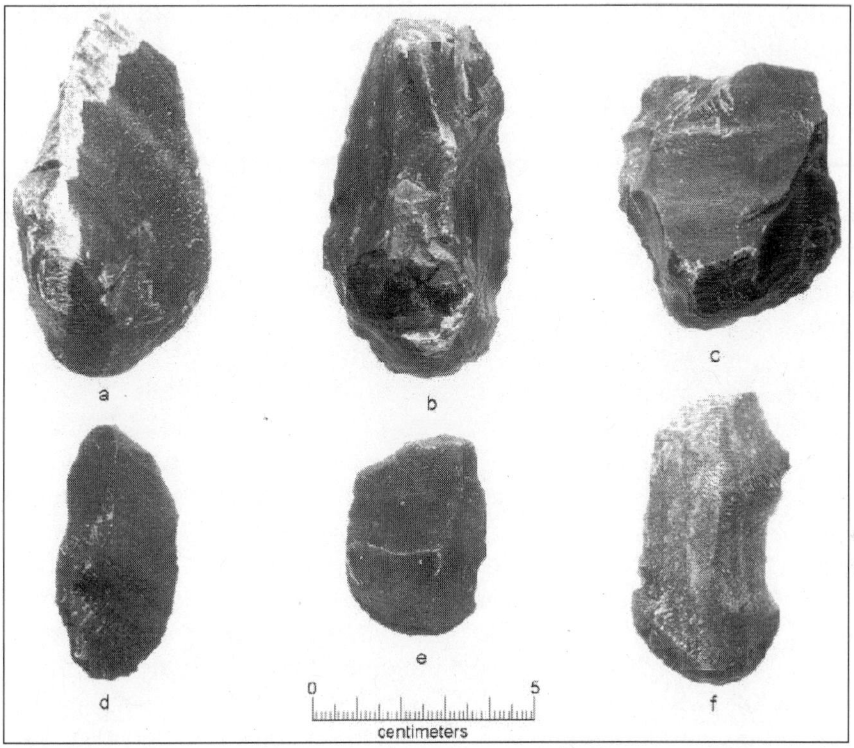

Figure 4.17. Type II end scrapers: (a-c) Type IIa end scrapers; (d-f) Type IIb end scrapers

ing of Coe's definition, would preclude their being included in this class. An examination of the specimens in Coe's analysis (e.g., Coe 1964:figure 65B), however, reveals that Type II end scrapers do display lateral edge retouch; although many specimens do not exhibit retouch as extensive as that present on Type I end scrapers.

Given the presence of lateral retouch, it proved harder to distinguish between Type IIb (n = 44) and some Type Ia end scrapers. I suggest that this difficulty is the result of the artificial separation of essentially one tool type. With the exception of tool length, the Type IIb end scraper is little different in form from Type Ia end scrapers. An examination of both quantitative and qualitative attributes illustrates their overall similarity. The occurrence of lateral retouch, for example, along with proximal thinning, and lateral notching indicates that the Type IIb end scrapers, like Type Ia end scrapers, were hafted (tables 4.2–4.4). Moreover, the only significant difference in tool dimensions between the two end scrapers is that of length (figure 4.16), which may be explained as a result of tool resharpening.

A similar explanation may account for the apparent significant differences in bit width between these two end scrapers. Median bit width (23.9 mm) for the Type IIb end scraper is significantly narrower than the bit width (29.3 mm) for the Type Ia end scraper (figure 4.15). This difference would be expected if the Type Ia end scraper was made on a relatively long narrow flake blank, where the distal end of the flake was narrower than its midsection. The bit would become wider as it approaches the middle of the flake blank through resharpening. That this is the case is evident from the fact that the median maximum width (30 mm) of Type IIb end scrapers is about 6 mm greater than its bit width. Maximum widths (32 mm) of Type Ia end scrapers, on the other hand, are virtually no different from median bit widths (29.3 mm).

The Type IIa end scraper (n = 87), however, is certainly made from a larger flake blank. Along with the Type III end scraper described below, it is the largest end scraper in the assemblage (figure 4.16). It was made from large block-derived flake blanks and exhibits a wide and often irregularly retouched bit. In fact, these tools have the second widest median bit width (38.5 mm) of all the end scrapers. Given its large size (particularly its width and thickness), it may have been hand held; however, many specimens exhibit some lateral retouch and proximal thinning suggesting hafting (tables 4.2–4.3).

As noted above, the lateral edge retouch present on these end scrapers is less uniform than similar retouch on Type I end scrapers and results in only a slight (if any) tapering back from the bit. Rather, the lateral retouch appears to shape the tool only minimally. Given the tools' relatively large size, this retouch in some instances may have been used to modify shape just enough to permit the tool to be hand held rather than hafted (cf. Gould 1980:127–129). Alternatively, this ambiguity may result simply from the fact that this tool was used either unhafted or hafted.

In any event, if some Type IIa end scrapers were hafted, they were undoubtedly hafted in a different size haft from Type I end scrapers. The extreme thickness of the tool in particular argues against the use of a hollow socket haft. Rather, their large width and thickness might reflect the use of wooden hafts.

With regard to hafting, Binford (1979:267) has noted that functionally similar tools may exhibit different hafting modifications that reflect their intended roles (i.e., long-versus short-term usage) in the technology. For example, curated gear may exhibit more design features related to hafting, whereas expedient tools used for similar functions may exhibit minimal and perhaps technically different hafting modifications. Given the minimal nature of lateral retouch, these tools may thus represent more expediently hafted tools intended primarily for use at Hardaway.

Figure 4.18. Type III end scrapers

Type III End Scrapers. Coe (1964:76) described the Type III end scraper as a "large and rough duplication of the more finely made Type I variety." It is a minority type among the end scrapers, as only six tools were identified by Coe (1964:76) and only nine specimens were observed in the present analysis (figure 4.18).

With the exception of tool thickness, Type III is virtually the same size as the Type IIa end scraper (figure 4.16) and was probably manufactured on a similar, albeit thinner, blank form. The Type III end scrapers, however, display more of the flaking qualities of the Type I end scrapers and exhibit the widest median bit value (42.4 mm) among all end scraper types (figure 4.15). Consequently, I view this tool as a large end scraper that needed more dorsal and lateral retouch to fit hafting requirements.

Type IV End Scrapers. The Type IV end scraper (n = 25) is a newly identified form (figure 4.19). I believe these tools were an unhafted, hand-held variety of end scraper. They display virtually no attempt to shape the flake blank beyond the manufacture of the bit. Tool bits exhibit careful regular unifacial retouch, and with the exception of the larger Type IIa and III end scraper forms, median bit width (49.7 mm) is slightly greater than in the remaining end scraper types (figure 4.15).

Over half of the specimens (52 percent) display no lateral retouch, and those that do exhibit a limited amount restricted to the edges near the bit (table 4.2). Furthermore, this retouch appears more related to isolating and defining the bit rather than shaping the lateral margins for hafting.

Although median tool length (50 mm) is not substantially greater than median tool width (49.7 mm) (figure 4.16), this group tends to display a high degree of morphological variability both in flake blank choice and bit placement. Evidence for blank variability can be seen in that 44 percent of the tools do not exhibit the triangular, trapezoidal, or plano-convex forms

Figure 4.19. Type IV end scrapers

that commonly characterize other end scrapers (table 4.1). The implication is that fewer restrictions were placed on blank choice for Type IV as compared with the other end scrapers.

An additional factor that contributes to this morphological variability is the placement of the bit in relation to the blank striking platform. Among the vast majority of end scraper types, maximum flake length parallels the axis of percussion, and bit placement is opposite the striking platform; however, this is not generally the case with Type IV end scrapers. Over half (56 percent, n = 14) of the Type IV specimens have their maximum length oriented at perpendicular or oblique angles to the axis of percussion, requiring bits to be placed laterally to the striking platform.

A final characteristic of this end scraper is the presence of a high incidence of tools with cortex (44 percent, n = 11). Moreover, when present, cortex appears to cover much of the dorsal surface. While this cortex may be fortuitous, it is tempting to speculate that the slightly roughened texture presented by it would have made it easier to grasp the tool.

In short, the variability in flake blank morphology, the absence of unifacial modification beyond bit manufacture, and the presence of cortex on a medium-sized flake blank all suggest a hand-held end scraper that was manufactured on an ad hoc basis, presumably for use in a specific and immediate task.

Type V End Scrapers. The Type V end scraper (n = 79) also appears to have been an unhafted end scraper (figure 4.20). Type V end scrapers were made on block-derived flakes with varied cross sections (table 4.1) comparable in size to Type IV specimens (figure 4.16).

This category is based upon bit size and placement, and a particular mode of lateral edge modification. First, it is distinguished by a relatively

Figure 4.20. Type V end scrapers

narrow, well-made bit that is usually asymmetrically placed at a corner of the blank. In other words, the bit is somewhat cantered toward the distal-lateral intersection of the flake blank, presumably to take advantage of the narrow point of this juncture. Consequently, this type has the narrowest median bit width (19.8 mm) of all the end scrapers in the assemblage (figure 4.15), despite the fact that its median tool width (42.7mm) is one of the highest.

Second, most specimens have straight to slightly incurvate retouched lateral edges that expand away from the bit. This retouch is generally well executed and continuous on one or more commonly both lateral edges. On specimens that exhibit bilateral edge retouch, one side tends to display more extensive and continuous retouch than the other and results in little to no marked juncture between the bit and lateral edges. In contrast, the lateral edges of most of the other end scraper forms tend to contract away from the bit, forming a distinct outline break. This break is also distinguished by differences in the size and steepness in edge retouch between the bit and lateral edges.

Although this tool is labeled an end scraper because of its distinctively retouched bit, its lateral edges may have been used as well. This inference reflects the observed similarity in the mode of retouch between its distal and lateral edges and the fact that lateral retouch was clearly not extensive enough to regularize the tool for hafting. As noted above, this retouch similarity sets this type apart from other end scraper types in the assemblage, which exhibit marked differences in modes of retouch between tool bits and lateral tool edges. If the lateral edge was functional, however, it was apparently used in a different task from the end scraper bit, since none of the lateral edges exhibited the edge rounding—similar to that noted on Type I end scrapers—that was noted on many of the accompanying bits. Another interesting characteristic of this tool type is the presence of double bits on four specimens, oriented at opposite ends from each other (figure 4.20c). Bit placement in this fashion is further indication of an unhafted tool—if we assume that a person would not haft a tool over a bit.

One of these tools is particularly noteworthy, as it appears to have been recycled from another tool type, a Type IV side scraper. Although this side scraper is detailed in the next section, it can be described briefly as having an oval shape with a steeply retouched, relatively thick bit that is broadly convex and parallel to the tool's long axis. Additional thinning opposite the bit is suggestive of hafting modifications. In this instance, an end scraper bit was fashioned on one corner of the former side scraper bit. This end scraper retouch resulted in a distinct break in tool plan view—presumably created to help narrow the corner of the side scraper to adapt to proper end scraper bit width. Further thinning was accomplished by ventral retouch on both a portion of the end scraper bit and its lateral edges.

In sum, given their variable blank morphology, the apparent absence of hafting modifications, and the presence of some tools with two bits, Type V end scrapers were probably also a tool that was expediently made and used. This end scraper type has not been described from any other assemblages in the Southeast. Ellis and Deller (1988), however, have recently identified a very similar type, labeled a "proximal end and side scraper," in Paleo-Indian assemblages from the Great Lakes region.

Functional Considerations. End scrapers have traditionally been interpreted as hide scrapers. Microwear in the form of edge rounding, striations, and polish suggest that many of the end scrapers from Hardaway may indeed be hide scrapers. The association of edge rounding and striations with hide working, of course, has been noted on ethnographic (Hayden 1979), archaeological (Kimball and Chapman 1977), and experimental (Keeley 1980:50) scrapers. A preliminary experimental use-wear study involving hide working with rhyolite tools reproduced edge rounding, striations, and polish similar to that found on a small sample (n = 3) of Type Ia end scrapers (McDevitt 1994). In addition, distinct edge rounding was noted on several end scraper bits during the analysis. In some cases this rounding was so marked that it could be seen with the naked eye. Coe too noticed this pattern when he stated that "nearly all of them [Type I end scrapers] have been used until their cutting edge has worn smooth" (1964:76).

Subsequently, all bits were examined under a minimum of 10× magnification for the presence/absence of edge rounding. Edge rounding appears to be most frequently associated with Type I varieties and occurs on 41.5 percent of Type Ib and 27.2 percent of Type Ia end scrapers. It occurs with much less frequency on Type V end scrapers (20.3 percent) and least of all among Types II and IV end scrapers (ca. 11–12 percent). No edge rounding was observed on Type III end scrapers, although sample size is low.

Moreover, the intensity of rounding was also noted to vary among individual specimens, although it was not systematically recorded. For example, some bit edges exhibited only a light degree of rounding that was confined to the dorsal-ventral bit edge junction, while others displayed a marked band of rounding that extended a millimeter or more up the dorsal face of the bit and virtually obliterated flake scars there. In fact, there is an indication that Type I, and to a lesser extent Type V, end scrapers have the more heavily rounded bits. Finally, some linear features resembling striations oriented transversely to the bit edge were also observed on at least five specimens.

Of particular interest too, is the influence that the condition of the hide (i.e., wet/fresh vs. dry) has on the intensity of edge rounding. In short, a drier hide results in greater amounts of abrasion on the tool edge (Keeley 1980:50; Hayden 1979:225), so that rounding and striations are more pronounced. Thus, if we may push my interpretation even further, many end scrapers appear to have been used on dry hides.

Bit edge angles were also recorded for all end scrapers. Mean bit edge angles were computed from averaging maximum and minimum values for each bit. Following Wilmsen (1970), bit edge angles in lithic analyses are often the basis for functional determinations. Wilmsen's (1970) work is presented in more detail with respect to the side scraper functional discussion; here I discuss only implications for end scraper functions.

Histograms of mean values for each end scraper type indicate that edge angles cover essentially the same range (figures 4.21–4.27). Edge angles are routinely high for each type (ca. 55 degrees to 85 degrees). Wilmsen (1970:73) has suggested a bone and woodworking function for these steep-angled scrapers; however, he also notes that such steepness may be a function of bit resharpening. In this case I view such steep angles as more a reflection of tool exhaustion and the presence of edge rounding as a more reliable indicator of tool function.

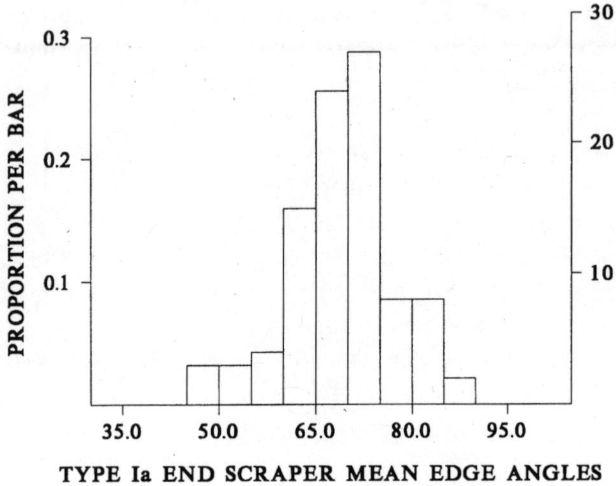

Figure 4.21. Histogram of Type Ia end scraper mean edge angles

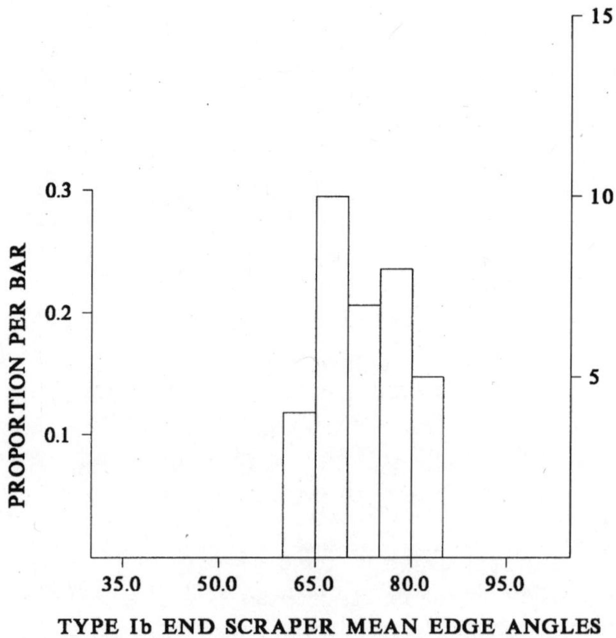

Figure 4.22. Histogram of Type Ib end scraper mean edge angles

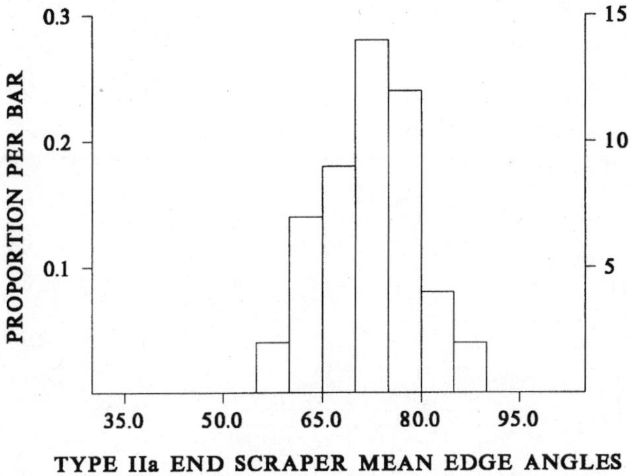

Figure 4.23. Histogram of Type IIa end scraper mean edge angles

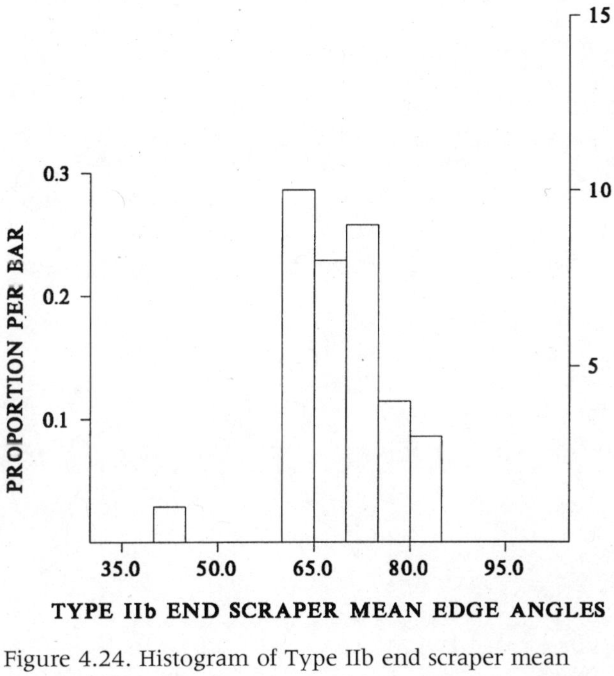

Figure 4.24. Histogram of Type IIb end scraper mean edge angles

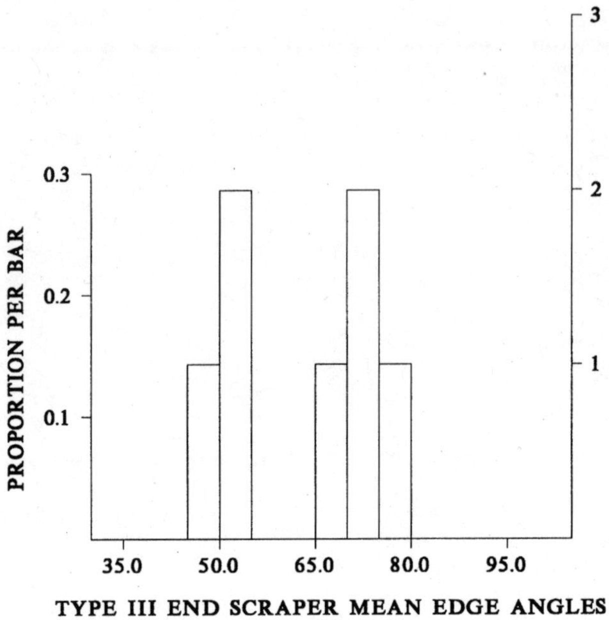

Figure 4.25. Histogram of Type III end scraper mean edge angles

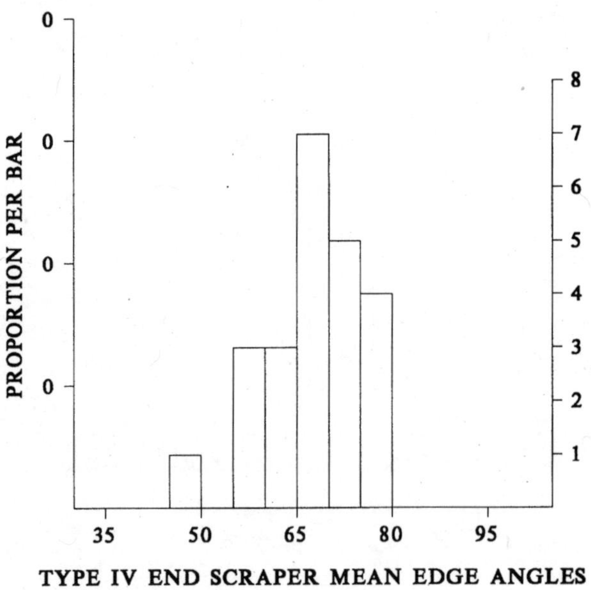

Figure 4.26. Histogram of Type IV end scraper mean edge angles

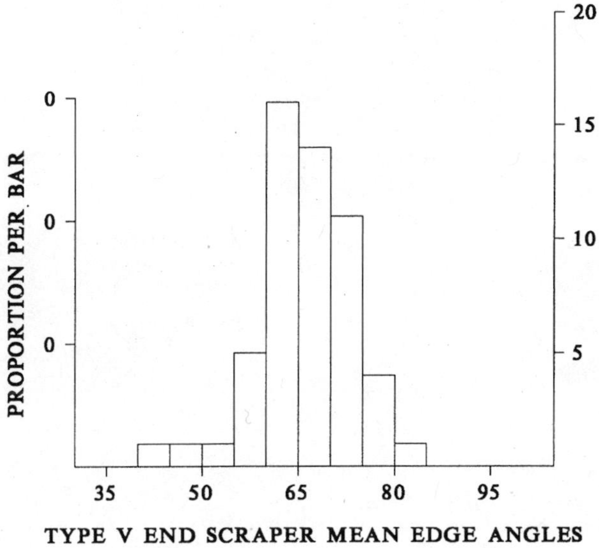

Figure 4.27. Histogram of Type V end scraper mean edge angles

In sum, a preliminary examination of microwear evidence in the form of polish, striations, and edge rounding permits some conjecture regarding tool use. In particular, the noticeable presence of edge rounding on many specimens suggests that, with the exception of the Type III end scraper, all end scraper forms were employed to some degree in hide-working activities. The relatively high frequency of edge rounding associated with the Type I end scrapers suggests that hide scraping was an important function of this tool. (Given a more sophisticated microwear analysis, this frequency may actually be higher.) The next highest incidence of edge rounding is present on Type V end scrapers, which may have been an unhafted but functionally equivalent version of the Type I scrapers. Although the presence of edge rounding on Types IIa and IV would indicate some hide scraping, the low occurrence of this wear pattern (coupled with the tools' less formalized shapes and larger bit sizes) suggests uses somewhat distinct from those of the smaller end scraper types. Along this line, Coe (1964:76) suggested that the Type IIa end scraper was most often used for working hard materials such as wood or bone.

Side Scrapers

Side scrapers are defined by the presence of one or more unifacially retouched working edges that parallel the long axis of the flake blank. A total

Figure 4.28. Type I side scrapers

of 409 side scrapers are present in the assemblage and have been divided into five types. Again, I have followed Coe's (1964) side scraper typology, with the addition of two new types. Side scraper types are identified on the basis of flake blank type, bit retouch, and overall tool morphology.

Type I Side Scrapers. Type I Side Scrapers (n = 20) are manufactured from relatively large, block-derived, oval-shaped flakes such that the working edge is perpendicular to the flake's axis of percussion (figure 4.28). As Coe (1964:77) states, most of these tools retain evidence of their striking platform. These scrapers tend to have offset triangular or flat trapezoidal cross sections, giving them a wide flat appearance (table 4.6). Tool bits exhibit well-executed, continuous retouch, forming working edges that are broad and slightly convex to straight (Coe 1964:77).

Along with the Type IV side scrapers, described below, Type I side scrapers are typically the largest side scrapers in the assemblage (figure 4.30) and could have been hand held, but their regularized shape also suggests a once-hafted tool (Keeley 1982). This possibility is elaborated upon below in the discussion of a morphologically similar tool: the Type IV side scraper.

Type II Side Scrapers. Coe (1964:79) defined Type II side scrapers as being made on "large irregular flake[s]" that possess bits displaying "no attempt to shape the working edge into any other form than what existed." Within this group I have separated two types based upon flake blank size (figure 4.29). The Type IIa side scraper (n = 221), which corresponds to Coe's Type II side scraper, exhibits bits placed on somewhat large flake blanks of various shapes; the Type IIb side scraper (n = 24) is essentially a much smaller version of the Type Ia (figure 4.30).

Table 4.6. Cross-Section Tabulation of Side Scrapers

Type	Triangular		Offset Triangular		Flat Trapezoidal		Convex Trapezoidal		Concave Trapezoidal		Plano-Convex		Other		Indeterminate		Total	
	n	%	*n*	%	*n*	%	*n*	%	*n*	%	*n*	%	*n*	%	*n*	%	*n*	%
I	1	5.0	5	25.0	4	20.0	1	5.0	2	10.0	2	10.0	5	25.0	-	-	20	100
IIa	37	16.7	48	21.7	36	16.3	7	3.2	12	5.4	27	12.2	47	21.3	7	3.2	221	100
IIb	2	8.3	11	45.8	3	12.5	-	-	1	4.1	3	12.5	4	16.7	-	-	24	100
III	26	21.1	33	26.8	28	22.8	2	1.6	6	4.8	16	13.0	12	9.8	-	-	123	100
IV	2	8.7	3	13.0	4	17.4	-	-	-	-	4	17.4	10	43.5	-	-	23	100

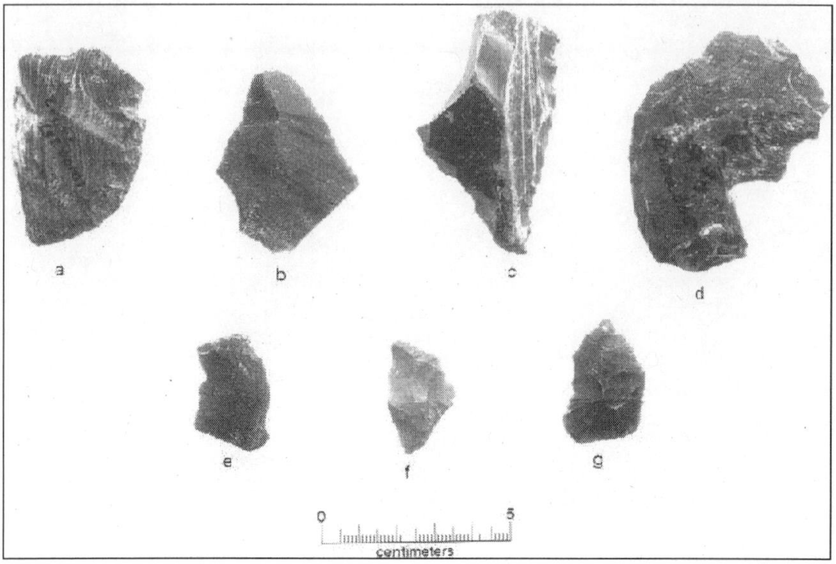

Figure 4.29. Type II side scrapers: (a-d) Type IIa side scrapers; (e-g) Type IIb side scrapers

The small size of the Type IIb side scraper may, in part, be related to its tendency to have been manufactured from a bifacial core rather than the block cores from which the Type IIa side scrapers were predominantly made (see the discussion of blanks in Chapter 5). Only a small number of these tools were identified, but this tool class may be underrepresented in the assemblage. Because of its small size and delicate nature, this tool could easily have passed through the 0.5 in screen during excavation. Moreover, given its delicate nature, it could have suffered postdepositional breakage, which would have made it more difficult to recover. In general, bits for both side scraper types are unifacially retouched lateral edges. A majority of both types have only one bit, but a small percentage (16–17 percent) of both Type IIa and Type IIb side scrapers have double bits (table 4.7). Moreover, the majority of both types exhibit retouch on the dorsal surface of the flake blank. Some Type IIa side scrapers (19.4 percent, n = 43) and Type IIb side scrapers (16.7 percent, n = 4), however, have at least one edge with retouch on the ventral surface. The significance of this mode of retouch, if any, is unknown.

Two Type IIa and one Type IIb side scrapers have bits that are slightly bifacially retouched. Although this bifacial retouch might technically exclude these items from being included in a unifacial class, the bifacial retouch is limited to the bit edge (i.e., it is not intended to thin the entire

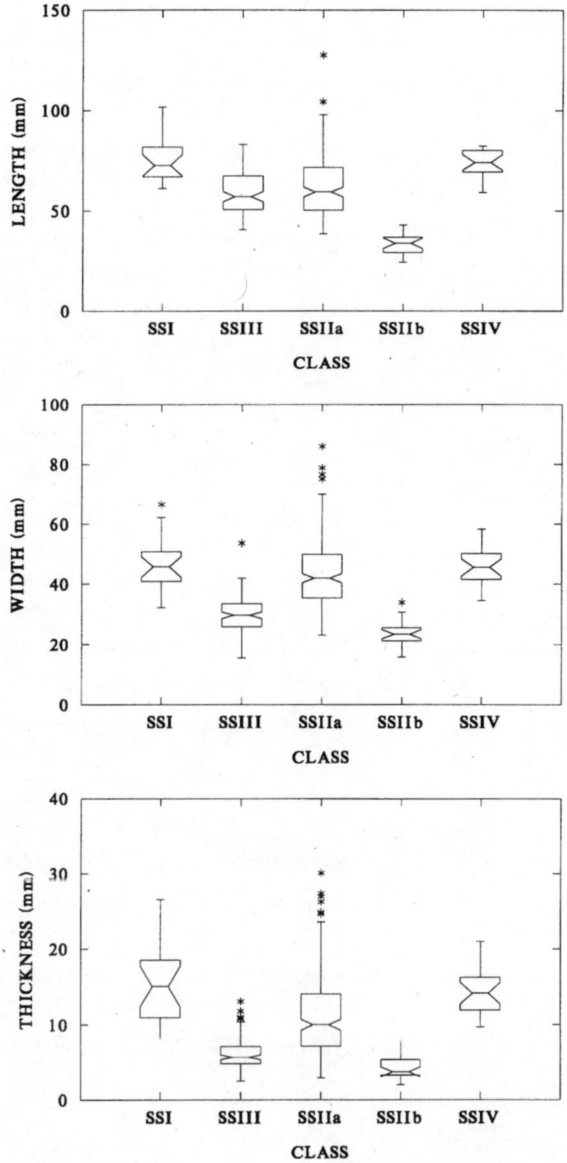

Figure 4.30. Box plots comparing dimensions of length (top), width (middle), and thickness (bottom) for all side scrapers

Table 4.7. Number of Bits for Type II and Type III Side Scrapers

	Single		Double		Indeterminate		Total	
	n	%	*n*	%	*n*	%	*n*	%
IIa	183	82.8	36	16.3	2	0.9	221	100
IIb	19	79.2	4	16.7	1	4.2	24	100
III	90	73.2	33	26.8	-	-	123	100

tool), and in overall morphology the tool is otherwise virtually identical to other side scrapers.

Bits of both scraper types tend to be slightly convex or straight in plan view, although this distinction is somewhat arbitrary because of the difficulty of differentiating these two shapes. Among single-edge Type IIa side scrapers, convex (61.7 percent) and straight (30.6 percent) edges dominate bit shapes (table 4.8). A similar pattern is noted for single-edged Type IIb side scrapers (table 4.9). The majority exhibit one straight and one convex bit edge (36.1 percent) or double straight (19.4 percent) edges, followed by lesser amounts of other bit shape combinations. With the small number of double-edged Type IIb side scrapers, it is hard to determine any significant patterning. It is possible that bit shape is at least partially related to tool function among these artifacts and this is discussed in more depth below.

Similarly, from a use-life perspective, it might be hypothesized that

Table 4.8. Cross-Tabulation of Type IIa Side Scraper Bit Shapes

	Number of Bits					
Bit Shape	Single		Double		Total	
Combination	*n*	%	*n*	%	*n*	%
Single-straight	56	30.9	-	-	56	25.3
Single-convex	113	62.4	-	-	113	51.1
Single-concave	5	2.8	-	-	5	2.3
Single-other	7	3.9	-	-	7	3.2
Double-straight	-	-	7	18.4	7	3.2
Double-convex	-	-	4	10.5	4	1.8
Double-concave	-	-	2	5.3	2	0.9
Straight-convex	-	-	13	34.2	13	5.9
Straight-concave	-	-	3	7.9	3	1.4
Straight-irregular	-	-	3	7.9	3	1.4
Convex-irregular	-	-	1	2.6	1	0.4
Concave-irregular	-	-	1	2.6	1	0.4
Double-other	-	-	4	10.5	4	1.8
Indeterminate	-	-	-	-	2	0.9
Total	181	100	38	100	221	100

Table 4.9. Cross-Tabulation of Type IIb Side Scraper Bit Shapes

Bit Shape Combination	Number of Bits: Single n	Single %	Double n	Double %	Total n	Total %
Single-straight	7	36.8	-	-	7	29.2
Single-convex	9	47.4	-	-	9	37.5
Single-concave	2	10.5	-	-	2	8.3
Single-indeterminate	1	5.3	-	-	1	4.2
Double-straight	-	-	1	25.0	1	4.2
Double-concave	-	-	1	25.0	1	4.2
Straight-convex	-	-	1	25.0	1	4.2
Straight-concave	-	-	1	25.0	1	4.2
Indeterminate	-	-	-	-	1	4.2
Total	19	100	4	100	24	100

double-edge side scrapers represent a more heavily worked single-edged variety. For example, in working with Mousterian assemblages, Dibble (1984, 1987b) has suggested that doubled-edged side scrapers represent a later stage in a continuum of reduction from single-edged side scrapers. According to this interpretation, double-edged side scrapers began their use life as single-edged scrapers but were subsequently converted when a second bit was manufactured on the opposing edge. This reduction model has important implications for interpreting side scraper variability beyond the middle Paleolithic. Due to the morphological similarity of all laterally retouched unifacial tools, the question of intensity of reduction is plausible for any assemblage and bears examination here.

If side scrapers in the Hardaway assemblage were part of a similar reduction sequence, then it would likely manifest itself in the attributes associated with tool size. Given that the lateral edges were retouched, for example, it would be expected that single-edged side scrapers would have greater widths (i.e., would exhibit the removal of less stone) than the double-edged variety, but this expectation is not met. A comparison of single-bit and double-bit tool median widths for Type IIa side scrapers shows similar values that are not significantly different (figure 4.31).

Similarly, an analysis of retouch intensity also does not support the reduction hypothesis. If double-edged side scrapers represent more heavily retouched single-edged scrapers, then they should display the removal of relatively more bit edge than single-edged scrapers. This characteristic was roughly monitored on Type IIa side scrapers by measuring both the minimum and maximum values of the flake scar lengths on side scraper bits. Contrary to the reduction hypothesis, no significant differences exist in median values (either minimum or maximum) between the right bits of

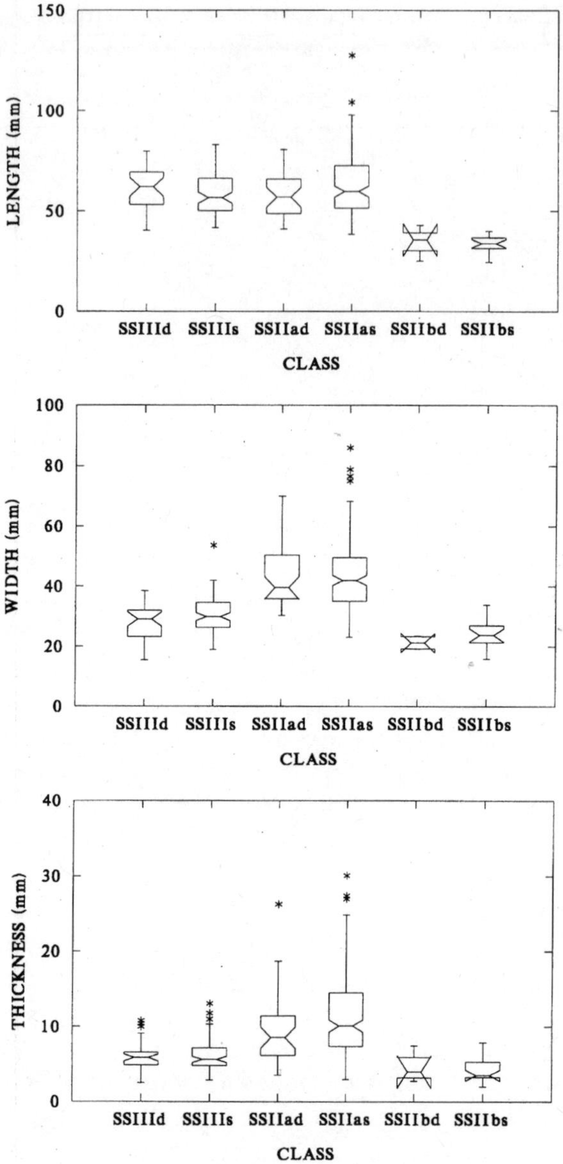

Figure 4.31. Box plots comparing Type II and Type III side scraper dimensions for single-bit (s) and double-bit (d) tools

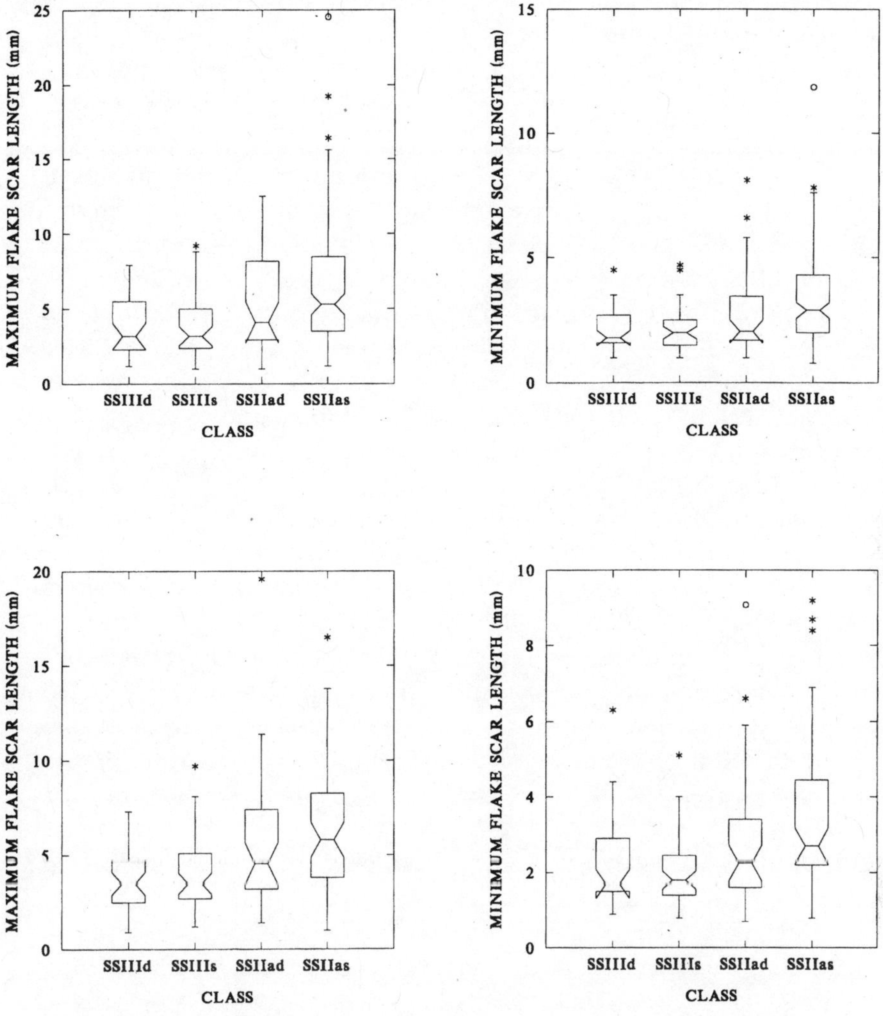

Figure 4.32. Box plots comparing bit retouch lengths of left (top) and right (bottom) bits for single-bit (s) and double-bit (d) Type II and Type III side scrapers

single- and double-edged side scrapers (figure 4.32). In fact, median values for scar length of double bit side scrapers are slightly *smaller* than single bit side scrapers—precisely the opposite of what is anticipated with the reduction model. Similar results are also reached from a comparison of the left bit edges between single- and double-bit side scrapers, except that median minimum retouch lengths are significantly different (figure 4.32).

Again, however, the median value of double-bit side scrapers is smaller than that of the single-bit variety.

Comparisons of tool width and retouch intensity, however, are only an indirect test of the reduction hypothesis, as they assume that both groups were manufactured on blanks of similar size. As Dibble (1987a:39) points out, a more direct test would be to measure how much reduction has taken place on the side scrapers relative to their original blank size. Controlled experimental work (Dibble 1985; Dibble and Whittaker 1981; Speth 1972, 1975, 1981) has shown that original flake size is largely a function of striking platform size; that is, striking platform size is positively correlated with flake size. The relationship between striking platform size and artifact size thus allows us to estimate the amount of reduction that the tool has undergone. On the average, blanks that are more reduced should exhibit smaller ratios of flake area to platform area than blanks less reduced from their original size.

Given this expectation, an estimate of tool reduction was derived on Type IIa side scrapers by dividing the remaining tool surface area (as estimated by the product of its length times width) by the surface area of the striking platform (as estimated by the product of its width times thickness). A comparison of the resulting ratios also produces results that conflict with the reduction hypothesis (figure 4.33). That is, single-edged Type IIa side scrapers have undergone more reduction (i.e., have smaller ratios) than the double-edged group. These results suggest that, if anything, single-edged side scrapers have undergone more reduction than double-edged side scrapers.

The rejection of this reduction hypothesis may be explained, at least in part, by side scraper blank morphology—in particular, the orientation of the striking platform in relation to the long axis of the blank. Side scrapers, by definition, have working edges that are parallel to the long axis of the tool. Most double-edged side scrapers (75 percent, $n = 27$) display striking platforms that are positioned perpendicular to the long axis of the tool, essentially freeing two lateral edges for bit production. On the other hand, only about half (55.7 percent, $n = 102$) of single-edged scrapers display striking platforms positioned in the above orientation. Instead, single-bit side scrapers have higher frequencies of platforms oriented at parallel or oblique angles (34.9 percent, $n = 64$) to the long axis than do double-edged side scrapers (19.5 percent, $n = 7$). Consequently, flake blanks with striking platforms oriented in this manner essentially leave only one edge suitable for bit production.

Given this explanation, the question remains: why do blanks with two available edges exhibit only one bit? The answer may lie in the consistency of median width between double-bit (40mm) and single-bit (42mm) Type

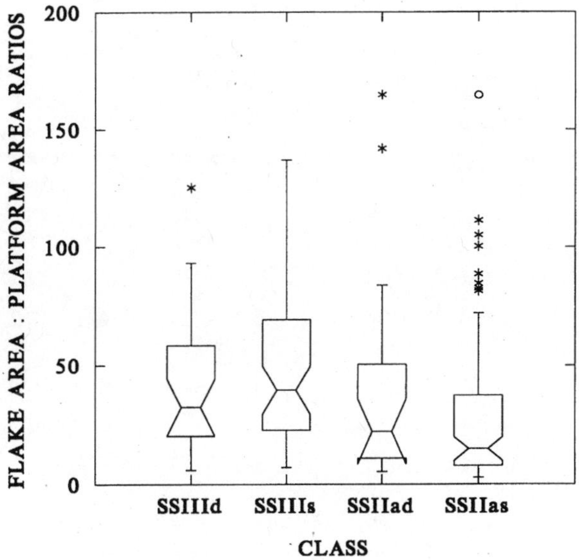

Figure 4.33. Box plots comparing tool reduction indexes for single-bit (s) and double-bit (d) Type II and Type III side scrapers

IIa side scrapers. Apparently, bit edges were retouched until a certain minimum width was attained, at which point the tool was discarded. If so, it was not the number of retouched edges but the width to which the tool was reduced that determined its use life. Presumably this width related to grasping requirements, since these side scrapers were probably unhafted (cf. Dibble 1987a:39).

In sum, the evidence given above suggests that few, if any, of the double-edged side scrapers at Hardaway were reworked from single-edged forms. While both kinds were apparently made on blanks of similar size, the variable shape of these blanks in combination with width restrictions resulted in the use of predominantly one edge for bit production.

Type III Side Scrapers. According to Coe (1964:79), Type III side scrapers were made from relatively thin, narrow flakes (figure 4.34). In fact, Type III side scrapers (n = 123) are bladelike in appearance, being about twice as long as they are wide, and with the exception of the Type IIb side scraper, they have the thinnest median width (5.7 mm) of any side scrapers in the assemblage (figure 4.30).

As with the Type II side scraper, these tools display single (73.2 percent) and double (26.9 percent) bits (table 4.7). Bits are relatively thin and are generally slightly convex to straight in shape (table 4.10). As with the Type II side scraper, too, there appears to be no evidence for an intentional re-

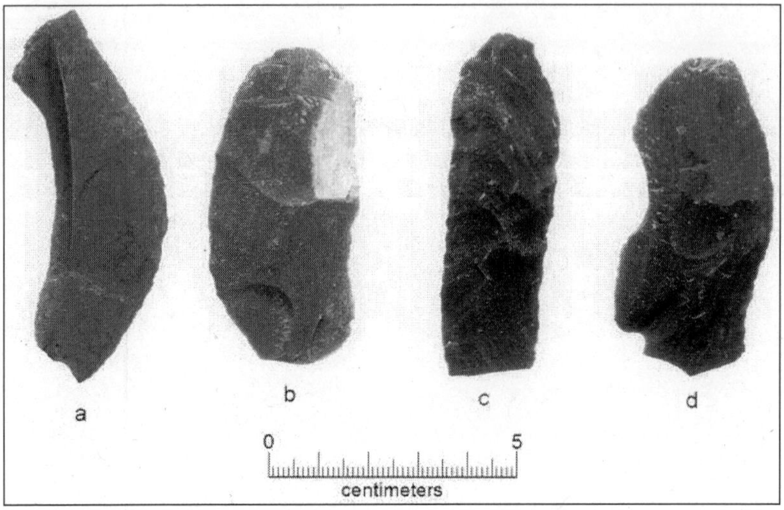

Figure 4.34. Type III side scrapers

duction sequence from single to double bits. No significant differences exist in tool dimensions between single- and double-bit Type III side scrapers (figure 4.31). As noted above, double-edged side scrapers would be significantly narrower in width than single-edged side scrapers if the reduction hypothesis were true. And although the median area ratio of double-edged side scrapers is less than that of the single-edged variety, this difference is not a significant one (table 4.10, figure 4.33). Similarly, the

Table 4.10. Cross-Tabulation of Type III Side Scraper Bit Shapes

Bit Shape Combination	Number of Bits: Single *n*	Single %	Double *n*	Double %	Total *n*	Total %
Single-straight	29	32.2	-	-	29	23.6
Single-convex	45	50.0	-	-	45	36.6
Single-concave	3	3.3	-	-	3	2.4
Single-other	13	14.4	-	-	13	10.6
Double-straight	-	-	9	27.3	9	7.3
Double-convex	-	-	4	12.1	4	3.3
Straight-convex	-	-	9	27.3	9	7.3
Convex-concave	-	-	1	3.0	1	0.8
Straight-irregular	-	-	1	3.0	1	0.8
Convex-irregular	-	-	5	15.2	5	4.1
Concave-irregular	-	-	2	6.1	2	1.6
Double-other	-	-	2	6.1	2	1.6
Total	90	100	33	100	123	100

Figure 4.35. Type IV side scrapers (obverse)

two groups do not differ significantly in retouch intensity either (figure 4.32). As with the Type II side scraper, the implication is that the width to which the tool was reduced and not the number of retouched edges determined tool use life.

Type IV Side Scrapers. I have identified a previously undefined type of side scraper in the Hardaway assemblage: a Type IV side scraper (figures 4.35–4.36). This type includes a total of twenty-three specimens that are very similar morphologically to the Type I side scraper except that they have a bifacial edge.

A comparison of the two scraper types reveals that there are no significant differences in length, width, and thickness (figure 4.30). Likewise, the Type IV side scraper has a relatively thick, broadly convex unifacial bit edge virtually identical to the Type I side scraper bit. Moreover, no significant differences are found in minimum or maximum bit thickness between the two scrapers, nor are there any significant differences in minimum or maximum bit flake scar length (figure 4.37).

The two side scrapers differ in the presence of a bifacial edge opposite the unifacial bit edge of the Type IV scraper on all but two of these tools. These latter two specimens, however, exhibit extensive unifacial thinning of the striking platform that is similar in nature to the bifacial thinning.

Figure 4.36. Type IV side scrapers (reverse)

Two explanations may account for this additional modified edge. First, this bifacial edge could have been functional, resulting in a multipurpose tool. The unifacial edge may have been used for scraping purposes, for example, while the bifacial edge may have been used for cutting activities. This interpretation, however, presents a problem. In order to use the unifacial edge, the tool must be held by its bifacial edge and vice versa. This mode of use is not very practical. Rather, I think the bifacial edge is the result of retouch intended to thin the tool for hafting—much like the proximal thinning present on end scrapers—while the unifacial edge was the actual working edge.

Additional support for this interpretation comes from an examination of the mode of bifacial retouch. The bifacial edge displays relatively large percussion flake scars that appear to have been struck more to thin the edge than to shape it. Moreover, these edges routinely lack small retouch flake scars that are typically the result of sharpening bifacial edges.

If we assume that this modification is designed to facilitate hafting, the question remains as to how the tool was positioned in the haft. I raise this issue because of the unusual orientation of the presumed hafting retouch in relation to the bit. As in the cases of the end scrapers and adzes mentioned earlier, retouch for hafting is located perpendicular to the bit; this

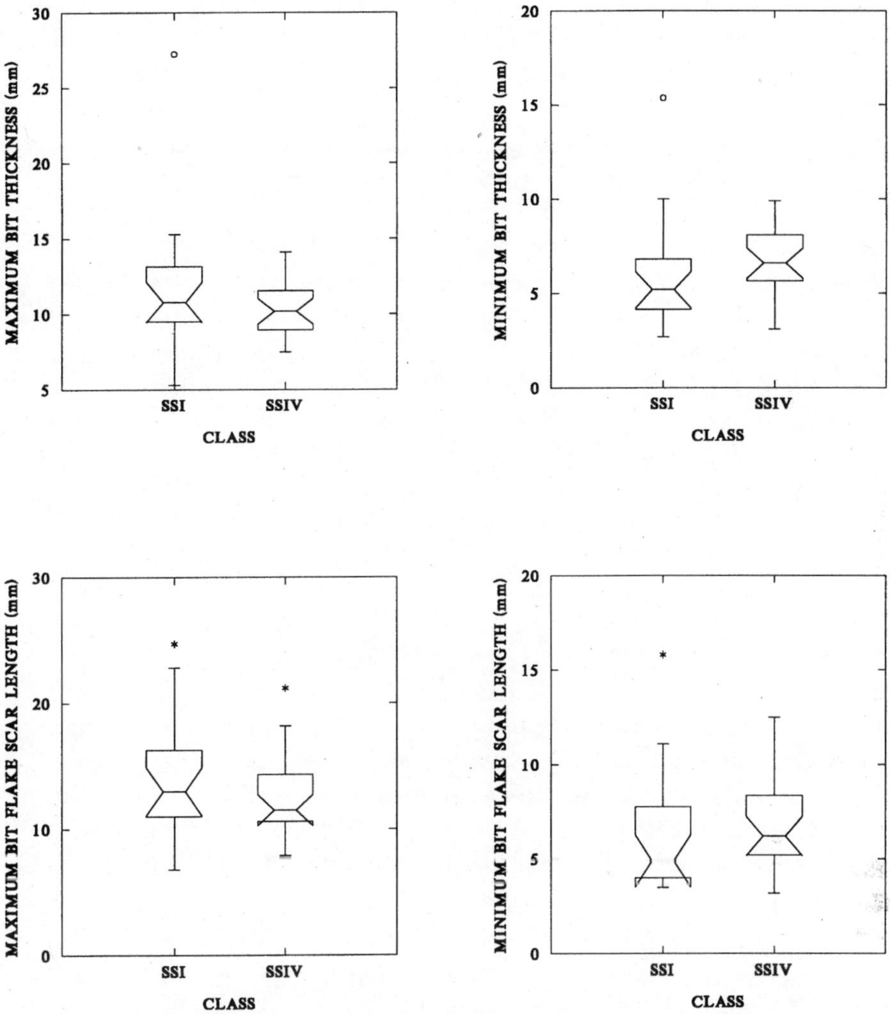

Figure 4.37. Box plots comparing bit thickness (top) and bit flake scar length (bottom) for Type I and Type IV side scrapers

is not the case for the Type IV side scrapers. As noted above, the hafting retouch is oriented parallel to the bit. If this interpretation is accurate, the tool may well have been hafted in such a way that it could have been used with both hands in a draw-knife fashion.

Although I have used hafting modification as an attribute important enough to separate this side scraper from the Type I form, the distinction may be more apparent than real. The absence of a bifacial edge on the Type I side scraper does not necessarily mean that it was not hafted. The tool blank for the Type I side scraper may have been sufficiently thin to begin with, eliminating the need for further thinning. The absence of any significant difference in median tool thickness between the two types suggests such a possibility (figure 4.30).

Functional Considerations. As with end scrapers, precise determinations of side scraper functions must await microwear analyses. Nevertheless, a variety of functions are probably represented among the side scrapers in the assemblage on the basis of their varying shapes and edge characteristics. Below I discuss some tentative inferences with respect to tool function on the basis of such criteria as bit edge angles and tool morphology. While we must be mindful of the problems inherent in assuming that "form equals function" (e.g., Odell 1981), routine morphological and technological analyses (see Ellis and Deller 1988) can produce certain insights into tool function.

Following Wilmsen (1970), edge angles are routinely reported in lithic analyses and are often the basis for functional determination. Wilmsen's (1970) study found patterning in edge angle distributions among Paleo-Indian scrapers and suggested that these distributions reflected functional categories. Wilmsen (1970:70–71) suggested, for example, that relatively acute angles (i.e., 26–35 degrees) were associated with cutting on soft materials such as meat and skin, while steeper angles (i.e., 66–75 degrees) indicated bone or wood working or heavy shredding. Middle-range values (i.e., 46–55 degrees), it was suggested, were associated with a broad array of activities such as skinning, hide working, the shredding of sinew and plant fiber, and heavy cutting. While an association between edge angles and tool functions is intuitively appealing, the link between the two still remains undemonstrated. And while a complete reliance on edge angles to determine tool function may be unwarranted, edge angles are probably associated with tool functions at some level, even if the functions remain unclear.

Frequency histograms comparing the distributions of mean bit edge angles for each side scraper type are displayed in figures 4.38–4.41. Excluding side scraper Types I and IV for the moment, a broad range of values from 25 degrees to 85 degrees is exhibited. The distribution of Type IIa side scrapers displays peaks at 65 degrees for both left and right bits, while Type II side scrapers have peaks at 55 degrees for left bits and 60 degrees for right bits. Perhaps more important, however, is the suggestion of multimodality within these ranges—particularly for the Type III side scraper. (The multimodality seen in the Type IIb side scraper may be spurious for two reasons, first, because the number of tools is small [n = 24] and, second, because the tools' small size make it hard to estimate edge angles accurately.)

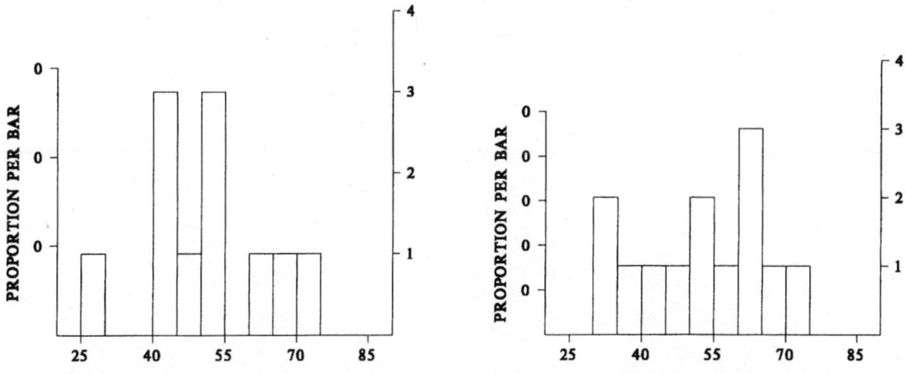

Figure 4.38. Histograms of left (left) and right (right) mean bit edge angles of Type IIb side scrapers

According to Wilmsen's classification, a number of different functional categories are present among Type II and III side scrapers. The possibility of multifunctional applications is also consistent with the varying bit shapes on these specimens that I noted earlier. Although tool functions among these scraper types probably overlapped, I speculate that the Type IIa side scrapers were probably used more often on harder materials than Type IIb or Type III side scrapers. This inference is based upon their larger size (thickness in particular), which makes them better suited for work on dense materials. Given their thinness and delicate nature, Type III side scrapers were probably employed on lighter materials, such as soft woods and meat. In short, morphological variability and wide range of edge angles all suggest that Type II side scrapers and Type III side scrapers were used to cut and scrape a variety of materials. Type I and IV side scrapers,

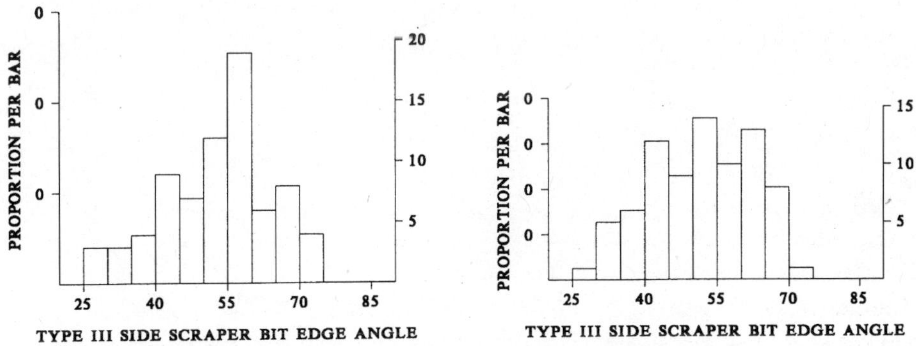

Figure 4.39. Histograms of left (left) and right (right) mean bit edge angles of Type III side scrapers

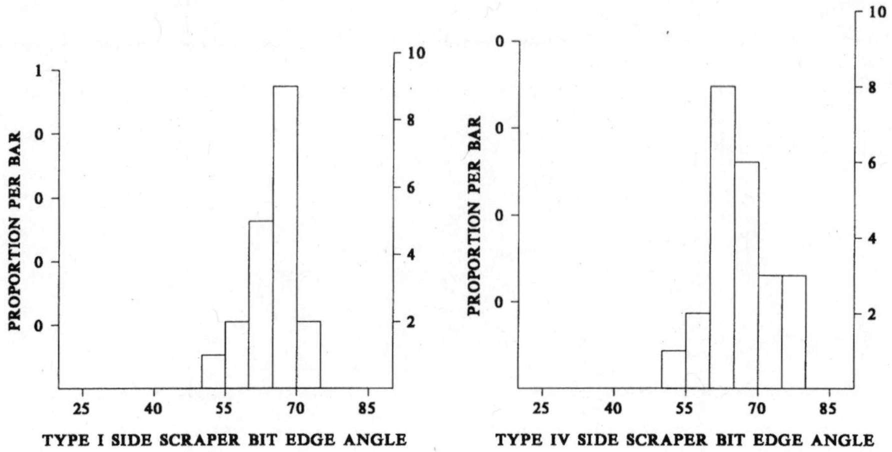

Figure 4.40. Histograms comparing mean bit edge angles of Type I side scrapers (left) and Type IV side scrapers (right)

on the other hand, have unimodal edge angle histograms that are much narrower in range (55–80 degrees) than those of the previous side scrapers. In fact, the edge angle distributions are more like those of end scrapers than other side scrapers. This similarity, however, does not indicate hide-working functions for these scrapers, since their bits show no evidence of edge rounding. Rather, the relatively steeper edge angles, the narrower range of edge angles, and the tools' morphology suggest heavy scraping activities consistent with their use as a draw knife.

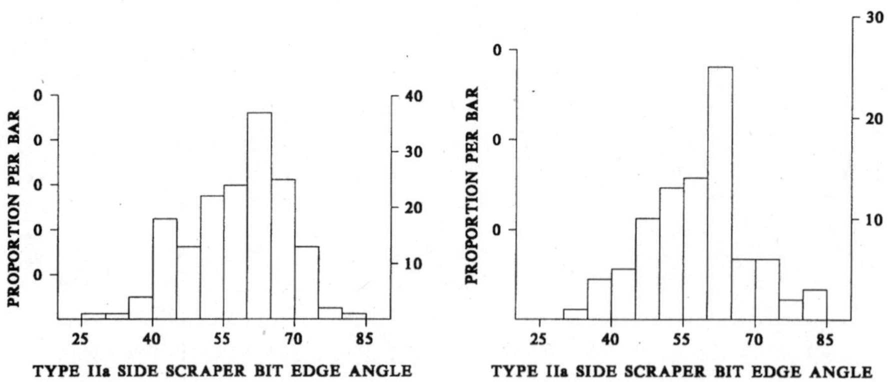

Figure 4.41. Histograms of left (left) and right (right) mean bit edge angles of Type IIa side scrapers

Figure 4.42. Other unifacial tools: (a-b) oval scrapers; (c, f) pointed scrapers; (d-e) miscellaneous scrapers

Other Unifacial Tools

The remaining flake tools in the assemblage include a variety of unifacial types. Some of these were previously reported by Coe (1964) (e.g., pointed scrapers, oval scrapers, and drills), while others (e.g., hafted spokeshaves, and denticulates) were not but have been found in other Early Archaic assemblages.

Oval Scrapers. Five oval scrapers are present in the assemblage (figure 4.42a–b). These tools exhibit well-executed, continuous retouch around the tool margins, so that there is a circular outline in plan view (Coe 1964:79). Although Coe (1964:79) noted that oval scrapers had been recovered from all levels of his excavations, he suggested that they were associated predominantly with the Hardaway component. Similar tools have been found in Dalton contexts in Arkansas (Morse 1973:27) and in Suwannee/Bolen contexts in Florida (Daniel and Wisenbaker 1987:69–70).

Morse (1973:27) has suggested that these tools may represent a hand-held version of the triangular end scrapers. While the specimens in the Hardaway assemblage were probably unhafted, they lacked the noticeable edge rounding that occurred on the end scrapers, and given their relatively thick bits and steep edge angles, they were probably used to scrape heavy materials.

Pointed Scrapers. Coe (1964:79) defined a pointed scraper as an "adaptation of the type II side scraper," produced "from a thick flake with two sides shaped to form a definite point." Nine such specimens were identified in the assemblage (figure 4.42c–d). I have divided pointed scrapers into two groups on the basis of a noticeable difference in flake blank size. Type Ia pointed scrapers were made on thicker flake blanks in line with Coe's definition. Type Ib pointed scrapers, however, were made on thinner flake blanks that do not strictly fit his original description. Nevertheless, they still display retouched edges that form a point and are included here on the basis of that criterion.

Of the nine tools, five have their points formed from the retouch of two straight lateral edges that converge distally; the remaining four specimens have one laterally retouched edge angled transversely across the flake blank until it reaches the opposite lateral edge—essentially forming a distal bit. In line with Coe's description, it might be concluded that pointed scrapers were modified side scrapers. That is, these pointed scrapers might represent a more heavily reduced Type IIa or Type III side scraper. The small number of these specimens makes this determination difficult. Whatever the case may be, the similarity with Type II and Type III side scrapers in bit attribute would suggest comparable tool uses.

Miscellaneous Scrapers. This class essentially represents a residual category of unifacial flake tools that could not be placed in any of the previous types. It includes seventeen tools exhibiting a variety of shapes and sizes (figure 4.42e–f). They exhibit at least two and sometimes three adjoining unifacially retouched edges that have straight, convex, and concave shapes. Given their variety of shapes and sizes, these were presumably hand-held tools manufactured for specific tasks on an ad hoc basis.

Indeterminate Scrapers. A total of 231 unifacially retouched artifacts are too broken or fragmentary to assign to any of the previous categories and are thus classified as indeterminate scrapers. In all likelihood, however, these specimens represent some type of side scraper.

Hafted Spokeshaves. This tool type was originally defined by Goodyear (1973, 1974) who noted its occurrence in Dalton contexts in Arkansas and possibly similar early contexts in Florida. Confirmation of this association

Figure 4.43. Hafted spokeshaves, denticulates, and Waller knife: (a–b) hafted spokeshaves; (c) denticulate; (d) Waller knife

in central Florida has come from excavations at Harney Flats, where they were recovered in Suwannee/Bolen contexts (Daniel and Wisenbaker 1987:85–86).

The Hardaway assemblage contained only two specimens, one of which has a missing bit (figure 4.43a–b). They were both made on a bladelike flake with marginal lateral retouch, so that there is a slight tapering toward the striking platform. The one complete specimen displays a slightly concave, steeply retouched working edge that is typical of this tool. It also exhibits a graver spur at one corner of the working edge. It may in fact have had two graver spurs, but damage at the other corner makes it impossible to tell. Goodyear (1973:40) has noted that these graver spurs often occur on both sides of the bit. Moreover, he also suggested that these small tools were hafted and used for scraping materials such as wood.

Denticulates. Two denticulates were identified in the assemblage (figure 4.43c). This tool class displays a series of regularly spaced small sharp projections along the working edge bit that results in a serrated or sawlike bit. One specimen, made on a relatively thin flake, exhibits a thin bit from which shallow flakes have been removed continuously along adjacent lateral and distal edges. The remaining denticulate was made on a thicker flake and displayed shallow but wider and steeper areas from which flakes have been removed along one lateral edge. Presumably these items would have been used in a cutting fashion on materials of soft to medium hardness.

Waller Knife. A single example of what appears to be a broken Waller knife is present in the assemblage (figure 4.43d). This tool class was originally noted in Florida (Purdy 1981:31–32; Waller 1971:173–174), where it was identified as a small unifacial tool with distinctive small side notches—presumably for hafting.

The specimen from Hardaway was made on a small flake with small U-shaped bifacially chipped notches. The blade, which is broken, exhibits very light unifacial retouch on the ventral surface of both lateral edges. Given its small size and delicate nature, this tool was probably used for cutting soft materials (Purdy 1981:31–32).

This tool type has been found in Early Archaic contexts in Florida (e.g., Bullen and Beilman 1973) and Mississippi (e.g., Geiger and Brown 1983) and has been observed in private collections from South Carolina (Goodyear et al. 1979). While this tool has been found in the Piedmont in places such as Rucker's Bottom in Georgia (Anderson and Schuldenrein 1985:292), it is much more commonly found in the Coastal Plain.

Drills, Perforators, and Gravers. Twenty-eight tools exhibiting flaked projections identified in the assemblage have been subdivided into two groups on the basis of bit shape. Eight specimens have been classified as drills/perforators on the basis of their relatively long pointed bits formed by either bifacial or unifacial retouch. The second group has much shorter "graver" projections formed by unifacial retouch. In both cases, this retouch is usually present at the lateral-distal juncture of the flake.

Within the first group, three of these tools could be classified as "drills," since they exhibit bifacial retouch forming a definite rodlike projection that is biconvex or diamond shaped in cross section (figure 4.44a–b). Only one artifact is complete, however, with the projection measuring 25 mm in length (figure 4.44a). Two of the specimens were probably hafted, as they are retouched along the flake's lateral margins beyond the bit. Given their sturdy appearance, these tools were probably used on dense materials.

The remaining five specimens have relatively long, thick bits formed by unifacial retouch and morphologically resemble perforators (figure 4.44c–d). Their bits are relatively thick and triangular in cross section. One exception is a specimen that is very well made except that it has a thinner, more delicate bit than the others (figure 4.44d). As such it appears more suited to punching holes in soft material such as hides. The other perforators, however, could have been used to bore holes in denser materials.

Gravers are characterized by a relatively short unifacially flaked projection that ranges from 3 to 5 mm in length (figure 4.44e–g). Twenty such tools were identified in the assemblage. Gravers have traditionally been interpreted as having been used to create fine engravings or small slots in bone or wood. Most of the specimens in the Hardaway assemblage exhibit

Figure 4.44. Drills, perforators, and gravers: (a-b) drills; (c-d) perforators; (e-g) gravers

relatively thick stubby bits capable of cutting into dense material such as wood, bone, or antler.

LARGE CHIPPED-STONE TOOLS

Two categories of large, roughly chipped stone tools are also present in the assemblage: choppers and cores/scrapers.

CHOPPERS

Twelve choppers were identified in the assemblage (figure 4.45a–b). These are large, roughly chipped stone tools that are oval to rectangular in plan view and tend to have a broad, crudely shaped convex working edge. Flaking is usually bifacial, although some are unifacially chipped

Figure 4.45. Choppers and core/scrapers: (a-b) choppers; (c-d) core/scrapers

and flaking is confined to the tool margins. Given their large size, these tools were probably used in heavy-duty chopping or digging activities.

Cores/Scrapers

This category includes six large, unifacially chipped artifacts that are somewhat smaller than choppers and are more regularly flaked (figure 4.45c–d). They tend to be plano-convex to trapezoidal in cross section and look like cores that were slightly modified into scrapers. All of these artifacts have a relatively large, flat, oval surface that served as the striking platform for all flake removals. In fact, two of these specimens actually resemble polyhedral cores.

CORES

In addition to the bifacial cores mentioned earlier, three additional core types are represented at Hardaway: a blocky, irregular-shaped core and two bipolar core forms. Included in this category are eighty-eight examples of cores and core fragments, and with one exception—an unusual small chunk of chalcedony—all are made from rhyolite and quartz. All of these artifacts are small and exhibit at least one negative bulb of percussion or are blocky chunks lacking any obvious flake characteristics, perhaps representing large pieces of shatter.

Block Cores

Six blocky-shaped rhyolite cores including five aphyric and one porphyritic variety are present in the assemblage weighing 110–265 g. These are medium-sized, blocky-shaped specimens displaying flake removal from different directions. An additional eighteen examples are all aphyric rhyolite chunks of 26–163 g. One small specimen is unusual for its raw material. It is a semitranslucent chunky piece of chalcedony with a waxy luster that varies from amber to reddish orange in color. The source of this stone is unknown. It is roughly rectangular in plan view with a diamond-shaped cross section and weighs only 21 g. Its small size has prevented much in the way of further reduction, with most of the flaking confined to one face located along one edge of the piece. Two other flake scars are present on the opposite face along the same edge at what may be an early attempt at bifacial flake removal.

Finally, small (10–188 g) blocky white quartz cores ($n = 30$) that display no more than one or two flake scars—as if the material was being tested for flaking quality—are also present in the assemblage.

Bipolar Cores and Pièces Esquillées

Another twenty-nine artifacts are quartz crystal. Most are the clear glassy type and have undergone bipolar flaking (figure 4.46a–d). These are small specimens, weighing 4–72 g; they tend to be thick and amorphous, with elongate flake scars originating from opposite directions on more than one face of the crystal, several of which retain remnants of the original faceted crystal surface (cf. Binford and Quimby 1963; Hayden 1980).

The small size and faceted surface of these crystals virtually precludes any flaking technique other than bipolar percussion. A bipolar technique—which involves placing the raw material on an anvil and repeatedly striking it with a hard hammer to produce small flakes—thus makes it possible to reduce these small pieces of raw material.

An additional four artifacts were identified as *pièces esquillées*—the more common formalized bipolar artifact class found in several Paleo-Indian and Early Archaic assemblages (e.g., Chapman 1975; Goodyear 1974, 1993; Lothrop and Gramly 1982; MacDonald 1968). No one attribute distinguishes pièces esquillées, but they are generally made on flakes, blade fragments, or exhausted tool fragments and are thin and squarish. This

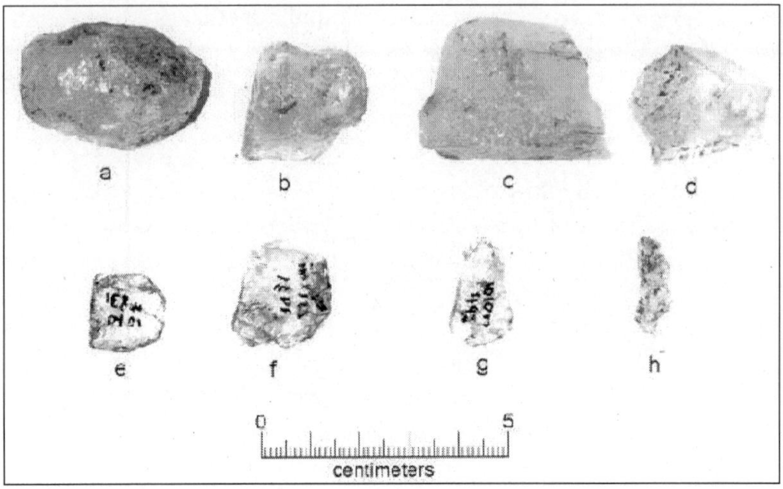

Figure 4.46. Bipolar cores and pièces esquillées: (a-d) bipolar cores; (e-h) pièces esquillées

form contrasts with the thick and blocky shape of bipolar cores. Moreover, pièces esquillées exhibit crushing (i.e., small flake removals) at two ends but lack the large colinear flake scars characteristic of bipolar cores. The four pièces esquillées from Hardaway were made from quartz crystal and are about 15 mm in size (figure 4.46e–h). They were probably derived from flakes, but this is difficult to determine because of their small size. Two specimens, being rather thin and squarish with crushing at opposite ends, are rather classic examples of this artifact (figure 4.46e–f). One of these artifacts, however, appears to have been split in half, while the other still retains a portion of the original crystal face along one edge. A third pièce esquillée is more rectangular in shape, and the final specimen may actually be a columnar fragment from a pièce esquillée (figure 4.46h). These are thin, columnlike fragments that sheared off from the edge of the specimen during flaking (Goodyear 1974:61–63; MacDonald 1968:86–87).

The functional interpretation of pièces esquillées in archaeological assemblages in the Eastern United States is the source of some debate. Following the lead of Old World archaeologists, who first identified this artifact class in Paleolithic assemblages, pièces esquillées have been interpreted largely as tools used as wedges or for slotting bone, wood, or antler (e.g., MacDonald 1968:88). Goodyear (1993), however, has taken exception to this interpretation—at least on northeastern Paleo-Indian sites. He argues, on the basis of ethnoarchaeological and technological data coupled with a spatial-statistical analysis of pièces esquillées at the Debert site, that these items are in fact bipolar cores where small, otherwise unusable bits of raw material (and sometimes tools) have been recycled to produce flakes.

The functional interpretation of the bipolar artifacts identified as pièces esquillées here is problematic. Although their size and shape does not preclude them from having been used as wedges, neither does it prevent them from having been cores as well (see Shott 1989c). If they were used as wedges, however, we must wonder why such tools appear to have been made only from quartz crystal. Given the abundance of nearby rhyolite, why were no rhyolite bipolar artifacts found? In fact, the question becomes: why bother to flake crystal quartz at all?

Assuming that rhyolite was the functional equivalent of quartz in a utilitarian sense, I can only suggest that there was something special about the quartz crystals themselves—some special property not directly related to a utilitarian function. Thus I speculate that the Hardaway pièces esquillées were probably used as cores to derive small flakes for use in some social or ritual context. This interpretation would also explain the presence of the other crystal quartz bipolar cores in the assemblage. Their thick and blocky (if not amorphous) shape would preclude their use as a wedge or slotting tool.

But given their small size, it might be argued that the flakes produced from these crystals would be too small to be of any practical use. Goodyear (1993), however, has cautioned against such a view. In reviewing both ethnoarchaeological and archaeological studies, he provides evidence that even small flakes (<20 mm) produced from bipolar reduction are almost routinely used. With respect to the cases of exceptionally small flakes—such as were likely produced at Hardaway—there is the possibility that they were hafted. Again, regarding the utility of small bipolar flakes, Hayden (1980:4) notes, "The vast majority of ethnographically recorded uses of small bipolar flakes concerns cutting flesh, either in ritual, butchering contexts or as barbs on spears." Moreover, with respect to cutting flesh, Hayden (1980:4) specifically notes the practice in Tanzania of the bipolar technique to obtain small "slivers of clear quartz in scarification activities." Unfortunately, a close inspection of the crystal quartz flakes in the assemblage revealed no evidence that any specimens had been derived from bipolar reduction. A cursory examination of flake scars on the quartz crystal cores indicate that flakes would have been less than 15 mm in length and very delicate. Most of the quartz debitage is either too large to be derived from the crystal specimens or was bifacially derived. Given the specimens' delicate nature, bipolar debitage may not have survived intact or could have been lost because a 0.5-in screen (circa 13 mm) was used.

The possibility also exists, of course, that the worked crystals themselves were the desired product; the bipolar technique being necessary to convert an otherwise unusable piece of raw material into a small tool with several sharp edges (MacDonald 1968:69). Many of the quartz specimens from Hardaway have sharp edges that could have been used, but this determination must await a microwear analysis.

STONE TYPES

A minimum of fifteen stone types are present in the Hardaway assemblage of flaked tools (table 4.11). Clearly, the dark gray aphyric rhyolite that is often flow banded dominates the assemblage (68.3 percent). The abundance of this stone is not surprising, given Hardaway's proximity to Morrow Mountain, which is the primary source of this stone. Among the major tool types, this rhyolite occurs in highest frequencies among bifaces (76.9 percent), followed by equal amounts in both end scrapers (66.5 percent) and side scrapers (66.7 percent), and slightly lower frequencies (60.6 percent) in points. Aphyric rhyolite also dominates among the remaining tool categories of adzes (100 percent), miscellaneous scrapers (58.8 percent), and a combined category of denticulates, drills, and gravers (83.3 percent). Cores and large chipped-stone tools are the only two tool types that are not dominated by aphyric rhyolite.

While Hardaway's proximity to Morrow Mountain is obviously an important factor in the presence of high frequencies of aphyric rhyolite in the assemblage, distance alone cannot entirely account for its abundance, as numerous porphyritic rhyolite quarries exist near Hardaway as well. In fact, several such quarries are even closer than Morrow Mountain (Chapter 3). I suggest that the intensive use of Morrow Mountain rhyolite is related to its better flaking quality relative to the porphyritic (and other metavolcanic) stone outcrops in the area.

This statement is at least partially supported by the results of an informal experiment in which samples of both rhyolite from Morrow Mountain and porphyritic rhyolite from nearby Falls Dam were given to several knappers, who were asked to reproduce a biface and to evaluate each stone type with respect to flaking quality. Without exception, each knapper clearly preferred Morrow Mountain rhyolite, which appeared to have an excellent conchoidal fracture. The flint knappers commented that the porphyritic rhyolite was much harder to knap. Presumably, the presence of phenocrysts in the porphyritic rhyolite negatively affected its flaking quality, although more rigorous tests are needed to verify this statement.

At 17.8 percent, rhyolitic tuff constitutes the second most commonly used raw material in the assemblage (table 4.11). As noted above, some of this raw material may originate in the rhyolitic tuff sources identified in

Table 4.11. Frequency Distribution of Chipped-Stone Raw Materials by Artifact Class

Raw Material	Points		Bifaces[a]		End Scrapers[b]		Side Scrapers[c]		Miscellaneous Scrapers[d]		Large Chipped Stone[e]	
	n	%	*n*	%	*n*	%	*n*	%	*n*	%	*n*	%
Aphyric rhyolite	86	60.6	579	76.9	280	66.5	274	66.7	20	58.8	7	38.9
Rhyolitic metatuff	47	33.1	93	12.4	87	20.7	92	22.4	8	23.5	8	44.4
Quartz	2	1.4	19	2.5	10	2.4	-	-	-	-	-	-
Green metasiltstone	5	3.5	2	0.3	21	4.9	20	4.9	3	8.8	-	-
Argillite	-	-	17	2.3	7	1.7	13	3.2	-	-	2	11.1
Quartz crystal	-	-	3	0.4	-	-	3	0.7	-	-	-	-
Plagioclase-quartz porphyritic rhyolite	-	-	22	2.9	7	1.7	1	0.2	1	2.9	-	-
Plagioclase porphyritic rhyolite	-	-	14	1.9	6	1.4	6	1.5	1	2.9	-	-
Quartz porphyritic rhyolite	-	-	-	-	-	-	1	0.2	1	2.9	-	-
Jasper	1	0.7	2	0.3	-	-	-	-	-	-	-	-
Ridge and Valley chert	1	0.7	-	-	-	-	1	0.2	-	-	-	-
Chalcedony	-	-	1	0.1	-	-	-	-	-	-	-	-
Other chert	-	-	-	-	2	0.5	-	-	-	-	-	-
Coastal Plain chert	-	-	-	-	1	0.2	-	-	-	-	-	-
Greenstone	-	-	-	-	-	-	-	-	-	-	1	5.6

[a]Includes Types I, II, and III bifaces.
[b]Includes all end scraper types.
[c]Includes all side scraper types.
[d]Includes oval scrapers, pointed scrapers, hafted spokeshaves, and Waller knives.
[e]Includes choppers and core scrapers

(continued)

Table 4.11 (continued). Frequency Distribution of Chipped-Stone Raw Materials by Artifact Class

Raw Material	Adzes		Gravers, Drills Denticulates		Cores		Pièces esquillées		Total	
	n	%	*n*	%	*n*	%	*n*	%	*n*	%
Aphyric rhyolite	2	100.0	25	83.3	23	27.4	-	-	1,296	68.3
Rhyolitic metatuff	-	-	2	6.7	-	-	-	-	337	17.8
Quartz	-	-	-	-	30	35.7	-	-	61	3.2
Green metasiltstone	-	-	2	6.7	-	-	-	-	53	2.8
Argillite	-	-	-	-	-	-	-	-	39	2.1
Quartz cyrstal	-	-	-	-	29	34.5	4	100.0	39	2.1
Plagioclase-quartz porphyritic rhyolite	-	-	-	-	1	1.2	-	-	32	1.7
Plagioclase porphyritic rhyolite	-	-	-	-	-	-	-	-	27	1.4
Quartz porphyritic rhyolite	-	-	1	3.3	-	-	-	-	3	0.2
Jasper	-	-	-	-	-	-	-	-	3	0.2
Ridge and valley chert	-	-	-	-	-	-	-	-	2	0.1
Chalcedony	-	-	-	-	1	1.2	-	-	2	0.1
Other chert	-	-	-	-	-	-	-	-	2	0.1
Coastal Plain chert	-	-	-	-	-	-	-	-	1	0.1
Greenstone	-	-	-	-	-	-	-	-	1	0.1

the northern Uwharrie Mountains approximately 30 km to the northeast of Hardaway near Asheboro.

The remaining thirteen raw materials all represent minority types in the assemblage. Occurring at about 3 percent, quartz and a green metasiltstone dominate the minority raw materials. Two types of porphyritic rhyolite, crystal quartz, and argillite constitute 1–2 percent of the assemblage, while the remaining seven stone types make up less than 1 percent of the total. This latter group primarily includes all "cherts" (i.e., Coastal Plain chert, Ridge and Valley chert, jasper, chalcedony, and other chert).

One specimen of Coastal Plain chert, a broken Type Ia end scraper, appears to be from the Allendale quarries (Albert Goodyear, personal communication 1992), whose source is over 300 km to the southwest of Hardaway. Two other specimens, a Palmer point and a Type IIa side scraper, appear to be made of Knox chert from the Ridge and Valley province over 300 km to the west of Hardaway. Jasper artifacts in the assemblage include two bifaces and one Kirk Corner-Notched point. As mentioned previously the origins of this stone are unknown, although a source could lie in the Piedmont. The one source described above, for example, is located about 120 km north of Hardaway.

The remaining four specimens include two Type Ib end scrapers made from "other cherts" and a core and biface made from two varieties of chalcedony. The sources of all these raw materials are unknown, but they probably originated outside the Piedmont.

It is interesting to find these examples of nonlocal cherts because they have traveled such a distance from their source. If the distance an artifact travels from its source reflects the use life of a tool from which it was made, then eight of the above ten chert tools include points, bifaces, or Type I end scrapers—all tool classes identified with extended use lives in earlier discussions. The remaining two tools include a core and a Type IIa side scraper. A closer inspection of these two examples, however, suggests that the side scraper may be an exception, since the blank for the this tool may have been derived from a bifacial, and likely curated, core.

Finally, some additional comments can be made concerning the origins of the siliceous green metasiltstone in the assemblage. Assuming that this stone would have been readily used where available, its relatively low percentage at Hardaway might suggest a distant source. As noted above, however, its petrologic similarity to argillite suggests a source relatively close to the site. This hypothesis is also supported by the relatively high frequencies of cortex pieces in the debitage (table 4.17). Similarly, although the collections survey identified only a very small number of points made from this material, the greatest number of recorded points were concentrated around Stanly County (Appendix C).

If true, then this stone's minor presence in the assemblage could be related to the "package size" in which the material occurs. As I mentioned in Chapter 3, argillite occurs in units with well-developed bedding planes that are less than 15 mm in thickness. If the green metasiltstone occurs as a unit in the argillite, such a structure would obviously pose restrictions in raw material procurement and tool manufacture.

Another factor contributing to this material's minor presence at Hardaway might be the geomorphic history of the Yadkin River Valley. Since argillite forms much of the lower volcanic-sedimentary sequence of the Yadkin River (Conley 1962:5), outcrops exposed very early in the Holocene may subsequently have been covered by floodplain deposits (cf. Goodyear, in press). In other words, it is possible that this stone had a limited temporal as well as spatial exposure during the Early Archaic, thereby restricting its availability for use.

Although the above scenario is speculative, a limited temporal use of this stone is also consistent with the observation that point types made of green metasiltstone rarely postdate the Early to Middle Archaic. I base this impression upon an examination of some 22,000 points in the research laboratories of anthropology collections (Davis and Daniel 1990) and upon my observations from examining numerous private collections as well.

In sum, the occupants of Hardaway used diverse raw materials, although they preferred rhyolite from Morrow Mountain. Additional exploited metavolcanic substances included porphyritic rhyolite and some unidentified metavolcanic stone. While the sources of the former are known, the latter are not; although they are most likely located in the Carolina Slate Belt—if not elsewhere in the Uwharries themselves. At least two metasedimentary stone types were also used: argillite and a metasiltstone. Both raw materials were probably obtained near Hardaway, although no specific quarries of either stone were identified. Similarly, quartz was probably obtained either locally or within the Piedmont. In contrast, several nonlocal cherts that are present in small amounts were probably obtained outside the Piedmont.

COBBLE AND TABULAR STONE TOOLS

A series of large stone tools primarily made on river cobbles and other large tabular pieces of stone are also present in the assemblage. Within this class, various categories have been constructed on the basis of artifact size, shape, and the nature and location of wear patterns (e.g., battering, pitting, grinding, etc.) that are used to reconstruct tool functions.

Hammerstones

There are fifty-three hammerstones in the assemblage, most of which are broken or small fragments. Cobbles identified as hammerstones are recognized by battering and extensive pitting present on ends, edges, or intermediate surfaces. Other noncobble masses of quartz and rhyolite were also used as hammerstones. Presumably these tools were used as percussors in stone tool production or as pounders in food processing.

Twenty-one quartz cobbles were used as hammerstones. Six of these are whole, spherical to elliptical in shape, ranging between 123 g and 205 g in weight. The remaining fifteen items include broken cobbles or small cobble fragments that exhibit hammerstone use. These tools range in weight from 7 g to 217 g. An additional eight specimens appear to be extensively battered masses or fragments of vein quartz rather than cobbles. They range in weight from 14 g to 194 g.

Twenty-one igneous cobbles, mostly of greenstone, also display hammerstone battering. They are small to medium-sized cobbles and are spherical to elliptical in shape. Three examples, however, are distinctly bar shaped. Whole specimens (n = 6) range in weight between 37 g and 466 g. Fifteen broken and fragmented examples range from 13 g to 654 g. One exceptionally large but broken hammerstone weighs 1350 g.

The remaining three hammerstones are made from rhyolite. Two examples were made from the aphyric variety, and one was made from the plagioclase-quartz porphyritic variety. The presence of flake scars partially obliterated by battering suggests that they may originally have been cores that secondarily functioned as hammerstones. They range in weight from 61 g to 161 g.

It should be mentioned that hammerstones, as well as other cobble tools, may be underrepresented in the assemblage. Coe (1964:79), for example, noted that while hammerstones were quite common on the surface (n = 536), they were quite scarce in the excavated levels (n = 30). Baker (1978:290) has suggested that this scarcity may result from the "size effect," according to which large artifacts predominate on site surfaces probably because tools are reused through time. That is, large artifacts are less likely to be buried by depositional processes, or are more easily exposed by erosion, than smaller artifacts. Where sites are repeatedly reoccupied, the higher visibility of larger artifacts may thus increase their potential for reuse. Binford (1979) has observed this process among the Nunamiut. "One process which I have observed with regard to site furniture has been discussed as the 'size effect'. . . . Upon arrival at a known site, one generally searches for the 'furniture' and pulls it 'up' out of its matrix for reuse.

Figure 4.47. Hammerstones/anvils and hammerstones/abraders: (a) hammerstone/abrader; (b-c) hammerstones/anvils

This means that large items of site furniture get continuously translated 'upward' if a deposit is forming" (Binford 1979:264).

A similar process probably took place at Hardaway, given its repeated occupation. If so, then hammerstones and other large cobble tools described below may have been more numerous in the early component than is now apparent.

Hammerstones/Anvils

Seventeen cobbles exhibit battering wear on their margins and percussion pitting or pecking on their flat faces (i.e., pitted cobbles) (figure 4.47b–c). Fourteen of these are quartz cobbles and three are greenstone cobbles. Only two quartz cobbles are whole, weighing 494 g and 596 g. The remaining broken pieces range in weight from 50 g to 594 g. Two greenstone cobbles are whole, weighing 478 g and 558 g, while one is broken and weighs 346 g.

Given the two patterns of wear on these cobbles, these specimens presumably functioned both as percussors (similar to the hammerstones described above) and as anvils—if we may judge from the pitting wear noted on the stones' flat faces. This wear may reflect use in bone, meat, or nut processing or in anvil-supported core reduction. The latter function is associated with the bipolar core use discussed previously.

Hammerstones/Abraders

In addition to hammerstone wear on their edges, two quartz cobbles display grooves worn on their flat faces. Only one cobble is complete, and it weighs 520 g. Three shallow grooves are lightly discernible, crisscrossing one face of the cobble and forming a starlike pattern (figure 4.47:a). They are about 4 mm wide and 1–2 mm deep where they are measurable. Although no grooves are present on the reverse side, it exhibits some abrasion and a wide, shallow depression across its face. The second specimen is a cobble fragment that displays hammerstone battering on its side and a portion of a groove on its flat surface. Abraders are a noted part of the Dalton tool kit; however, those from Arkansas were made from sandstone (Goodyear 1974:69–73; Morse 1971:18). Similarly, grooved sandstone abraders have been recovered from an early context in Florida (Daniel and Wisenbaker 1987:90–92). Suggested activities for abraders include the manufacture of bone implements such as pins and foreshafts; abraders are also thought to have been used in grinding the lateral edges of adzes. Although of different material, the specimens from Hardaway could have performed similar functions.

Grinding Stones/Anvils

Twelve flattened cobbles and tabular pieces of igneous rock were identified as combination grinding stones and anvils. These tools were defined by the presence of abrasion on the stone's flattened faces and were sometimes accompanied by light pecking. Furthermore, this class is almost always distinguished by a shallow concavity or basin on a working face (figure 4.48).

Abrasion usually occurred in the form of striations or "scoring" of the stone surface that resulted in a light to moderate smoothing, although some portions of the altered surface remained roughened. A slightly polished surface was observed to accompany striations on the face of one specimen.

Two of the more complete examples were made of tabular pieces of greenstone and granite. They are roughly rectangular in shape, approximately 100 by 90 mm in size and weigh about 500 g; one is 30 mm thick, while the other is 51 mm in thickness. Both flat surfaces on both specimens display grinding wear in the form of light to marked linear scratches or striations.

One stone also has a marked concavity along the center of one edge and a similar concavity on the reverse face. Some light pecking accompanies both concavities. Light pecking is also present on both flat surfaces of the other stone, but it lacks any noticeable concavities. Extensive battering occurs on three corners of this specimen and may reflect the use of a hammerstone or the shaping of the stone.

One large (180 mm × 132 mm × 20 mm) piece of tabular greenstone

Figure 4.48. Grinding stones/anvils

also displays extensive anvil use in the form of heavy pitting (i.e., slits or gouges in the stone) on one flat surface and weighs 765g. In addition, a portion of one edge of this surface appears abraded; faint scratches run the length of the edge. A slight concavity is also present along this edge.

Four cobbles also display grinding wear. The first is a large igneous rock (probably greenstone) that weighs 1134 g. One surface is relatively flat and appears smoothed, with a small lightly pitted depression located just off center. The remaining three flattened quartz cobbles are broken. Two are very similar to each other and display marked concavities associated with some light pecking. One displays marked concavities on two faces, while the other has only one worked face.

The remaining quartz cobble is plano-convex in shape with a somewhat different wear pattern. While its flat face displays an abraded surface with a pecked concavity similar to the previously described examples, its more convex reverse face displays abrasion and pecking localized on the top of its rounded surface. This wear may have resulted from anvil use, but the localization of this wear on a convex surface also suggests a mano function. Furthermore, some extensive battering, suggestive of hammerstone use, is also present along one edge.

Figure 4.49. "Engraved slate"

Finally, the remaining five artifacts are all greenstone fragments that display some evidence of grinding. They range in weight from 27 to 296 g. The pecking damage observed on these artifacts may reflect technological modification or some light pounding of food materials in the grinding process or both. Suggested functions for these artifacts include grinding or pulverizing plant or nut resources. The more extensive pitting noted on the one greenstone specimen, however, may result from use on harder materials such as in bipolar core reduction.

Anvil

A single flattened broken cobble exhibits some extreme crushing and pitting on its flat surface, suggesting that it was used as an anvil.

"Engraved Slate" and Pebbles

Several puzzling pieces of what Coe (1964:81) called "engraved slate" are present in the assemblage (figure 4.49). Three of these are actually tabular fragments of argillite, and one platy fragment of greenstone. They range in weight from 21 g to 90 g. Two other pieces include an engraved pebble and an engraved broken cobble that weigh 25 and 202 g, respectively.

With one exception these artifacts display a series of fine incisions or scratches randomly placed across one or both flat surfaces of the stone. The single exception, however, displays a more deliberate design of simple cross-hatching (figure 4.49a).

While these specimens were quite numerous on the surface at Hardaway (213 engraved pieces of slate and 46 engraved pebbles), only 16 engraved slate fragments and 5 engraved pebbles were found in the excavated levels from Hardaway (Coe 1964:81). Although no exact distribution is given, they were apparently found in all levels at the site. Similar engraved specimens were also found in almost all levels at the nearby Doerschuk site, some with complicated geometric designs (Coe 1964:53).

The function of these artifacts is unclear. Coe (1964:53) suggested that they were used as cutting boards; however, as he also notes, many of the more complex incised designs belie this interpretation. It may also be significant that this artifact class is not widespread in the Piedmont (Coe 1964:53) and is apparently unknown in any other sites in the Southeast that date to the Archaic period.

Other Worked Stone

This category includes crudely modified cobbles or pebbles whose functions are uncertain. Three of these are small, flat, elliptically shaped greenstone cobbles. They are about 85 by 45 mm in size and 11–15 mm in thickness. They exhibit crude flaking around their margins and somewhat resemble the atlatl weight blanks identified by Coe (1964:figures 45, 70). While the items that Coe illustrated are clearly unfinished atlatl weights, the three specimens here are less certainly identifiable because of their small size and crude flaking (early stage?). In addition, all of the previously excavated atlatl weights are from a Middle Archaic (i.e., Stanly) context, both at Hardaway (Coe 1964:81) and at Doerschuk (Coe 1964:52–53). These three specimens were all recovered from early contexts: two from Zone 4 and the other from the top of Zone 3.

The two remaining roughly shaped pieces are a thin oval pebble with one crudely flaked edge and a thin piece of marginally shaped phylite, similar in size and shape to the possible atlatl blanks described above. Given the raw material and its thinness (10 mm), this was probably not intended to become an atlatl weight.

Finally, this category also includes a broken portion of a large cobble with at least five lightly pecked and incised parallel lines that probably extended around the circumference of the cobble. Moreover, these lines appear to be decoration rather than the products of use. Four of the lines form a group and are regularly spaced 4–5 mm apart; the fifth line is separated from the group by a distance of 14 mm. Portions of the lines are obliterated by some battering that was apparently caused by anvil use, which may have been a secondary function after it was broken. There is no clear indication of this specimen's original function.

Cobbles and Other Stones

This category ($n = 41$) primarily includes whole cobbles, cobble fragments, and large pebbles that exhibit no obvious use-wear damage. Both quartz and igneous stone are present among the cobbles and may represent unused or minimally used specimens with undetected damage. Similarly, the fragments may be unused portions of cobbles that fractured during use. This category also includes a broken piece of tabular quartzite and one relatively large piece of tabular argillite. The latter specimen is similar in size and form to the examples of "engraved slate" discussed earlier; however, it exhibits no evidence of incisions or other obvious modifications.

GROUND STONE ARTIFACTS

Only a single, indeterminate ground stone artifact is present in the assemblage. Such artifacts are extremely rare in Early Archaic contexts, and as mentioned below, the association of this artifact with the Early Archaic component should be viewed with caution.

One very small (0.8 g) ground stone fragment was identified in the assemblage. Given its fragmentary condition, precise identification cannot be made, but it may have been part of a pendant. Although this artifact was found in the bottom of Zone 3, its very small size would make it susceptible to vertical movement, and it could have migrated down from a later occupation.

FLAKE ANALYSIS

The stone debitage was analyzed in terms of an hypothesized reduction trajectory. When coupled with the previous tool analysis, the flake analysis assisted in identifying the stage at which tools and cores arrived at and left the site. This classification categorized the relative amounts of early and late stages of lithic reduction by monitoring the presence and absence of flakes exhibiting cortex. Flakes with cortex reflected the initial removal of material from the natural weathered surface of rock. Conversely, flakes without cortex signaled a later stage of reduction. Although somewhat simple, when combined with measurements of relative flake

Table 4.12. Stone Flake Totals

Raw Material Type	Count *n*	Count %	Weight (g) *n*	Weight (g) %
Metavolcanic	64,974	97.9	201,523	97.1
Quartz	856	1.3	4,020	1.9
Green metasiltstone	351	0.5	1,524	0.7
Quartz crystal	135	0.2	294	0.1
Chalcedony	18	<0.1	29	<0.1
Coastal Plain chert	12	<0.1	36	<0.1
Ridge and Valley chert	2	<0.1	1	<0.1
Jasper	4	<0.1	4	<0.1
Other chert	1	<0.1	1	<0.1
Total	66,353	100	207,432	100

size, this technique provided some measure of the reduction activities undertaken at Hardaway.

Initially, all flakes from the eighty units containing the undisturbed Early Archaic component identified in Chapter 2 were sorted by raw material. All rhyolite and other metavolcanic and metasedimentary rock types were lumped into a single category labeled metavolcanic stone (table 4.12). The flakes were subsequently screened through 0.5 and 0.25 in hardware cloth to provide a rough measure of flake size. Despite the fact that only 0.5 in screen was used during the excavations, a substantial number of small flakes were recovered (i.e., flakes small enough to pass through 0.5 in mesh) (table 4.13). The very small amount of material that passed through the 0.25 in screen appeared to be tiny fragments of debris resulting from bag storage. This material was collected and weighed but does not figure in the analysis here.

Once the flakes were sorted by raw material type and mesh size, a rather simple key of flake types was used for the analysis. Flakes were divided into five categories primarily upon the presence/absence of cortex and their condition (i.e., whole or broken): whole nondecortication flakes, broken nondecortication flakes, whole decortication flakes, broken decortication flakes, and shatter.

Flakes that exhibited any amount of cortex were classified as decortication flakes; those without cortex were classified as nondecortication flakes. Flakes were then divided into whole or broken categories principally on the basis of the presence or absence of a striking platform. All flakes exhibiting a complete or partial striking platform with relatively intact margins were classified as whole; all remaining flakes (excluding shatter) were classified as broken. Broken flakes tended to be relatively flat thin pieces that lacked any definable bulb of percussion or striking platform. Shatter,

Table 4.13. Metavolcanic Flake Totals

	Count				Weight (g)			
Flake Type	½" Screen	¼" Screen	Total	%	½" Screen	¼" Screen	Total	%
Whole	22,288	8,465	30,753	47.3	92,090	5,372	97,462	48.4
Broken	12,604	11,509	24,113	37.1	34,843	5,963	40,806	20.2
Whole decortication	5,256	761	6,017	9.3	44,671	684	45,355	22.5
Broken decortication	2,670	858	3,528	5.4	12,772	708	13,480	6.7
Shatter	424	139	563	0.9	4,191	247	4,438	2.2
Total	43,242	21,732	64,974	100	188,567	12,974	201,541	100

the final flake category, represents all the angular, chunky fragments (regardless of the presence of cortex) that do not exhibit the characteristic flat morphology of thinning flakes.

Although not systematically examined, the vast majority of the debitage could be classified as biface thinning flakes (House and Ballenger 1976:89–90). This identification was based on the relatively complicated dorsal flake scar patterns, faceted platforms, and flake curvature in profile. A very few flakes, however, were noted that could be described as uniface retouch flakes (Shafer 1970). That is, they exhibited a flat unfaceted striking platform that served as the ventral aspect of the unifacial tool from which they were struck. These flakes are believed to result from either unifacial tool manufacture or resharpening.

All stone debitage was sorted according to the above categories, and counts and weights were obtained for each raw material type by provenance. Summary totals for debitage by raw material and flake type appear in tables 4.14–4.17.

At this point it should be remembered that only 0.5 in screen was used during the excavations, so that there was undoubtedly some bias in flake size recovery. Nevertheless, the analysis revealed that a substantial amount (n = 22,290, or 34 percent of the total count) of small flakes were recovered in the 0.25 in mesh. The vast majority of these flakes, however, were recovered during the 1970s excavations (n = 21,267).

Moreover, a clear difference exists in the frequencies of flake counts by mesh size between the 1950s and 1970s excavations. A significantly greater percentage of the 0.25 in flakes (n = 21,267, or 32.1 percent of the debitage total) were recovered during the 1970s as compared with the 1950s (n = 1,023, or 1.5 percent of the debitage total). While it is possible that this larger quantity may reflect spatial differences (i.e., activity areas) within the site, I believe that it most likely reflects changes in attitude with the passage of two decades regarding the importance of recovering stone debitage.

Metavolcanic and Metasedimentary Flakes

Lithic reduction was clearly an important activity at Hardaway. A total of over 66,000 flakes weighing over 207 kg is present in the debitage (table 4.12). As with the tools, the vast majority of the debitage—between 97 and 98 percent by count and weight—is either metavolcanic or metasedimentary stone. Clearly, most of this debitage comes from nearby Morrow Mountain: it is a gray fine-grained aphyric metavolcanic rock with a slight flow banding discernible on many specimens. A few other metavolcanic

Table 4.14. Quartz Flake Totals

	Count				Weight (g)			
Flake Type	½" Screen	¼" Screen	Total	%	½" Screen	¼" Screen	Total	%
Whole	221	59	280	32.7	1,649	67	1,716	42.6
Broken	105	143	248	29.0	465	113	578	14.4
Shatter	202	126	328	38.3	1,586	144	1,730	43.0
Total	528	328	856	100	3,700	324	4,024	100

Table 4.15. Quartz Crystal Flake Totals

	Count				Weight (g)			
Flake Type	½" Screen	¼" Screen	Total	%	½" Screen	¼" Screen	Total	%
Whole	47	25	72	53.3	161	18	179	60.7
Broken	16	21	37	27.4	68	10	78	26.4
Shatter	6	20	26	19.3	23	15	38	12.9
Total	69	66	135	100	252	43	295	100

and metasedimentary stone types were also observed in the debitage, including porphyritic rhyolite, argillite, and a green metasiltstone. These other raw materials were only minority types, however. We recorded the presence of the green metasiltstone but not that of the other metavolcanic types.

That the majority of the these flakes lack cortex (n = 54,866, n = 84.4 percent) suggests that late-stage reduction predominated in the tool manufacturing sequence at Hardaway (table 4.13). Nevertheless, a substantial number by count (n = 9,546, or 14.7 percent) and even more by weight (58,835 g, or 29.2 percent) are decortication flakes (table 4.13), suggesting that the stone was transported to Hardaway in only partially reduced form.

Further indications that not all of the stone production was conducted at the quarry are apparent from the tendency for decortication flakes to be large and heavy—presumably cortex removal was completed at Hardaway. Among whole decortication flakes, for example, the vast majority (n = 5,256, or 87.4 percent) are large (retained in the 0.5 in screen). Moreover, this group accounts for only 8.1 percent of the metavolcanic debitage count but 22.2 percent of the total debitage weight. (These results presuppose that the bias against small flakes in the assemblage is not affected by cortex type.)

The Remaining Debitage

The discussion here will focus on the identification of the nonmetavolcanic minority raw material types represented in the debitage. Among these, the most abundant is quartz, although it accounts for only about 1 percent of the debitage. The remaining stone types include several varieties of cryptocrystalline stone, and all constitute only a fraction of the debitage total (table 4.12). Furthermore, they tend to be small nondecortication flakes, virtually all of which are biface thinning flakes.

Despite the low frequency of the cryptocrystalline materials, it may be of some significance that most of them probably originated from distant sources located outside the Piedmont. In fact, some of these same materials are also represented in the tools (which are discussed in the following chapter), although no refits between any flakes and tools could be made. Nevertheless, the chalcedony flakes match a tan chalcedony biface so closely in color and texture that the flakes could have been knapped from the same biface. If they were, the spatial relationships between the flakes and the biface are particularly interesting. That is, most of the flakes clustered in one part of the site, while the biface was located about 40 ft away

Table 4.16. Chert Flake Totals

Raw Material/Flake Type	Count		Weight (g)	
	½" Screen	¼" Screen	½" Screen	¼" Screen
Coastal Plain chert				
Whole	3	2	12	1
Whole decortication	1	-	1	-
Broken	1	4	1	2
Broken decortication	1	-	19	-
Ridge and Valley chert				
Whole	1	1	1	<1
Other chert				
Whole	-	1	-	1
Chalcedony				
Whole	5	5	12	3
Whole decortication	2	2	6	2
Broken	3	1	8	<1
Jasper				
Whole	1	2	1	2
Broken	1	-	1	-

(see discussion in Chapter 6). The geologic source of this chalcedony is unknown.

At least two varieties of chert, however, appear to have their sources outside the Piedmont. Two dark bluish gray chert flakes are likely Knox chert (Larry Kimball, personal communication 1992), while another fourteen flakes appear to be from the Allendale sources (Albert Goodyear, personal communication 1992). The only other "chert" specimen in the debitage is a translucent bluish green, somewhat grainy stone that actually may be a variety of quartz from Virginia (Larry Kimball, personal communication 1992). It has been placed in the "other chert" category in tables 4.13 and 4.16.

Jasper is also present in the debitage; its source is unknown, but it may have originated in the Piedmont (table 4.16). Three of the four flakes are a dark brown, very homogeneous stone that could have come from the same specimen. The fourth item is a waxy, mottled brownish green material.

Finally, the flake analysis also offers some insight into the source of the unique green metasiltstone mentioned earlier. Although this material was not particularly numerous in the assemblage, a relatively high frequency by count (12.8 percent, $n = 45$) and by weight (37.7 percent, 574 g) exhibit cortex (table 4.17). In fact, the percentage by count of this material is very

Table 4.17. Green Metasiltstone Flake Totals

	Count				Weight (g)			
Flake Type	½" Screen	¼" Screen	Total	%	½" Screen	¼" Screen	Total	%
Whole	134	69	203	57.8	767	40	807	52.9
Broken	43	58	101	28.8	102	32	134	8.8
Whole decortication	16	12	28	8.0	534	7	541	35.5
Broken decortication	11	6	17	4.8	29	4	33	2.2
Shatter	1	1	2	0.6	9	-	9	0.6
Total	205	146	351	100	1,441	83	1,524	100

close to that of cortex flakes in the metavolcanic debitage (14.7 percent), while the percentage by weight of the metasiltstone flakes is even greater than that of the metavolcanic flakes (29.2 percent). Thus if cortex frequencies reflect distance from source, a relatively close source is indicated for this metasiltstone. A similar conclusion was reached in Chapter 3 with regard to the local geology of the site.

SUMMARY

The sample of stone artifacts from the Early Archaic component at Hardaway constitutes one of the largest such assemblages recovered from a single site in the Southeast. The lanceolate and side-notched Daltons, as well as corner-notched Palmer and Kirk points, document repeated occupation at Hardaway throughout the Early Archaic. A wide variety of other tool types including both expedient and curated unifacial tools are also present. And while these tools are made from a variety of raw materials, the assemblage is dominated by a single rhyolite type—aphyric rhyolite. The Early Archaic complex at Hardaway is thus characterized by a diversity of tools made of a distinctive stone procured from a nearby outcrop. These two assemblage characteristics have important implications for site function at Hardaway, a topic that I will address in Chapter 5.

5

The Organization of an Early Archaic Technology

Assemblage Composition and Site Function at Hardaway

Thus far I have detailed the classification of the chipped-stone tools found at Hardaway. In this chapter, I investigate site function at Hardaway by examining the composition of the site's stone tool assemblage. This examination involves placing morphological types in the assemblage into functional and organizational (i.e., curated vs. expedient) categories to understand the range and frequency of activities undertaken at the site. The identification of site function, in turn, has implications for understanding Early Archaic settlement adaptations, a topic that I also address briefly. First, however, the question of tool use life in the assemblage is examined as it relates to the functional and organizational classification that follows.

TOOL USE LIFE

The question of tool use life has been an important theme of this analysis and is particularly relevant to several archaeological issues. First, tool use life is directly linked to the concept of curation: the manufacture and maintenance of tools in anticipation of their use among different settlements. Originally advanced by Binford (1973, 1977, 1979), the notion of curation is an important organizational concept in many lithic studies. In the wake of arguments by Binford (1979:267–268), upon which many others have elaborated (e.g., Bamforth 1986; Keeley 1982; Shott 1989a), tool curation has been inferred in archaeological assemblages on the basis of factors such as the relative rarity and high quality of stone types (e.g.,

Goodyear 1979), formalized tool morphologies (e.g., Keeley 1982), and the staging of tool manufacture and use (e.g., Goodyear 1974). Recently, however, more objective methods have been introduced to measure tool use life quantitatively in archaeological assemblages (e.g., Dibble 1987b; Kuhn 1992; Shott 1989b) on the basis of experimental replication (Dibble and Whitaker 1981; Kuhn 1990).

These methods assign case-specific rates of tool reduction to archaeological specimens along a continuous scale. Following these methods, two measures of tool reduction were used here. The first method follows Kuhn's (1990) experimentally derived geometric index of scraper reduction. The second method is a measurement based upon the ratio of flake surface area to striking platform area (Dibble 1985; Dibble and Whittaker 1981; Speth 1972, 1975, 1981).

Kuhn's (1990) index is a ratio between the maximum centerline thickness of the tool and thickness of the tool bit. This ratio is based upon a simple assumption concerning the cross-section geometry of flake tools: the center of a flake blank is thicker than its edges. Bit thickness (i.e., the thickness of a retouched edge) thus approaches tool centerline thickness as a tool is more intensively reduced; hence, the index theoretically ranges between near 0 (unretouched) and 1 (heavily retouched). (In practice, however, some values slightly exceed 1.0 because of vagaries of tool blank cross-section thickness [see also Kuhn 1992:119].)

Figure 5.1 compares these tool reduction indexes by type. The results support the inferences regarding tool curation that I presented in Chapter 4. For example, among end scrapers, the classes with the three highest median values are Type Ib (0.87), Type III (0.86), and Type Ia (0.79). (In fact, the Type Ib end scraper value is significantly higher than any other end scraper value except Type III.) I suggested that all three of these scrapers were curated (and hence more intensively used) tools. Similarly, the three lowest median values belong to specimens identified as more expedient scrapers: Type IIb (.66), Type IV (.66), and Type V (.47) (figure 5.1). In fact, the Type V end scraper exhibits a median value that is significantly lower than that for any other end scrapers. The middle rank of the final end scraper—Type IIa—is interesting in light of the discussion in Chapter 4 concerning its potential use life and the ambiguity concerning a determination of whether this tool type was ever hafted. Although it exhibits a value of 0.76—midway among the seven end scrapers—this index is not significantly different from the values of some curated end scrapers (e.g., Type Ia) or some expedient (e.g., Type IIb) specimens. This middling value illustrates nicely the nature of the curation continuum. It was suggested in Chapter 4, for instance, that this end scraper exhibited hafting modifications technically different from the smaller forms and likely represented

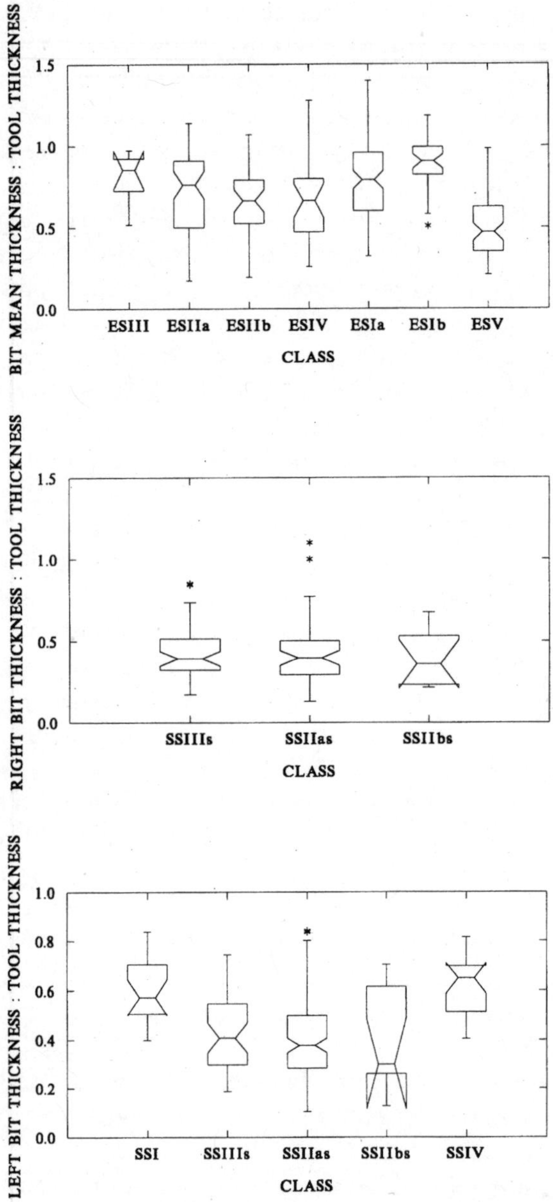

Figure 5.1. Box plots comparing tool reduction indexes (bit thickness:tool thickness) for end scrapers (top) and side scrapers (middle and bottom)

a response to more situational contexts related to specific tool designs needed for tasks at Hardaway. Thus its index midway among the end scrapers might suggest that its use life was intense relative to the site occupation (i.e., relatively longer than that of Type IV and Type V end scrapers) but that the tool was probably not transported and employed beyond its use at Hardaway (as opposed to the Type I and Type III end scrapers).

Similar trends are noted in the reduction values for side scrapers (figure 5.1). Type I and Type IV side scrapers display the highest indexes, 0.57 and 0.65, respectively, among all the side scrapers. These values are, in fact, significantly higher than those from any other side scraper forms. The values for the remaining side scrapers range from 0.31 to 0.41 (for both left and right bits), with no significant differences among these values. Thus these results also support the conclusions concerning tool use life that I discussed in Chapter 4. That is, it appears that the Type I and Type IV side scrapers were used more intensively than the other side scrapers at Hardaway, an inference that is consistent with their interpretation as hafted tools. As such, these specimens might have been curated items.

The second measure of reduction—the flake area:platform area ratio—gave somewhat mixed results. It will be recalled from Chapter 4 that the amount of relative blank reduction can be estimated by comparing the remaining surface area of the tool (the product of length times width) with the surface area of the intact platform (platform width times platform thickness). These ratios have been used with success in measuring tool reduction in Mousterian assemblages (e.g., Dibble 1987a, 1987b) and were employed here.

The box plots comparing flake area:platform area ratios indicate virtually no difference among the end scraper types (figure 5.2). Moreover, the median values for both Type Ia end scrapers (19.3) and Type Ib end scrapers (25.1) as well as Type III end scrapers (26.1) suggest that these curated tools underwent less reduction than their expedient counterparts, Type IV (18.5) and Type V (14.4) end scrapers. A closer examination of the data and certain assumptions concerning the ratio measurement, however, indicates that these results may be spurious.

The area-ratio method assumes that the platform area of the tool remains relatively constant, while flake area (i.e., tool length and/or width) is reduced. As I previously noted, hafting modifications (in the form of proximal thinning) have undoubtedly reduced original platform size on some of the hafted end scraper forms, so that an integral assumption of the method is obviously violated. This modification has likely resulted in greater platform area reduction relative to flake area reduction. Hence the higher ratios for these end scrapers are not surprising.

A further examination of the outlying values in figure 5.2 illustrates

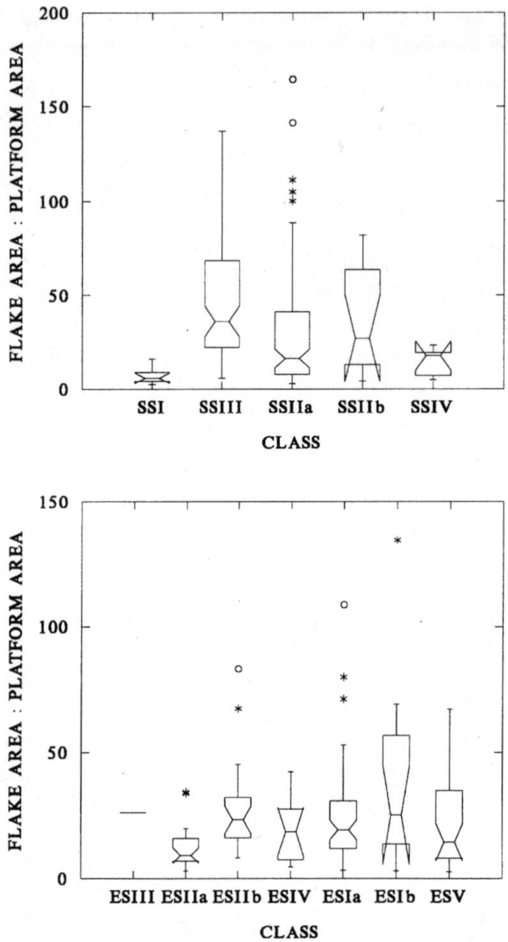

Figure 5.2. Box plots comparing tool reduction indexes (flake area:platform area) for side scrapers (top) and end scrapers (bottom)

this point. Inspection of all of the specimens represented by outliers revealed substantially modified striking platforms. Moreover, only end scraper types that are thought to have been hafted exhibit outliers. I conclude that the first index discussed above is a more reliable measure of tool reduction among end scrapers.

The area-ratio rankings for side scrapers, on the other hand, are more consistent with the geometric index rankings (figure 5.2). Type I side scrapers exhibit the lowest median value (6.0), which is significantly lower (i.e., more reduced) than that for other side scrapers. The Type I side scraper is followed by Type IIa (16.6) and Type IV side scrapers (18), respectively, although there is no significant difference between their median values. Finally, Types IIb (27.1) and III (36.2) side scrapers exhibit the highest median values (i.e., are the less reduced), a finding that is consistent with their interpretation as expediently used tools.

The relatively high ranking of the Type IV side scrapers appears inconsistent with the geometric index rankings but is likely spurious. As with the hafting modifications on the end scraper types, discussed above, the bifacial modification of the platform area of Type IV side scrapers probably accounts for the type's relatively high value. Similarly, platform modification also largely accounts for the five outlier values for the Type IIa side scrapers in figure 5.2. Three of these specimens have their platforms reduced by lateral (i.e., bit) retouch, while the remaining two simply have very small striking platforms.

In sum, this quantitative analysis tends to support the conclusions advanced concerning tool use life on the basis of the qualitative consideration of morphology. The small, formalized Type I end scrapers were generally the most intensively used unifacial tool in the assemblage. The results of these analyses also identified more expediently made and used end scrapers. Side scrapers were the least reduced unifacial tools and were expediently used. Two exceptions, however, may be noted. Types I and IV side scrapers were more intensively used than the other side scraper forms but exhibit values suggesting that they were within the range of the expedient end scrapers. While these tools were likely hafted, it remains unclear whether they were curated much beyond their use at Hardaway.

Primarily because of small sample size, no attempt was made to examine the other flake tools in a similar manner. Except for hafted spokeshaves and drills, however, the remaining tools are morphologically similar to the unhafted side scrapers and thus were probably expedient tools. It remains uncertain to what degree the hafted spokeshaves and drills were curated.

ASSEMBLAGE COMPOSITION AND SITE FUNCTION

Three interrelated factors were examined in interpreting assemblage composition as it related to site function. These factors included: (1) the relative frequencies of functional groupings of tool types; (2) the organizational roles (e.g., curated vs. expedient) of individual tool types; and (3) the proximity of Hardaway to stone resources.

Tool types in the Hardaway assemblage were sorted into nine functional groups on the basis of their inferred predominant function as outlined in Chapter 4 (table 5.1). While some inferred tool uses were fairly precise, and the tools were assigned to specific functional groups (e.g., hunting

Table 5.1. Summary of Proposed Functional Classes at the Hardaway Site

Functional Class/Artifact Class	Organizational Context	*n*	%
Hunting and Butchering			
Projectile points[a]	personal gear	280	11.0
Hide scraping			
End scraper Ia	personal gear	136	
End scraper Ib	personal gear	41	
End scraper IIa	personal gear	87	
End scraper IIb	personal gear	44	
End scraper III	personal gear	9	
End scraper IV	personal gear	25	
End scraper V	personal gear	79	
Subtotal		421	16.5
Light scraping and cutting			
Side scraper III	situational gear	123	
Side scraper IIb	situational gear	24	
Denticulate	situational gear	2	
Waller knife	situational gear	1	
Pointed scraper	situational gear	9	
Subtotal		159	6.2
Heavy scraping and cutting			
Choppers	site furniture	14	
Side scraper I	personal gear	20	
Side scraper IV	personal gear	23	
Side scraper IIa	situational gear	221	
Hafted spokeshave	personal gear	2	
Oval scraper	situational gear	5	
Core scraper	situational gear	6	
Miscellaneous scraper	situational gear	17	
Subtotal		308	12.1
Heavy chopping			
Adzes	personal gear	2	0.1
Boring and scoring			
Drill	personal gear	3	
Perforator	situational gear	5	
Graver	situational gear	20	
Subtotal		28	1.1
Tool Manufacture			
Hammerstone	site furniture	53	
Hammerstone/abrader	site furniture	2	
Hammerstone/anvil	site furniture	17	
Anvil	site furniture	1	
Biface	personal gear	900	
Core	situational gear	84	
Pièces esquillées	situational gear	4	
Subtotal		1,061	41.6
Plant Food Processing			
Grindingstone/anvil	site furniture	12	0.5
Indeterminate			
Indeterminate ground stone	?	1	
Engraved stone	?	6	
Indeterminate scraper	situational gear	224	
Other worked stone	situational gear	6	
Unmodified cobble\stone	site furniture	41	
Subtotal		278	10.9
Total		2,549	100.0

Note: Data tabulated from tables 2.1, 2.3, and 2.4.

[a] Data for Early Archaic point totals tabulated from CBM, Zones 3 and 4.

and butchering or hide scraping), other tools were assigned to broader functional categories (e.g., light and heavy scraping and cutting).

In addition to their functional tasks, each tool type in the Hardaway assemblage was considered in one of three possible organizational roles: personal gear, situational gear, or site furniture (table 5.1). This scheme was used to reflect the fact that tools were not only designed to meet the functional requirements of particular tasks but were also organized to fulfill certain roles within a settlement system (Binford 1977, 1978, 1979). The distinction between personal gear and situational gear, for example, is based largely upon the idea that tools were organized with variable use lives that condition various aspects of their manufacture, use, maintenance, and discard.

Personal gear is that part of the technology which each individual carries in anticipation of future conditions or activities (Binford 1979). Personal gear is heavily curated; implements are recycled and reused and incur many maintenance expenditures (Binford 1977:33–34). Examples of such gear include bone cutters, discoidal cores, axes, flints for fires, needles, a quiver for arrows, and flake knives (Binford 1979:262–263).

The second category, situational gear, consists of items put together to carry out specific activities on an ad hoc basis. Situational gear is expediently made and used and is usually limited by the available raw material (Binford 1977). Raw material is acquired from caches, personal gear modified for reuse, material resources from the immediate environment, or material scavenged from previous occupations.

The last organizational category, site furniture, encompasses items that are site specific and are generally cached in anticipation of reuse (Binford 1978:339, 1979:263–264). Common examples of these items include relatively large or bulky objects such as hearthstones, anvils, and lithic raw material (Binford 1979:264).

This organizational scheme has important implications for understanding assemblage composition. The distinction between personal (curated) gear and situational (expedient) gear, for example, suggests that while assemblages should reliably reflect tool use involving expedient tools, the same may not be true for curated tools. Since curated tools are transported from site to site, the frequencies with which they occur in an assemblage may not accurately reflect the intensity of their use at any one site. Indeed, curated tools should enter the archaeological record more often at locations where they are replaced, which is not necessarily where they were used (Binford 1977:34).

It should be clear from the functional categories listed in table 5.1 that a variety of activities were probably undertaken at Hardaway. Moreover, given the preceding discussion, it should also be apparent that basing a determination of site function at Hardaway solely on a traditional qualitative and quantitative analysis of tool frequencies might be misleading. End scrapers, for example, account for 16.5 percent of the assemblage total, and on the basis of this measurement alone, hide scraping would constitute the second most abundant functional category at Hardaway (table 5.1). Given that this functional group consists largely of curated tools, however, and given Hardaway's proximity to the quarry source at Morrow Mountain, an alternative interpretation must be considered. As personal gear, the curated end scrapers recovered at Hardaway were probably used elsewhere in the settlement system and were brought to Hardaway in anticipation of being replaced. This interpretation, of course, takes into account the final factor relevant for an interpretation of assemblage composition at Hardaway—raw material availability (Bamforth 1986). The abundance of nearby rhyolite undoubtedly exerted a major influence on the assemblage at Hardaway, especially in the abundance of both expedient and curated tools. In fact, it is difficult to consider the presence of curated or expedient tools at Hardaway apart from their source. That is, given the abundance of nearby rhyolite and the mix of both curated and expedient tools at Hardaway, it seems probable that most of the curated tools recovered there were not used at the site but rather were discarded and replaced by newly manufactured ones.

The presence of curated end scrapers in the assemblage may thus reflect retooling activities as much as the activity of hide scraping. The actual degree of hide working undertaken at Hardaway is probably better reflected in the expedient end scraper tool types, which constitute only 6.1 percent (n = 157) of the total—less than half the initial hide-scraping frequency. Likewise, additional tool classes classified as personal gear at Hardaway may have been discarded as a result of retooling (table 5.1). In particular, retooled artifact classes would have included points and adzes. Points, of course, reflect hunting and butchering activities and constitute 11 percent of the assemblage total. While such activities were probably associated with the site occupation, point retooling was probably undertaken at Hardaway as well. The presence of exhausted and broken points as well as point preforms in the assemblage is also consistent with the notion of retooling. Similarly, the occurrence of adze preforms in the assemblage is also suggestive of adze replacement at Hardaway.

More direct evidence of retooling (or at least of gearing up) can be found in the assemblage in the presence of hammerstones, anvils, and cores, which, along with bifaces, compose the tool manufacturing group (41.6 percent). Tool manufacture is the dominant activity represented in the assemblage, with bifaces (35.3 percent, n = 900) accounting for the vast majority of items assigned to this functional group. Bifaces make efficient portable cores and were thus probably manufactured at Hardaway to be used elsewhere in the region.

BIFACE AND BLANK PRODUCTION

The idea that bifaces served as portable cores is a common theme in many models of hunter-gatherer technology (Cable 1982; Goodyear 1979; Keeley 1980:161; Kelly 1988). The preponderance of bifaces at Hardaway indicates that this was the raw material form in which other portions of the settlement region were provisioned. As is commonly noted, bifaces provide the maximum amount of flake return for the amount of stone carried and thus serve as an ideal portable source of raw material; this function does not, however, prevent the biface from being a long use-life tool itself (e.g., Kelly 1988). But bifaces alone were not the only form by which stone was introduced into Hardaway. Below I suggest that large flake blanks, also roughed out at the quarry, accompanied bifaces into Hardaway.

This conclusion is suggested by the fact that while most of the unifacial tools in the assemblage were made from block-derived blanks, virtually no block cores were recovered at Hardaway. The reader will recall that the tool descriptions in Chapter 4 emphasized blank size, shape, and modification. Remnant blank attributes examined here allowed unifacial tools in the assemblage to be placed into either a biface- or a block-derived category (or an indeterminate category) on the basis of an examination of striking platform type and angle.

Block-derived blanks, for instance, have relatively large and flat striking platforms with more obtuse striking angles; blanks in the later stage of reduction may also exhibit some platform faceting. Similarly, block-derived blanks have less complex and more unidirectional dorsal surface flake scar patterns than biface-derived blanks. Finally, the thick angular nature of block cores yields blanks with relatively thicker cross sections and more diverse shapes than bifacially derived flakes. The cores from which these flakes were produced were probably angular stone masses, squarish in shape, that had been quarried directly from the bedrock outcrop.

Biface-derived blanks, on the other hand, usually exhibit a faceted platform (i.e., retain remnants of the edge of the biface) along with platform preparation remnants such as grinding or some other modification usually required for proper bifacial thinning. Moreover, bifacial flaking also results in relatively small lipped platforms with relatively acute striking platform angles. Biface-derived blanks also have relatively more acute striking platform angles than block-derived blanks. In addition, biface-derived blanks display more complicated dorsal surface flake scar patterns resulting from previous flake removals. Finally, bifacially derived flakes tend to have rounded cross sections with pronounced ventral surface curvatures.

Blank type and platform angle are illustrated in figure 5.3. Striking platform angles on tools with measurable platforms display a bimodal distribution with peaks at 70–75 degrees and 80–85 degrees. Moreover, individual histograms for block- and biface-derived blank platform angles reveal the separate nature of these two populations. In fact, box plots of these data (figure 5.4) indicate that a significant difference exists in median striking platform values between block- and biface-derived blanks (80 degrees and 65 degrees, respectively).

Block-derived blanks are far more common, comprising 67.7 percent of the unifacial tools in the Hardaway assemblage, as compared with only 8.4 percent for biface-derived blanks (table 5.2). While a substantial number (23.9 percent) of tools could not confidently be assigned to a blank type, the box plot in figure 5.4 suggests that most of those with measurable platform angles were probably block derived as well.

Because bifaces, including projectile points, were more reduced, blank remnants were not as readily observed on them. Although this absence precluded the sort of analysis that was performed on the unifacial tools, some tentative conclusions concerning the derivation of biface blanks can be drawn on the basis of cursory observations made within the biface class discussed in Chapter 4. That is, bifaces appear to be produced most often from large block-derived flakes and less frequently from relatively large angular masses. Yet many Type I bifaces appeared to have originated in the latter group. This inference is made primarily on the basis of their relatively thick, blocky cross sections. Some Type I bifaces, and virtually all of those of Types II and III, however, were probably produced from large block-derived flakes. Portions of an unflaked ventral surface on some specimens verified their flake origin, and their relatively large dimensions probably precluded a bifacial derivation.

In sum, these results indicate that block cores were the primary source for deriving tool blanks in the Hardaway assemblage. In fact, only one tool type—side scraper Type IIb—had higher frequencies of biface-derived blanks than of block-derived blanks (table 5.2). As previously noted, these are fairly small tools that may reflect largely the opportunistic use of debitage produced during biface manufacture. Given that most of the tool blanks from the Hardaway assemblage were derived from block cores, it seems unlikely that blank production took place at Hardaway itself. Rather, it seems reasonable to suggest that tool blanks were produced at the quarry in the form of large flakes and were transported to Hardaway in unmodified or minimally retouched form. Furthermore, since some of the scrapers

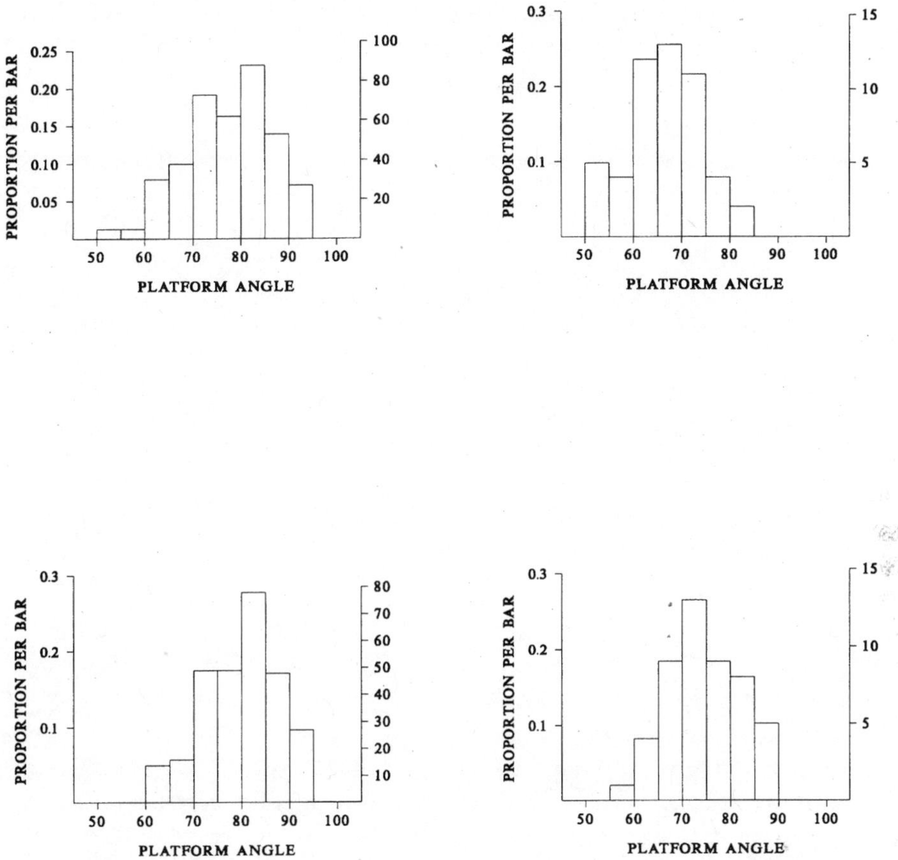

Figure 5.3. Histograms of striking platform angles on tool blanks: total sample (top left), biface-derived blanks (top right), block-derived blanks (bottom left), and indeterminate blank specimens (bottom right)

in the assemblage are relatively large (e.g., Type IIa end scrapers and Type IV side scrapers) and would have required a fairly large core as a parent material, it seems more likely that this activity would have been performed at the bedrock source. Moreover, if block cores were being brought to Hardaway in appreciable amounts, greater numbers of exhausted specimens and core remnants would be expected. These artifacts simply do not exist.

Three related behaviors, however, may have masked the former presence of block cores at Hardaway and therefore demand consideration. First, these cores may have suffered from the "size effect" described earlier. That is, a relatively large item such as a block core might have been scavenged repeatedly—as hypothesized for the hammerstones—when a site was reoccupied. Second, rather than being reduced until they were exhausted,

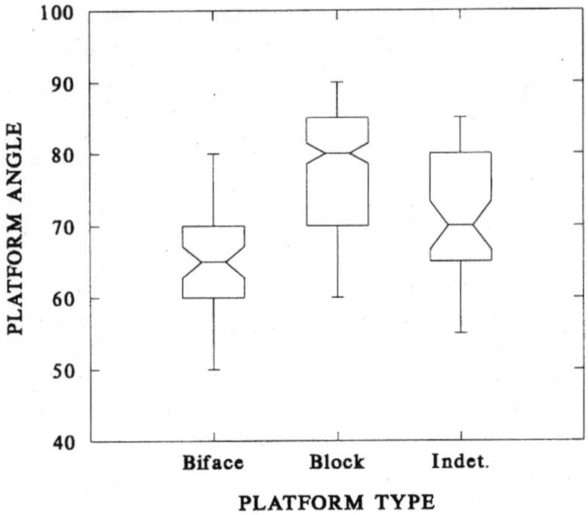

Figure 5.4. Box plots comparing platform angles of biface- and block-derived blanks and indeterminate blanks

block cores may simply have been recycled into large tools such as the core/scraper form described in Chapter 4. Third, block cores may have been only partly reduced at Hardaway and may have been transported from the site for use elsewhere.

While the first two explanations—scavenging and recycling—are plausible, they are still not sufficient in themselves to account for the virtual absence of block cores at Hardaway. The need to scavenge or recycle stone is more likely to manifest itself at locations where raw material is scarce; this, of course, was not the case at Hardaway. Finally, the third explanation—the transportation of block cores from Hardaway—seems least likely to account for their absence at the site. It is economical to use block cores only when stone sources are abundant. As has often been noted, block cores (i.e., mostly unmodified angular masses rectangular to squarish in shape, used with little regard for platform preparation and removal of subsequent flakes) generally produce much more waste than usable blanks (e.g., Goodyear 1979; Kelly 1988; MacDonald 1968:66; Parry and Kelly 1986). For mobile groups who spend considerable time away from stone sources, bifacial forms are a much more economical source of raw material than block cores and are thus more likely to be transported. Therefore, if block cores were present in any significant amount at Hardaway, they should have stayed there.

This procurement and production strategy of manufacturing tool blanks and roughing out bifaces at the quarry would have reduced the amount of stone to be carried to Hardaway and would have made it pos-

Table 5.2. Frequency of Block-Derived Versus Biface-Derived Blanks Among Unifacial Tools

	Block		Biface		Indeterminate		Total
Tool Type	*n*	%	*n*	%	*n*	%	
End scraper Ia	57	41.9	9	6.6	70	51.5	136
End scraper Ib	13	31.7	-	-	28	68.3	41
End scraper IIa	67	77.0	1	1.1	19	21.8	87
End scraper IIb	38	86.4	2	4.5	4	9.1	44
End scraper III	6	66.7	-	-	3	33.3	9
End scraper IV	22	88.0	-	-	3	12.0	25
End scraper V	62	78.5	5	6.3	12	15.2	79
Side scraper I	19	95.0	-	-	1	5.0	20
Side scraper IIa	177	80.1	23	10.4	21	9.5	221
Side scraper IIb	3	12.5	14	58.3	7	29.2	24
Side scraper III	94	76.4	17	13.8	12	9.8	123
Side scraper IV	16	70.0	-	-	7	30.0	23
Pointed scraper Ia	3	100.0	-	-	-	-	3
Pointed scraper Ib	3	50.0	1	16.7	2	33.3	6
Oval scraper	3	60.0	-	-	2	40.0	5
Denticulate	1	50.0	-	-	1	50.0	2
Perforator/drill	5	55.6	-	-	4	44.4	9
Graver	6	31.6	2	10.5	11	57.9	19
Other scraper	9	52.9	1	5.9	7	41.2	17
Hafted spokeshave	2	100.0	-	-	-	-	2
Waller knife	1	100.0	-	-	-	-	1
Total	607	67.7	75	8.4	214	23.9	896

sible—a luxury—to select only the most suitable tool blanks and bifaces. In fact, such a strategy has been observed ethnoarchaeologically, as indicated by the following description of two Alywara men at work in a stone quarry. "It was explained that shaping the core was the 'big job,' and was always done in the quarry, where all the big chunks and 'mistakes' could be thrown away before one had to carry anything. Jacob noted that once one got a 'good one,' that is, a well-prepared core, 'everybody hit 'em off as many as you can get before you make mistakes'. . . . The comments by the informants made it clear that the manufacture of blades as demonstrated by Sandy was normally done in the quarry. The resulting blanks would then be introduced to the residential site as manufactured items" (Binford and O'Connell 1984:415). In sum, while it is possible that some blanks were also finished into tools at the quarry, the vast amount of production debris at Hardaway indicates that tool manufacture was probably not a significant activity at the quarry itself.

SITE FUNCTION AND SETTLEMENT ADAPTATION

Stone tool assemblages reflect more than simply the tasks for which they were designed. As such, archaeologists are now viewing stone tool assemblages as reflecting the organized use of prehistoric landscapes. That is, stone tool assemblages reflect the larger contexts of the locations and conditions under which they were produced, used, maintained, and discarded. Moreover, the perspective of technological organization—the concept that stone tool technologies were spatially, temporally, and functionally organized—is now being used as a method of understanding nonmaterial aspects of cultural systems such as settlement adaptations (e.g., Binford 1977, 1978, 1979).

With respect to the Hardaway assemblage, tool types were designed to fulfill certain *roles* in the settlement system as well as certain functional *tasks*. That is, tools were not only made to be used for a particular function (or range of functions) but were also designed with respect to long- versus short-term usage, to be used at specific times and places in the settlement system. In fact, this form of organization meant that tools designed for different roles in the assemblage were used for the same tasks.

The distinction between roles and tasks is nicely illustrated with regard to the various end scrapers identified at Hardaway. As I noted in Chapter 4, edge rounding was observed on the bits of virtually every type of end scraper in the assemblage. Assuming that this use-wear trait largely reflects a single function (i.e., hide scraping), then the function crosscuts tool form. The end scrapers were created to be used for similar functions but under different conditions. Expedient end scrapers were manufactured for immediate use at Hardaway, while the curated forms were made primarily for transport and use elsewhere in the region. Binford has anticipated this variability in the context of tool use. "We can expect many such tool-design parallels, that is tools of very different design being used for identical tasks; but this is not to say that they are functionally isomorphic, since they are clearly designed for very different intended roles within the technology" (Binford 1979:269).

Thus, given the abundance of nearby rhyolite outcrops, the mix of both curated and expedient tools at Hardaway is consistent with the model: expedient tools were used at sites near stone sources, while curated tools were made and conserved for use elsewhere. "If a group is occupying a site near a source of lithic raw material, they may prefer to employ expedient implements while conserving or even ignoring hafted tools. The assemblage at such a site would contain large amounts of waste and a relatively large number of big, minimally retouched tools. . . . In addition, a group about to leave a site with abundant lithic raw material may extensively retool in anticipation of future shortages of suitable stone at sites occupied next in their seasonal round" (Keeley 1982:803–804).

While tool manufacturing was emphasized at Hardaway, the presence of hide working, a bone- and woodworking industry, butchering activities, and plant processing indicates that the site was not occupied exclusively to replace tool kits. These activities are reflected in the situational gear present in most of the functional tool groups in table 5.1. Tools categorized as situational gear are abundant in the functional groups of light scraping and cutting (6.2 percent) and heavy scraping and cutting (12.1 percent); quite possibly these activities would have included wood and bone working and even butchering (table 5.1). Finally, that plant food was processed is also suggested by the presence of site furniture in the form of grinding stones (0.5 percent). Plant food processing, however, is probably underrepresented in table 5.1, since perishable materials or cobble tools (e.g., hammerstones/anvils) could also have been used for this activity. Taken together, these activities presumably reflect routine maintenance tasks associated with a residential base camp. It therefore appears that Hardaway can be characterized as a quarry-related base camp. In fact, tool kits are most often refurbished during longer-term occupations within a settlement system (Keeley 1982:804).

Finally, although retooling may have been the primary economic activity undertaken at Hardaway, social or ritual functions may have been carried out at the site as well. This possibility is raised by the presence of three unusual tool classes: quartz crystal pièces esquilleés, bipolar quartz crystal cores, and engraved stone. The exact functions of these tool classes remains unknown, but as I indicated earlier, I speculate that they were not used in utilitarian tasks. The unique nature of the crystal itself may have prompted it to be used in some social or ritual functions. Engraved stone also represents another unusual artifact category; it too may have some social or ritual significance.

In any case, as a quarry-related base camp, Hardaway probably performed a unique role in the settlement system. Early Archaic groups likely visited Hardaway as a regular part of their settlement round. These visits were scheduled to replace depleted tool kits, and camping at Hardaway provided access to stone of the best quality in the region. Rhyolite was procured and initially processed at Morrow Mountain and was then brought to Hardaway primarily in the form of bifaces and flake blanks. Some of this stone was made into expedient tools that were used to sustain a group during its stay at the site. Other tools were produced and stockpiled for future use elsewhere in the region where there was no ready access to stone sources. This latter assemblage—including points, bifaces, and hafted unifacial tools—replaced the remnants of depleted tool kits brought to the site and then discarded in anticipation of gearing up at Hardaway. In addition, relatively large unmodified flake blanks were probably also transported with the finished tool kit as insurance against situational contingencies not initially anticipated in the tool kit inventory.

This organizational strategy did not lack adaptive significance for the Early Archaic inhabitants of the Piedmont. In fact, it was vital to survival in the region once the group left Hardaway. That is, the organization of the technology at Hardaway was an adaptive response by mobile Early Archaic groups, which essentially focused on Uwharrie rhyolite as an economic source for stone tools but which otherwise employed a geographically wide-ranging settlement round that necessitated spending considerable distance or time (or both) away from knappable stone.

6

Intrasite Spatial Analysis

The analysis of the spatial distributions of artifacts has led to important insights concerning the spatial structure of several early prehistoric hunter-gatherer sites in North America. In particular, the analyses of the spatial distributions of stone artifacts on northeastern Paleo-Indian sites have been successful in identifying discrete clusters of artifacts. Moreover, these artifact clusters have been interpreted to represent the remains of short-term habitation episodes by small social groups (e.g., Gramly 1982; Grimes et al. 1984; Lothrop 1988; MacDonald 1968). In fact, the evidence of refitted broken artifacts among these clusters supports the possibility that different areas on the same site were contemporaneously occupied.

It has been more difficult to identify and interpret spatial patterning on early sites in the Southeast, however. This difficulty may be related, in part, to longer-term habitation or greater site reoccupation in the Southeast. In any event, spatial analyses have been conducted on only two Paleo-Indian sites in the Southeast: Thunderbird (Gardner 1974) and Harney Flats (Daniel and Wisenbaker 1987). Several Dalton and Early Archaic sites, however, have received attention, including Brand (Goodyear 1974), Haw River (Claggett and Cable 1982), Rucker's Bottom (Anderson and Schuldenrein 1985), George S. Lewis (Anderson and Hanson 1988), and Rose Island (Kimball 1993). Attempts at spatial analysis on these sites have involved both visual inspection of artifact distributions as well as more formal, quantitative techniques. In this chapter I examine the spatial distributions of stone artifacts at Hardaway.

ANALYTICAL APPROACHES

The spatial analysis in this chapter has two parts. First, I compare simple density distributions of various artifact groups across the site. These artifact distributions include various tool groups (i.e., "functional classes") as well as debitage and raw material classes. The primary purpose of the analysis is to represent the patterning of artifacts visually across the excavated block and to afford some basis for the identification of potential activity areas.

Second, I analyze spatial distributions of the same functional classes using Whallon's (1984) "unconstrained clustering" technique. This technique detects significant spatial variation and patterning in assemblage composition among grid squares across the site and avoids many of the questionable assumptions for which other techniques have been criticized (see Whallon 1984).

To facilitate the analysis I have lumped all the artifact types described in Chapter 4 into eight "functional" categories. It is important to note, however, that while tool types with similar presumed functions have been combined into single categories, the term "functional" is not defined solely by specific tool uses. Rather, the term is employed in a broad fashion to include other factors (such as curation rates) that affect conditions under which a tool was made, used, and discarded. In this regard, the organizational categories outlined in Chapter 5 have been used to create the functional groupings. The resulting classes are described below.

All point types and unidentifiable point fragments have been combined under "projectile points." (Since temporal distinctions can be made within this group, maps have also been generated on the basis of individual point types to examine variation in site use through time.) Biface manufacture was clearly an important activity at Hardaway, and all biface and preform types were lumped into a single "bifaces" category. All hafted end scrapers (Types Ia, Ib, IIb, and III) and side scrapers (Types I and IV) were combined into a category called "hafted scrapers." The two adzes were also included in this group, because they too were once hafted. These curated tools were combined here, since they were probably discarded at the site where they were replaced rather than where they were used (see Keeley 1982). In contrast, expedient tools probably accumulated at or closer to the place of their last use (Binford 1979), and several expedient tools in the assemblage were combined to reflect this discard pattern. Given their presumed functional differences, several expedient end and side scraper types were combined into two general classes: "expedient end scrapers" (Types IIa, IV, V) and "expedient side scrapers" (Type IIa, IIb, and III). This latter category also included all indeterminate scraper fragments.

"Miscellaneous flaked tools" is a residual category that comprises the remaining minority of chipped-stone tools, representing a variety of functions. This group includes gravers, drills, core scrapers, hafted spokeshaves, pointed scrapers, oval scrapers, other scrapers, denticulates, and Waller knives; most of these classes represent expedient tools.

The category "site furniture" includes artifacts identified as such in table

5.2: hammerstones, hammerstones/abraders, hammerstones/anvils, anvils, grinding stones/anvils, choppers, and unmodified cobbles. In addition, I have somewhat arbitrarily included the unidentified ground stone fragment and the engraved "slate" in site furniture. Since the engraved slate has rarely been identified in sites beyond Hardaway, an argument could be made for its being site specific. Finally, the category "cores" includes all core types and pièces esquillées.

ARTIFACT DENSITY DISTRIBUTIONS

The computer program SURFER was used to generate contour maps based upon artifact counts for each unit; artifact counts were totaled for Zone 3 (or CBM) and Zone 4 for each 5 ft square. These data were smoothed using a cubic spline interpolation algorithm (SURFER 1987) and essentially depict artifact densities across the excavated block. Because zone thickness varied, the density maps were generated on the basis of artifact counts per cubic foot of excavated soil. Pothunting, of course, had disturbed many of the units from the 1970s excavations. Therefore, artifact counts were computed on the basis of the undisturbed portion of the square. These estimates, along with the procedure used to derive them, appear in Appendix B.

A contour map of the total tool count indicates that tools are well distributed across the excavated block, with several tool concentrations 5–10 ft (1.5–3 m) in diameter of greater than three tools per cubic foot (figure 6.1). Moreover, these tool concentrations are all connected by a less dense but continuous tool scatter. The most distinct concentration lies near the center of the block; using a density contour of 3 tools/ft^3 as a boundary, it is about 15 ft (4.5 m) in diameter.

While it is tempting to view each of these tool concentrations as activity areas (i.e., locales of refuse deposited as a result of domestic or communal activities), this interpretation is suspect for at least two reasons. First, the question of site formation, which remains to be resolved, bears on the interpretation of artifact concentrations at Hardaway. A comparison of the contour map of tool density with a similar map of soil volume, for example, reveals that concentrations of tools roughly parallel the volume of excavated soil (figure 6.1). This comparison suggests that tool density is at least partially related to soil volume at Hardaway. In Chapter 2, I suggested that natural processes may have played a more significant role in site formation than originally thought. If so, then artifact densities may not be completely related to cultural processes.

In any case, the behavioral interpretation of at least one tool concentration—the large dense tool cluster noted above—can be questioned, since

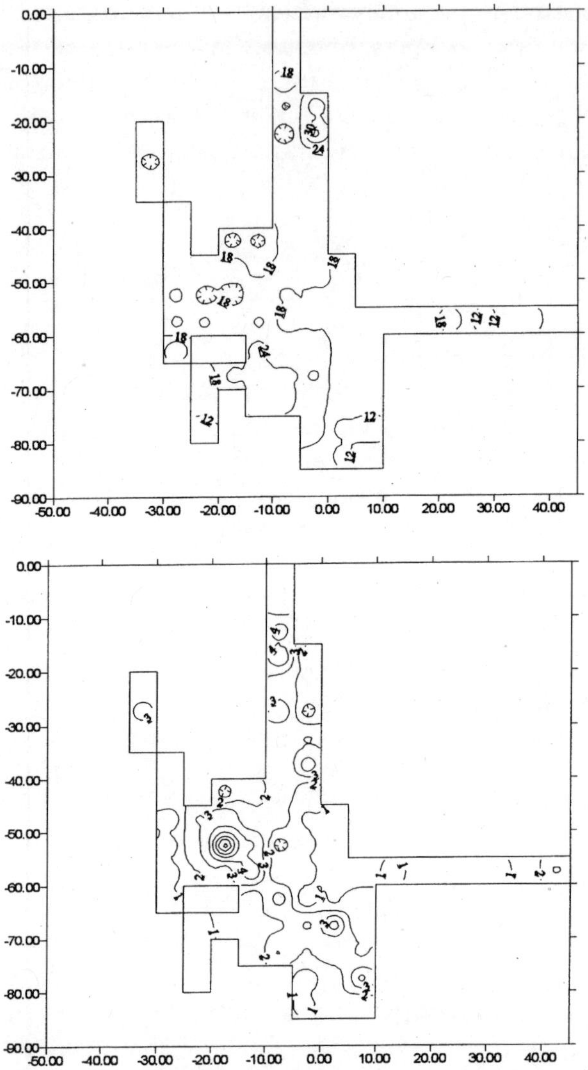

Figure 6.1. Contour map comparing soil volume (ft^3) for the CBM, Zone 3, and Zone 4 (top), with total tool density (count/ft^3) (bottom)

it relates to two features (Feature 40 and Feature 41) with questionable cultural origins. That is, both of these features were probably naturally filled depressions (see Chapter 2). If true, this fact would obviously belie any interpretation of this artifact concentration as an activity area.

But even if the question of site formation is disregarded, no readily interpretable pattern is evident. Moreover, these concentrations are unlike other material clusters that have been identified as activity areas either archaeologically (e.g., Gramly 1982; Grimes et al. 1984) or ethnoarchaeologically (e.g., Binford 1983; O'Connell 1987; O'Connell et al. 1991; Yellen 1977) in hunter-gatherer campsites. Material clusters in these ethnoarchaeological sites are often characterized by artifact concentrations that are spatially discrete from one another. Instead, spatial patterning at Hardaway exhibits a relatively large continuous artifact distribution containing smaller areas of relatively high artifact densities. Such a pattern suggests numerous and perhaps intense reoccupations created by a series of overlapping tool deposits.

Site reoccupation, of course, is consistent with the range of Early Archaic point types recovered from Hardaway. And while some loose clustering of point types is present—represented by groups of contiguous squares containing similar point types—the occurrence of several point types from the same square is just as common (figures 6.2–6.6). In short, this evidence suggests that the site structure manifested by several temporally discrete artifact clusters may not have existed or may not have survived at Hardaway as a result of site reuse through the millennia. A similar conclusion may be drawn from an examination of the spatial distribution for each of the functional tool groups described above (figures 6.7–6.14). That is, almost every functional class exhibits several relatively high concentrations connected by a continuous, less dense scatter of tools. In short, no "functionally" discrete artifact clusters are discernible in the spatial patterning at Hardaway either.

Turning to the spatial patterning of flakes, we also see a few small areas of relatively high densities scattered among a continuous area of lower densities (figures 6.15–6.16). Moreover, the highest flake densities consistently occur south of the –45 line (figure 6.15). It is unlikely, however, that this pattern has any spatial significance. Rather, the higher flake densities in the southern half of the block almost certainly relate to the greater emphasis given to flake recovery in the 1970s excavations (see Chapter 4).

Also occurring south of the –45 line is a noticeable concentration of flakes both by count (from 100 to more than 200 flakes/ft^3) and weight (from 200 to 700 g/ft^3). This flake cluster coincides with the tool concentration discussed previously that was associated with Features 40 and 41. As in the case of the tool distribution, it is unlikely that any distinct activity areas can be identified in the flake distributions. Rather, even accounting for the biases in flake recovery, the pattern of small areas of flake concentrations scattered among a continuous distribution of flakes suggests that the flake distribution at Hardaway was also influenced by site reoccupation.

In an attempt to minimize the effects of site reoccupation, I examined

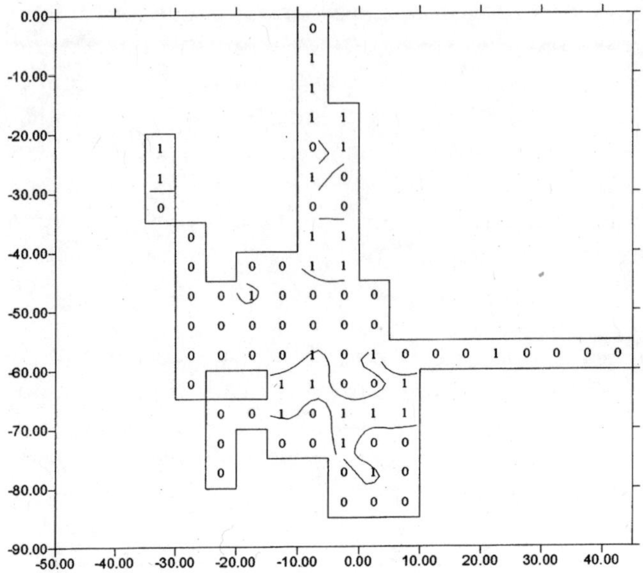

Figure 6.2. Spatial distribution of units containing Hardaway-Dalton points

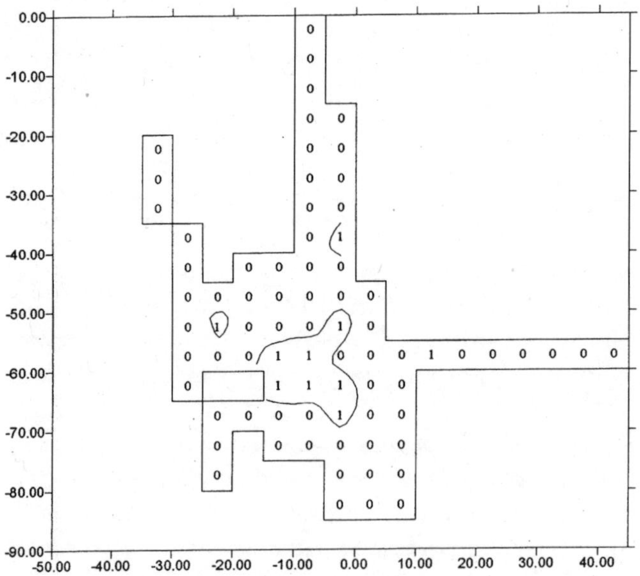

Figure 6.3. Spatial distribution of units containing Hardaway Side-Notched points

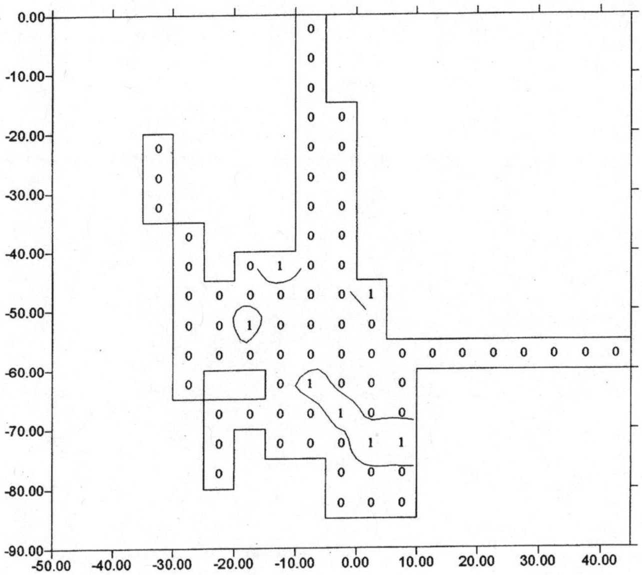

Figure 6.4. Spatial distribution of units containing small Dalton points

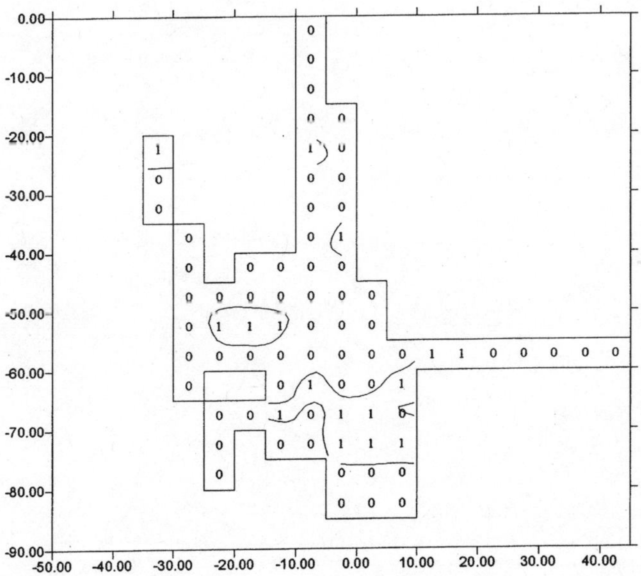

Figure 6.5. Spatial distribution of units containing Palmer Corner-Notched points

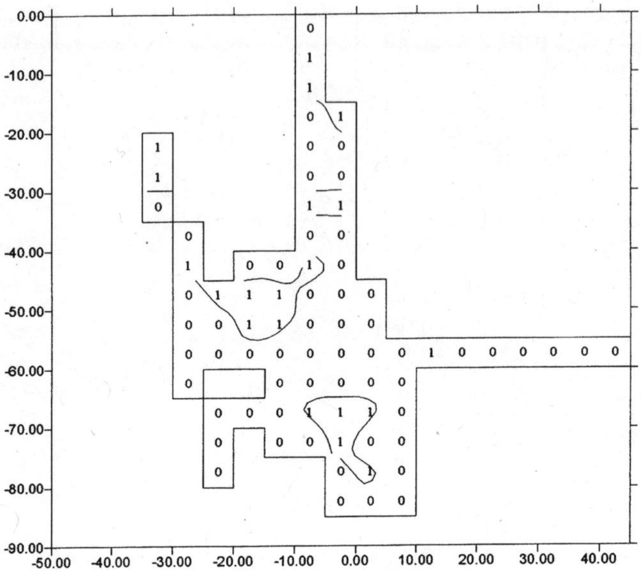

Figure 6.6. Spatial distribution of units containing Kirk Corner-Notched points

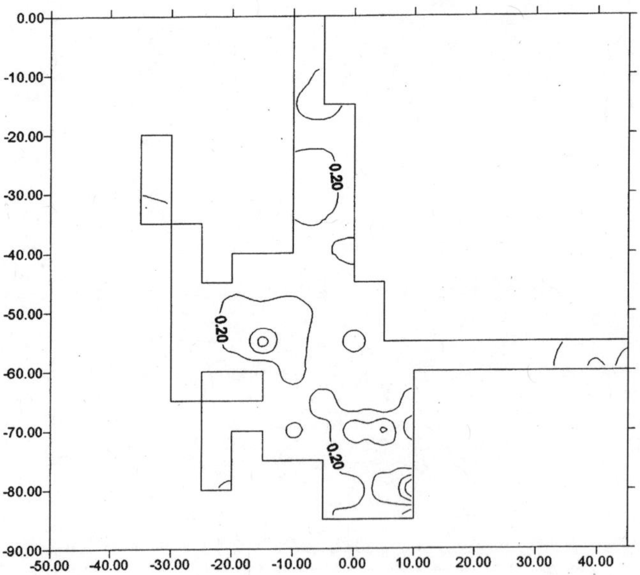

Figure 6.7. Density maps for points (count/ft^3)

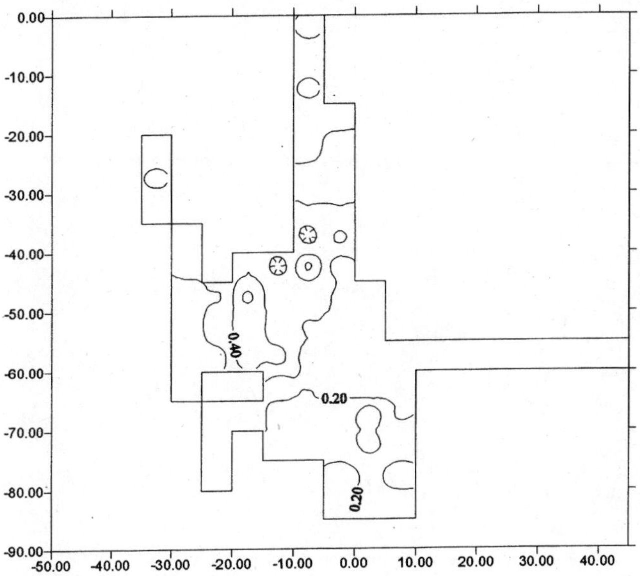

Figure 6.8. Density maps for hafted scrapers (count/ft^3)

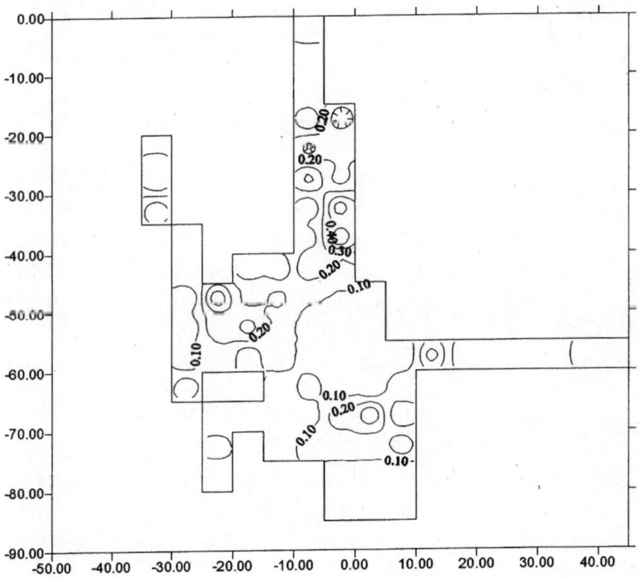

Figure 6.9. Density maps for expedient end scrapers (count/ft^3)

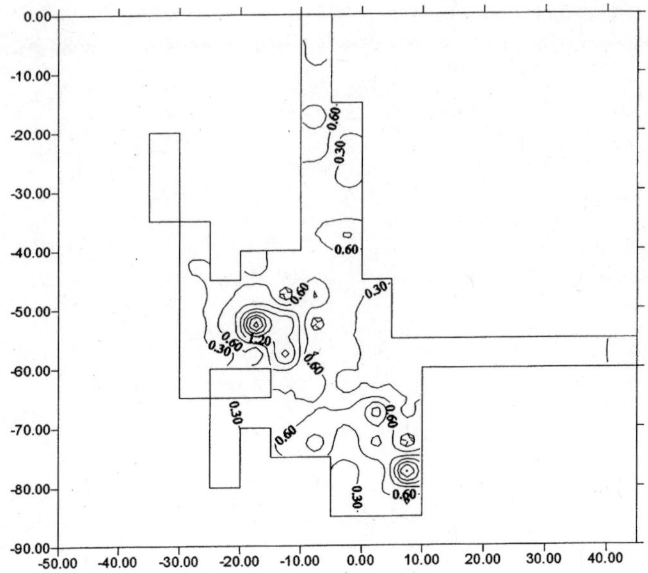

Figure 6.10. Density maps for other side scrapers (count/ft^3)

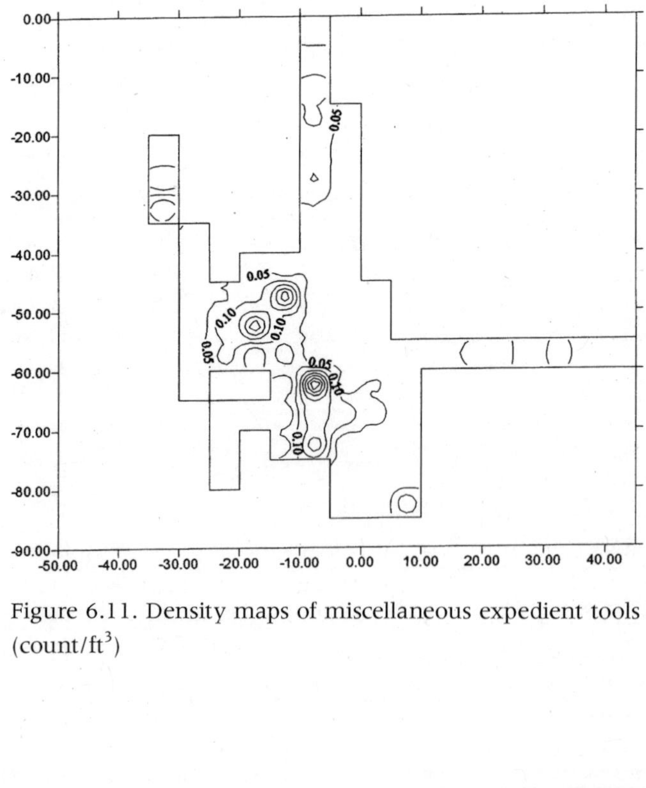

Figure 6.11. Density maps of miscellaneous expedient tools (count/ft^3)

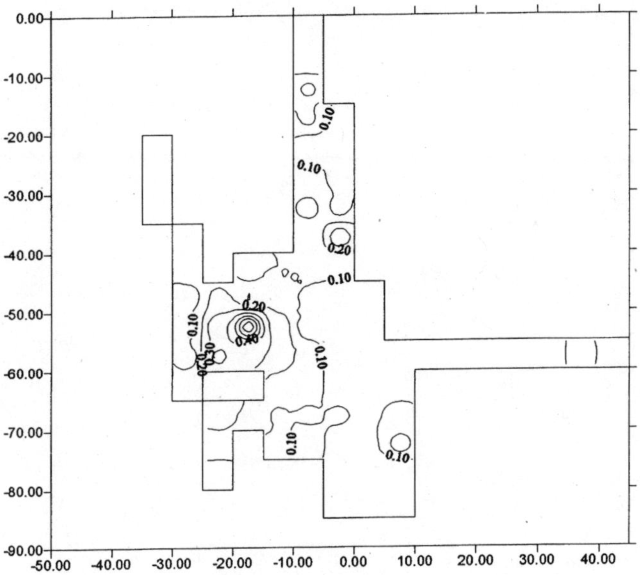

Figure 6.12. Density maps of site furniture (count/ft^3)

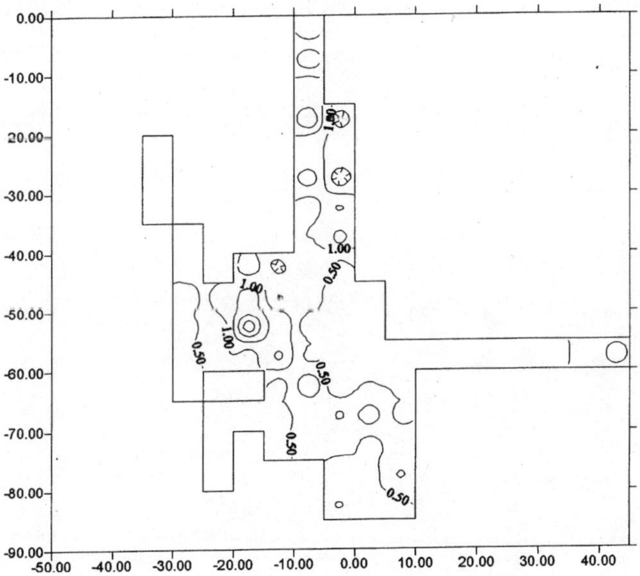

Figure 6.13. Density maps of bifaces (count/ft^3)

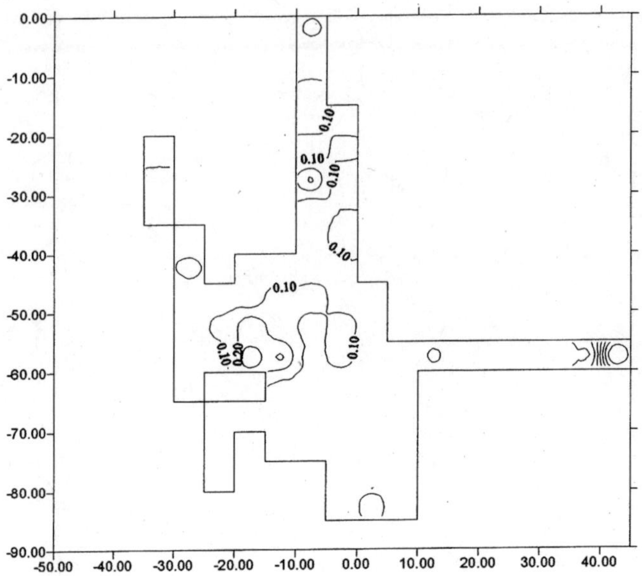

Figure 6.14. Density maps of cores (count/ft^3)

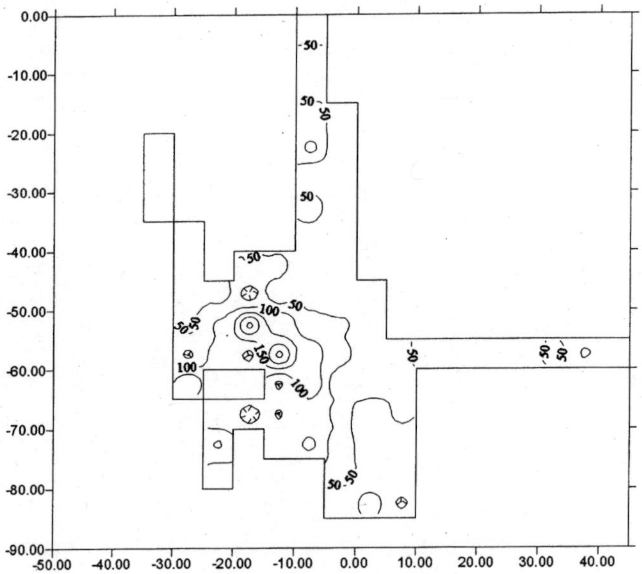

Figure 6.15. Density maps of total flake counts (count/ft^3)

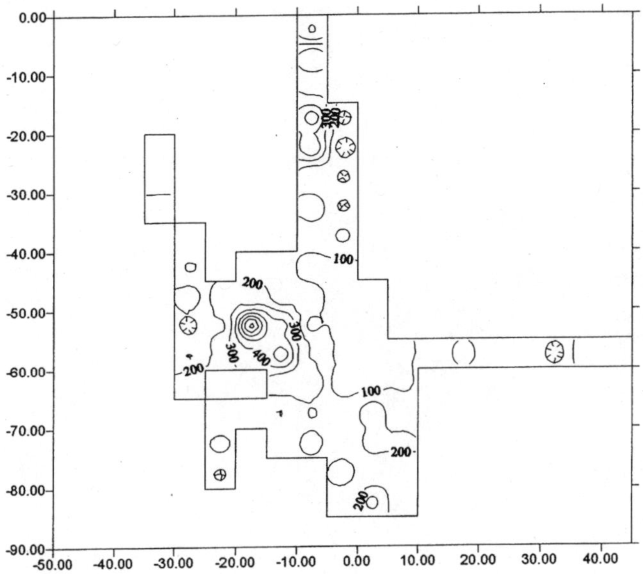

Figure 6.16. Density maps of total flake weight (g/ft^3)

the spatial distributions of the frequencies of nonrhyolitic stone (i.e., quartz, crystal quartz, green metasiltstone, and chert) in the assemblage. Given the low frequencies of these raw materials, I reasoned that their output on the site was more likely to be associated with relatively short-term episodes that might more easily be identified spatially in comparison with the more ubiquitous rhyolite. As expected, the densities of these raw materials are uniformly low (often less than 1/ft^3). Some clustering exists, but tool and flake concentrations often do not overlap. While the spatial distributions of these minority raw materials are provocative, any interpretations assigned to them must take into account the variation in flake recovery methods noted earlier, especially since most of the minority raw material flake clusters were located in the southern half of the block.

This bias notwithstanding, such patterning might suggest that tool reduction (i.e., tool manufacture and/or maintenance) was spatially separate from the location of tool discard. Green metasiltstone flakes and tools, for example, are continuously scattered across the excavated area, but there is only one location where clusters of both tools and debitage overlap (in the west-central portion of the block) (figure 6.17). There is even less spatial correspondence between tools and debitage of quartz crystal (figure 6.18). Similarly, quartz flakes are concentrated in the southern and particularly the southwestern portion of the excavated block, while concentrations of

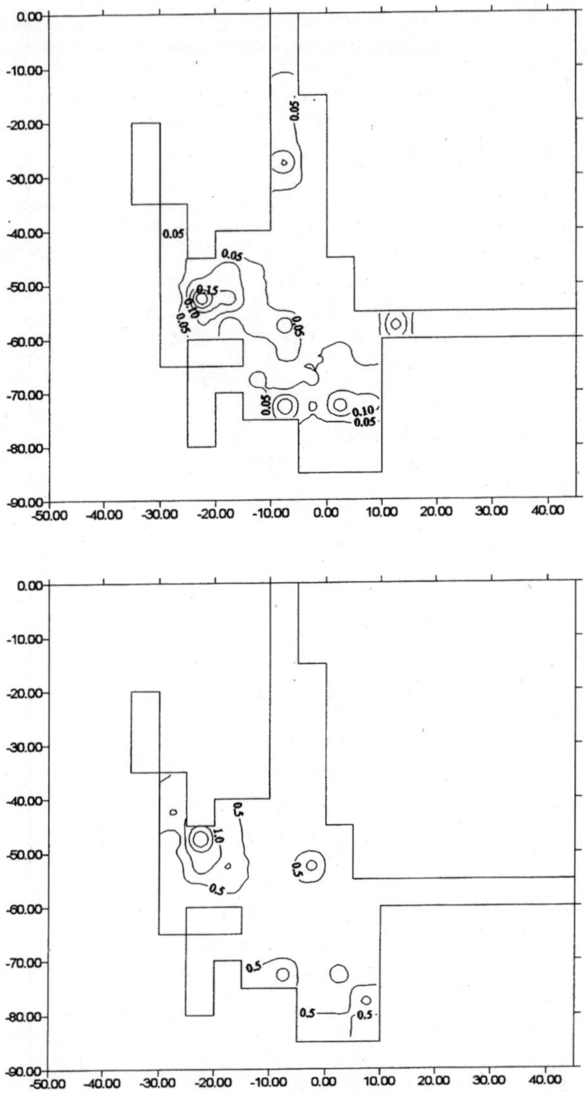

Figure 6.17. Density map of green metasiltstone: tools (top); flakes (bottom) (count/ft^3)

quartz tools are primarily located in the northern portion of the block (figure 6.19).

Last, another marked separation exists between chert flakes (i.e., chalcedony, jasper, and all other cherts), which are highly clustered in the east central and southern portion of the excavated block, and chert tools, which are also highly clustered to the south and are somewhat clustered to the

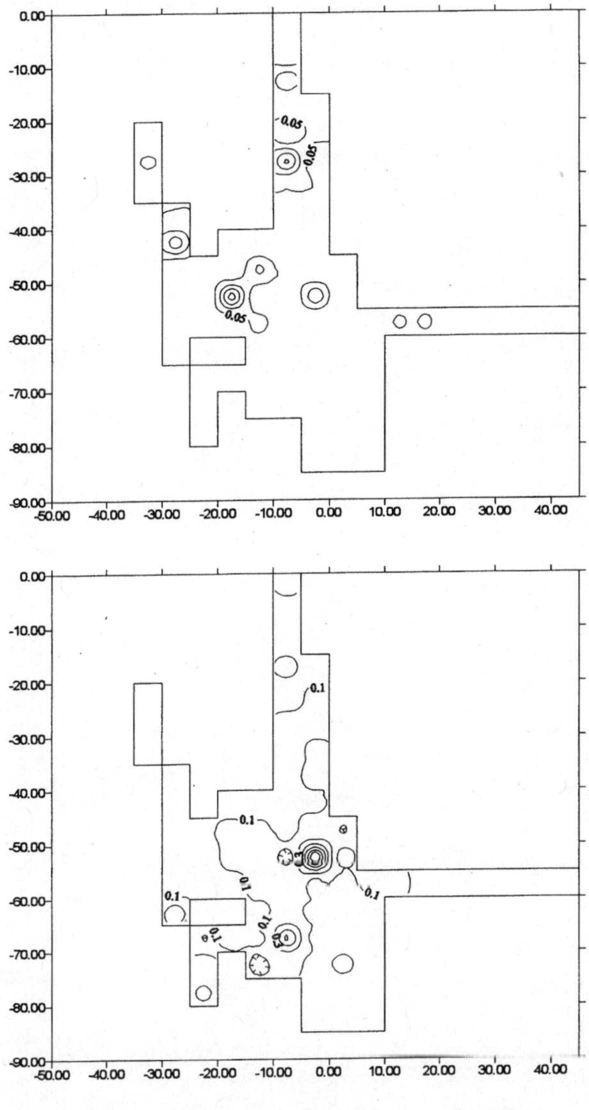

Figure 6.18. Density map of quartz crystal: tools (top); flakes (bottom) (count/ft^3)

north (although some overlap is present between tools and debitage in the southern part of the block) (figure 6.20). It is interesting to note that although this category includes a variety of cryptocrystalline raw materials, these stone types are clustered together. The close spatial association might reflect some temporal association in the use of these cherts at Hardaway. In any event, the question of separate but contemporaneous use of selected

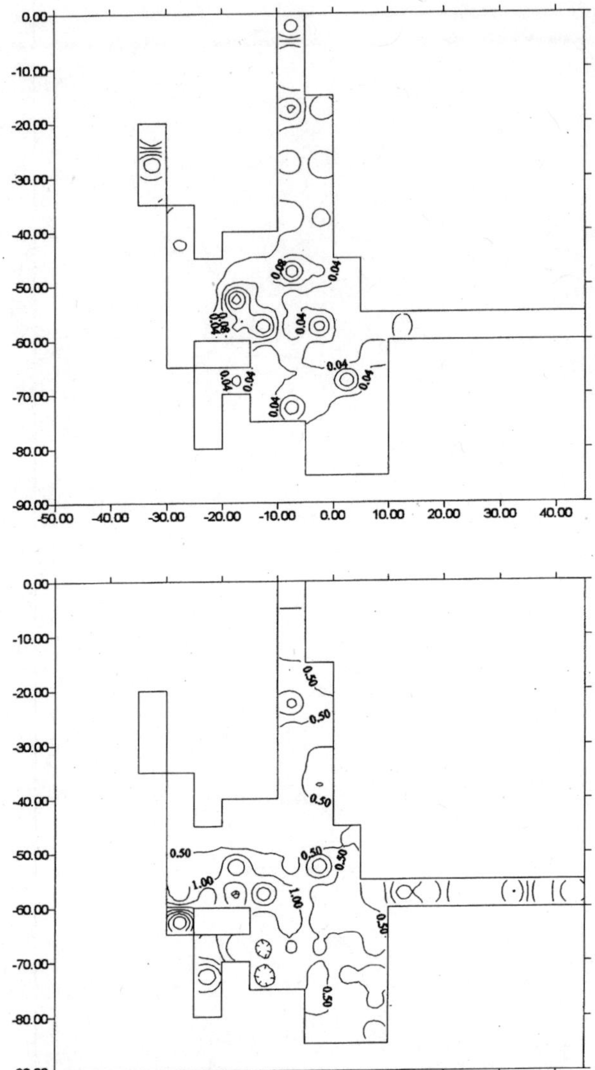

Figure 6.19. Density map of quartz: tools (top); flakes (bottom) (count/ft^3)

areas at Hardaway can be further addressed by an artifact refitting study (e.g., Cahen et al. 1979). If tools were made or maintained in areas separate from areas where they were discarded, then some artifacts should have cross-mends or flake refits from different areas of the site. Although no serious attempts at refitting were done in this study, a group of chalcedony flakes were found in the east-central chert cluster in figure 6.20, while a

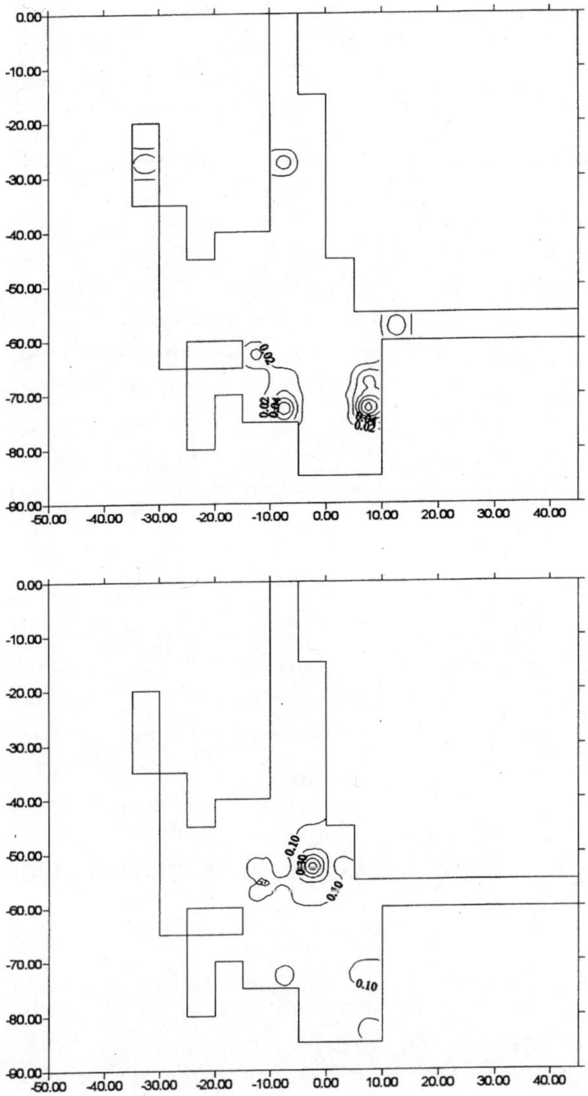

Figure 6.20. Density map of chert: tools (top); flakes (bottom) (count/ft^3)

chalcedony biface was recovered about 40 ft (12 m) to the northwest. Unfortunately, no refits could be made among the flakes and biface, but the distinctiveness and rarity of this raw material strongly suggests that these flakes were derived from the biface. Refitting among the rhyolite artifacts, of course, could also provide additional insight into site structure. (In view of the amount of material, however, I can't imagine a more tedious task.)

In sum, an attempt has been made to identify site structure at Hardaway by examining patterning in artifact density distributions. At least one conclusion can be drawn from these patterns: no readily distinguishable activity areas can be identified at Hardaway. The continued reuse of Hardaway appears to have produced a palimpsest of artifact distributions, essentially masking any clear signs of spatial structure. While I have emphasized the complicating effects of site reoccupation, other factors undoubtedly contributed to the artifact distributions at Hardaway, including the size and composition of the resident group, length of occupation, and aspects of technological organization such as raw material availability, curation, and discard rates. Given this complexity, the absence of apparent spatial patterning in a visual examination of artifact densities should not be surprising. I therefore used another, more quantitative technique as well to detect spatial patterning at Hardaway. As I note below, however, this analytical technique essentially supports the conclusions reached here.

CLUSTER ANALYSIS

There has been a rapid increase in the number of quantitative techniques available to archaeologists for spatial analysis during the last decade (e.g., Hietala 1984; Kent 1987; Kroll and Price 1991). The growing technical sophistication has been accompanied by an increased understanding of the processes, both cultural and natural, involved in the formation of spatial patterning on archaeological sites. At the same time, however, there has also been an increased awareness of the problem of congruence between the application of these analytical methods and the processes that are believed to form the archaeological record. Whallon (1984), for example, has noted that activity areas can vary in size, shape, densities, and assemblage composition and that many quantitative techniques (e.g., nearest neighbor) are not congruent with such expectations.

Fortunately, Whallon (1984) has also designed an approach that obviates such assumptions. This approach, known as "unconstrained clustering," determines whether clearly definable differences in assemblage composition exist across a site. If so, the distribution and composition of these groups are plotted and provide the basis for the interpretation of spatial patterning.

This method uses cluster analysis to find activity areas by examining the variation in the relative frequencies of artifact classes across a site. As applied here to grid count data, individual grid units comprise the observations, while the proportions of different artifact types within each unit form the variables to which the clustering algorithm is applied.

A *k*-means clustering algorithm was chosen because of its nonhierarchical nature. That is, clusters formed at one level can be independent from clusters joined at another. The specific cluster program used was the *k*-means procedure discussed by Kintigh and Ammerman (1982; Kintigh 1991). The *k*-means analysis attempts to minimize the sum-squared-error (SSE) statistic, which is used in interpreting the *k*-means results. The SSE is a measure of within-cluster variation: the sum of the squared distances between each point in the cluster and its centroid. As the number of clusters increases, the SSE decreases. Moreover, the better clustered the points are, the more rapidly the measure drops.

Using this statistic, Kintigh's (1991) program also provides a method by which the degree of data clustering can be evaluated. Although the analyst determines the maximum number of clusters, the procedure allows the researcher to compare the degree of clustering observed in the actual data with clustering observed with comparable randomized data. In essence, this procedure proposes a "significant" cluster level or levels for closer inspection by the analyst. This determination is made by plotting the SSE percentage from both the actual and random data runs against clustering stage. In this case, the SSE is expressed as a percentage of the total SSE of a single cluster divided by the SSE of any particular cluster configuration (Kintigh and Ammerman 1982:44–46). If the SSE based on the actual data falls within the range of the SSE generated by the randomized runs, then no significant clustering is indicated. On the other hand, if there is a strong difference between the actual and random SSE plots, then significant clustering is indicated.

For the Hardaway data, the plot of SSE percentage against the number of clusters for assemblage composition indicates no significant difference between plots of the actual data and five randomized data runs (figure 6.21). Nevertheless, a slight divergence is present at three, five, and nine clusters, and each of these groups was more closely examined for evidence of spatial patterning. Neither the mapping nor the composition of each of these solutions, however, revealed any clear evidence of interpretable clustering.

A discussion of the three-cluster solution illustrates the result. Figure 6.22 shows the assignment of each of the grid units to the three-cluster solution. The vast majority of the units belong to either Cluster 1 or Cluster 3; only two units comprise Cluster 2. Spatially, Clusters 1 and 3 are uniformly spread across the excavated block. Cluster 3 forms an amorphous area covering most of the center block but is heavily interfingered with Cluster 1 units. Some isolated Cluster 3 units are also present along the edge of the excavated area. The two isolated Cluster 2 units lie in the southern and southwest corner of the block. In short, no clustering can be detected here.

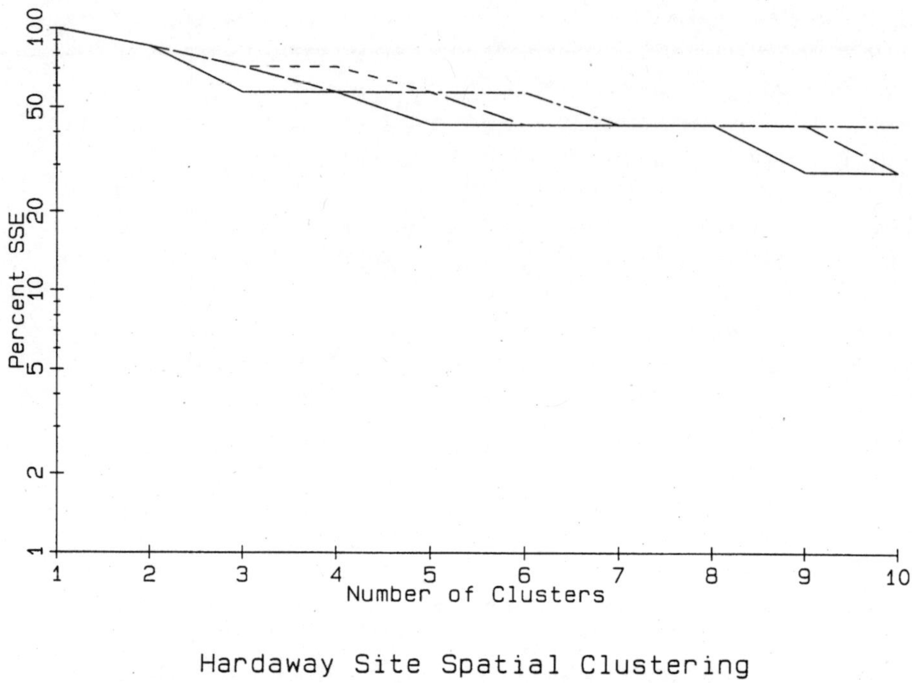

Figure 6.21. Plot of sum squared error percentage for *k*-means clustering comparing runs of input data (solid line) and randomized data (broken lines)

This lack of patterning is reinforced by an examination of the material composition of each cluster (table 6.1). The assemblage composition of each defined cluster is expressed by the means and standard deviations of the relative densities of all material classes over the item included in each cluster.

Cluster 1 constitutes almost 60 percent of all the units in the analysis. In composition, it represents an assemblage made up mostly of bifaces (42 percent), followed by lesser amounts of expedient side scrapers (16 percent), hafted scrapers (12 percent), and points (10 percent). In the latter two types, the standard deviations, which are near the mean score, suggest some variability of occurrence. The remaining functional classes are represented to a minor extent (i.e., less than 10 percent), although in almost every case their standard deviations are greater than their means, a reflection of extreme variability in their proportions.

The above characterization is generally true of Cluster 3 as well. The major difference between Cluster 1 and Cluster 3 is that bifaces and other side scrapers are reversed in ranking, with a slight change in their mean

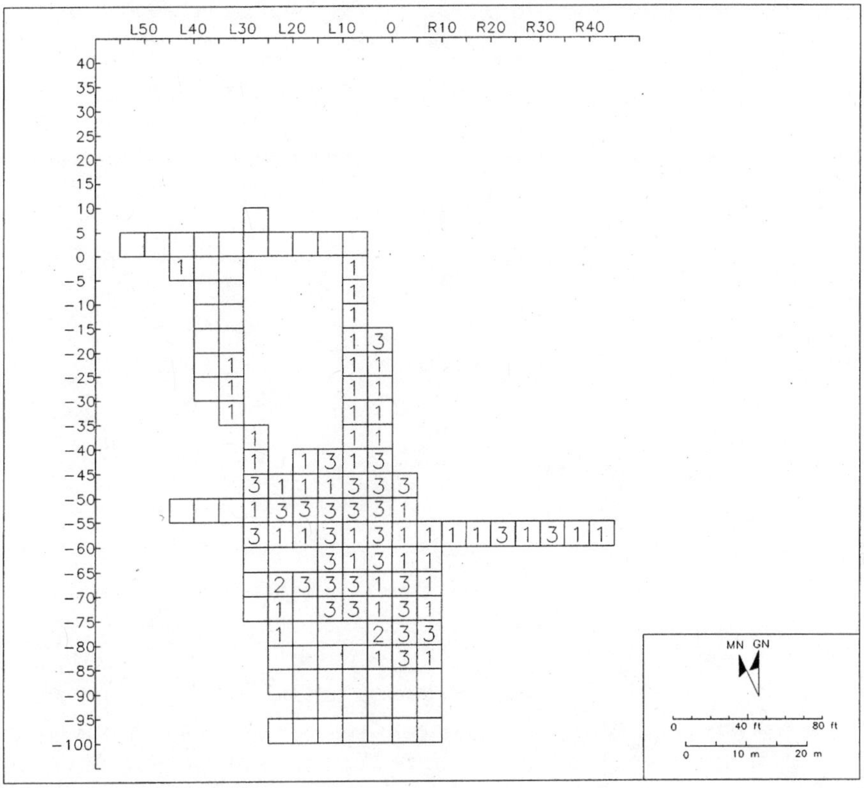

Figure 6.22. Distribution of three-cluster *k*-means solution

densities. Otherwise, the two clusters are similar in content, although there are slight differences in the rank order of some of the other items as well.

Finally, Cluster 2 represents two isolated units that are made up of only two functional classes: site furniture (79 percent) and expedient side scrapers (21 percent). These two squares could represent small specialized activity areas, but it is difficult to say what such an activity or activities might be, given the unusual assemblage composition. Nevertheless, it should be noted that these relatively small, low-artifact-density areas are potential examples of activity locations that are overlooked using "global" techniques (e.g., searching for high-density areas) such as those discussed above in my analysis.

Although the above discussion focuses on the actual relative frequencies within the 5 ft units, a similar analysis was also performed on a smoothed version of these data. The smoothed version was produced by a

Table 6.1. Means and Standard Deviations of Relative Densities by Unconstrained Cluster for the Hardaway Site

	Cluster					
	1		2		3	
Type	Mean	SD	Mean	SD	Mean	SD
Bifaces	0.42	0.12	-	-	0.25	0.11
Hafted scrapers	0.12	0.11	-	-	0.11	0.09
Expedient end scrapers	0.08	0.07	-	-	0.04	0.07
Cores	0.04	0.06	-	-	0.03	0.04
Miscellaneous expedient scrapers	0.02	0.03	-	-	0.02	0.04
Points	0.10	0.09	-	-	0.12	0.13
Other side scrapers	0.17	0.08	0.21	0.21	0.38	0.10
Site furniture	0.06	0.07	0.79	0.21	0.05	0.05

Note: SD = standard deviation.

two-dimensional running median, smoothed over a 10 × 10 ft area at 5 ft intervals. In order to facilitate this procedure, a few peripheral units were removed from the analysis. Smoothing was undertaken in order to remove the effects of local variation in artifact frequencies (see Gregg et al. 1991:158). In addition, relative frequencies were standardized to prevent the most common classes (e.g., bifaces and side scrapers) from having disproportionate influence on cluster solutions. The results of both smoothing and standardizing produced no difference between actual and randomized data in plots of SSE percentage versus the number of clusters.

DISCUSSION

Both the density distributions and cluster analysis failed to reveal any significant patterning. Essentially, the pattern displayed in both spatial analyses is one of uniform material distribution. With respect to the cluster analysis, all functional classes occur with virtually the same relative frequencies locally and are uniformly spread over the block. In fact, the most striking feature of both the composition and distribution of the clusters is their overwhelming homogeneity. Moreover, the cluster analysis indicates that little difference exists in assemblage composition between the concentrations identified previously in the density maps and the artifact distributions in the remaining block area. Thus, even though artifact concentrations can be identified on the basis of high tool density, the proportions of tool types within these areas are no different from those in areas of low tool density (at least at the 5 ft scale). The ubiquitous distribution of stone artifacts exhibiting within it localized areas of higher densities, then, could be the result of refuse outputs followed by a "smearing and blending" (Ascher 1968) of such clusters by human (or natural) processes through time, so that the discreteness of the clusters was partly obscured. While the following ethnoarchaeological description of Alyawara settlements refers to relatively intense occupations, it is not difficult to imagine the same effect resulting from repeated habitations. "Because refuse accumulation is continuous, and because hearths, roasting pits, and structures are frequently repositioned, clusters of facilities (i.e., hearths, roasting pits, structural remains) and refuse should grow in size through time. In general, the longer a site is occupied, the more likely clusters of facilities and refuse will have begun to coalesce, gradually becoming indistinguishable as separate entities. . . . this process may occur within a relatively short time, no more than a few months after a site is first occupied. . . . Under such circumstances, the clustered distribution of hearths, roasting pits, and refuse is likely to be preserved only in less intensively occupied areas, generally along the margins of the site" (O'Connell 1987:90–91).

While intensity of occupation was probably a factor in site formation at Hardaway, we can only guess at its exact nature on the basis of the density of lithic material. The evidence for site reoccupation, on the other hand, is less ambiguous, given the recovery of a wide range of Early Archaic point types spanning some 1,500 years of intermittent occupation. In any event, the cluster analysis could be interpreted as reflecting summations of multiple, spatially overlapping occupations.

Finally, while the search for spatial patterning within archaeological sites is often an end in itself, the analysis here has been particularly important because of its implications for the interpretation of site function. While the results have been more suggestive than conclusive, I believe that the apparent absence of clear site structure in combination with the high artifact density is best explained as a result of repeated residential occupations, probably for extended periods of time. This interpretation is also consistent with the base camp interpretation inferred from the assemblage analysis in Chapter 5.

7

Uwharrie Rhyolite and Early Archaic Settlement Range in the Carolina Piedmont

An important aspect of this study has been the identification of the sources of rhyolite so abundant at Hardaway (Chapter 3). In this chapter, the results of an extensive artifact collections survey documents the widespread movement of rhyolite beyond the Hardaway site. Given the quarry-related function of Hardaway, tracing the movement of Uwharrie rhyolite from its source allows the site to be viewed from a regional perspective.

PROBLEMS ADDRESSED

As a part of this research I surveyed Early Archaic point and raw material collections to test the watershed-based settlement adaptation posited in the band-macroband model for the Yadkin–Pee Dee River (Anderson and Hanson 1988:figure 3). I examined the distributions of raw materials among Early Archaic points, as in the study of the frequencies of stone raw materials along the Savannah River (Anderson and Hanson 1988:280), both along the Yadkin–Pee Dee and across several drainages through the eastern Piedmont. In addition, I compared the geographic patterns of Hardaway-Dalton and Hardaway Side-Notched point distributions with Palmer and Kirk Corner-Notched point distributions. Although Anderson and Hanson's (1988) study focused on Palmer and Kirk Corner-Notched point distributions, the inclusion of earlier points from the Hardaway complex allowed me to document possible temporal changes in raw material distributions.

I paid particular attention to a comparison of the archaeological distributions of Uwharrie rhyolite both along and across the Yadkin–Pee Dee. If Early Archaic settlement adaptation was largely confined to the Yadkin–

Pee Dee drainage, then the use of Uwharrie rhyolite should have been restricted primarily to that river valley. That is, relatively high frequencies of Uwharrie rhyolite should extend from its source in the Piedmont along the river down into the Coastal Plain. Moreover, this pattern should be associated with a significant decrease in the occurrence of Uwharrie rhyolite across the Yadkin–Pee Dee. On the other hand, if the occurrence of Uwharrie rhyolite along the Yadkin–Pee Dee is not significantly different from that across the eastern Piedmont, then group adaptation may have encompassed more than a single drainage.

COLLECTIONS SURVEY

Data on the raw materials used to make Early Archaic points (i.e., Hardaway-Dalton, Hardaway Side-Notched, Palmer Corner-Notched, and Kirk Corner-Notched) were recorded in collections from counties forming two transects: the first (cutting across several major drainages, including the Yadkin–Pee Dee) I call the "eastern Piedmont transect," and the second (roughly paralleling the course of the Yadkin–Pee Dee River) the "Yadkin–Pee Dee transect" (figures 7.1–7.4). The minimum level of provenance that I recorded was county location, although specific site locations were noted for many artifacts.

A total of 3,140 points from twenty-five counties in both North and South Carolina form the sample for this analysis (Appendix C). Approximately 50 percent (n = 1,580) of these artifacts came from the extensive North Carolina collections curated by the Research Laboratories of Anthropology. The remaining portion of the sample came from private collections in both states. Of this portion, I recorded 609 points (20 percent) from twenty-seven private collections in both states. The remaining 951 points (30 percent) were recorded by Charles's inventory of private collections in South Carolina (Charles 1981, 1983, 1986); this material comprises an additional twenty-five collections from six counties along the Pee Dee River that Charles has graciously allowed me to incorporate into the present analysis.

Data from Appendix C are summarized in tables 7.1–7.4 and are illustrated in figures 7.1–7.4. Before I discuss these figures, however, I must comment on their construction. For the purposes of this analysis, point types were combined into two groups: Hardaway-Dalton and Hardaway Side-Notched form one group, and Palmer Corner-Notched and Kirk Corner-Notched form a second group. For the Hardaway point group (n = 197), the eastern Piedmont transect included thirteen counties that covered a linear distance of approximately 300 km (figure 7.1). Similarly, the eastern Piedmont transect for the Palmer and Kirk Corner-Notched group

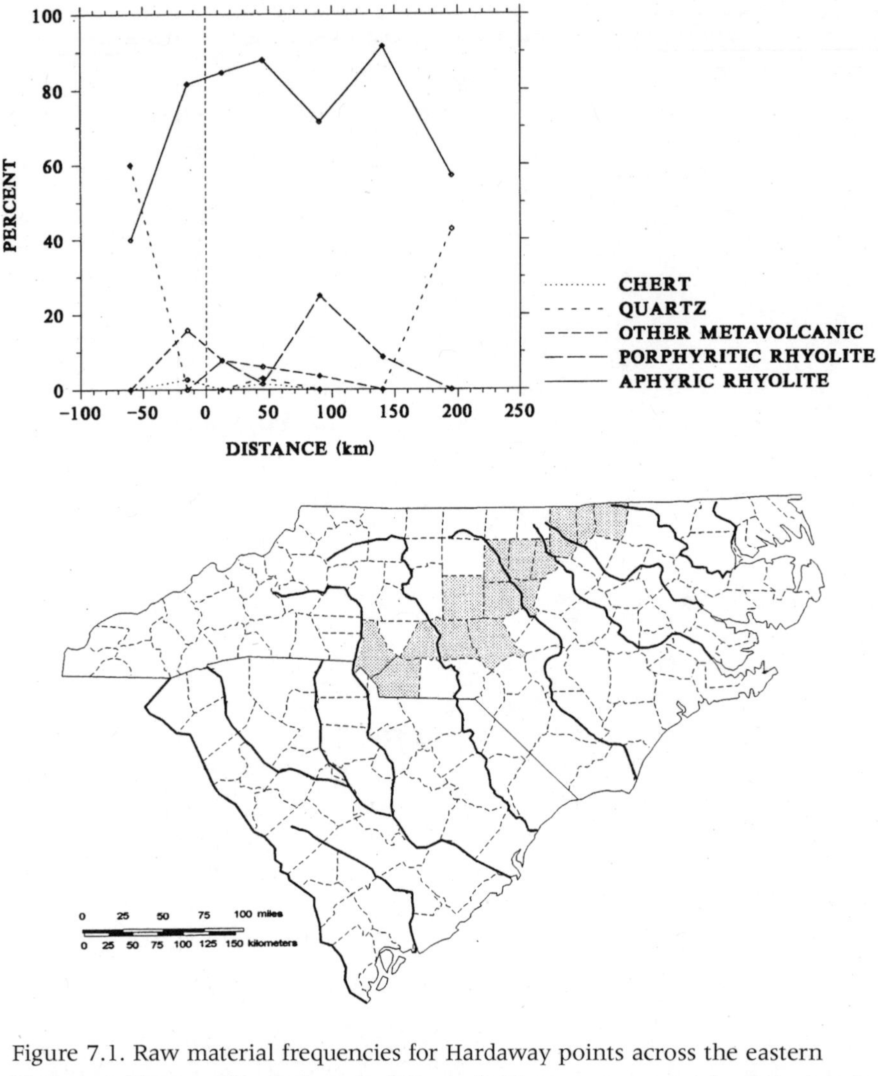

Figure 7.1. Raw material frequencies for Hardaway points across the eastern Piedmont. Morrow Mountain is at distance 0. Distances are west (negative) and east (positive) of Morrow Mountain. Shaded areas on the map represent the counties composing the transect.

(n = 1,015) encompassed eleven counties, covering a linear stretch just under 300 km. The Yadkin–Pee Dee transect for the Hardaway group (n = 263) included fifteen counties, while the Palmer Kirk Corner-Notched (n = 1,925) group included sixteen counties. These counties bordered both sides of the river and covered a linear stretch of approximately 290 km (figure 7.2).

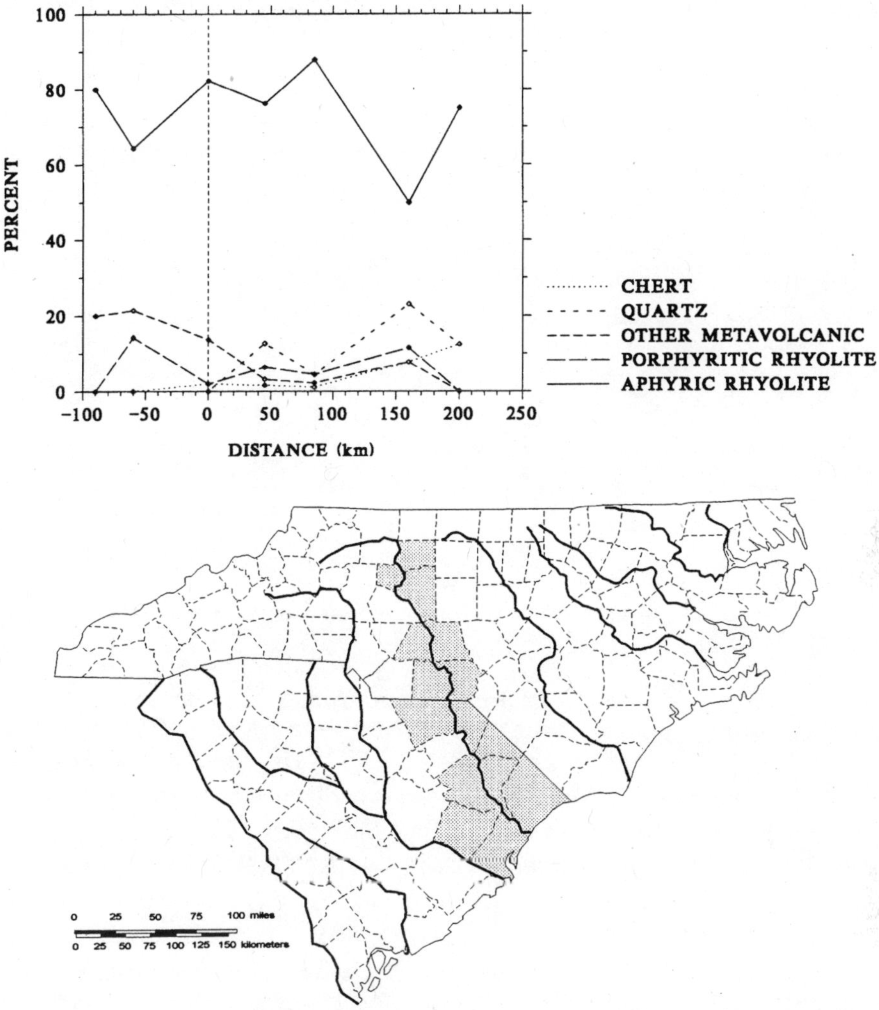

Figure 7.2. Raw material frequencies for Hardaway points along the Yadkin–Pee Dee drainage. Morrow Mountain is at distance 0. Distances are north (negative) and south (positive) of Morrow Mountain. Shaded areas on the map represent the counties composing the transect.

Each figure was generated by calculating and plotting the percentages of raw material types by county, using the linear midpoint of each county along the transect as the graphical reference point. In some instances, adjacent counties were combined to increase sample size and the graphical midpoint was adjusted accordingly.

Furthermore, several raw material types previously discussed in Chap-

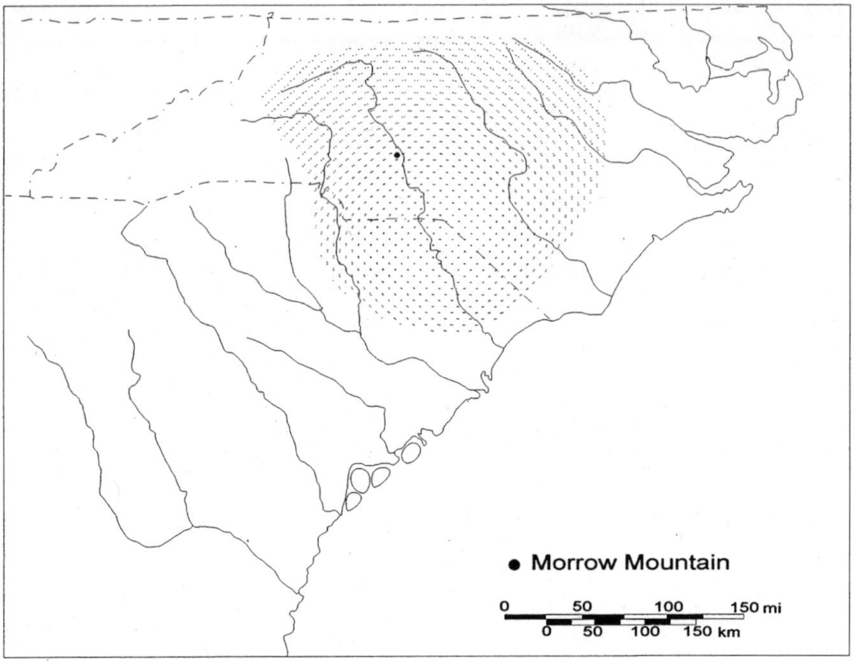

Figure 7.3. Geographic range of high frequencies of Early Archaic points made from Uwharrie rhyolite

ter 3 were combined into five categories for the sake of clarity (tables 7.1–7.4). These groupings were based upon typological similarity or similarity in their source location. Generally speaking, a range of raw materials similar to that in the Hardaway assemblage was observed in the collections survey. In the collections survey, however, unlike the Hardaway assemblage, highly weathered metavolcanic points were often encountered. These artifacts displayed a grayish white to buff-colored surface that made more specific identification problematic. I listed these artifacts as "weathered metavolcanic" in Appendix C, but these items were very probably weathered specimens of "aphyric rhyolite." I believe this to be the case, since numerous examples of these artifacts displayed breaks that, almost without exception, exposed fresh surfaces revealing a dark gray, fine-grained metavolcanic stone virtually identical to Morrow Mountain rhyolite. I have therefore included weathered metavolcanics with the category "aphyric rhyolite" (tables 7.1–7.4).

In any event, it is unlikely that the weathered specimens were porphyritic rhyolites, because phenocrysts weathered differently from the surrounding groundmass and thus remained visible. In fact, weathered porphyritic specimens were often easier to identify than unweathered

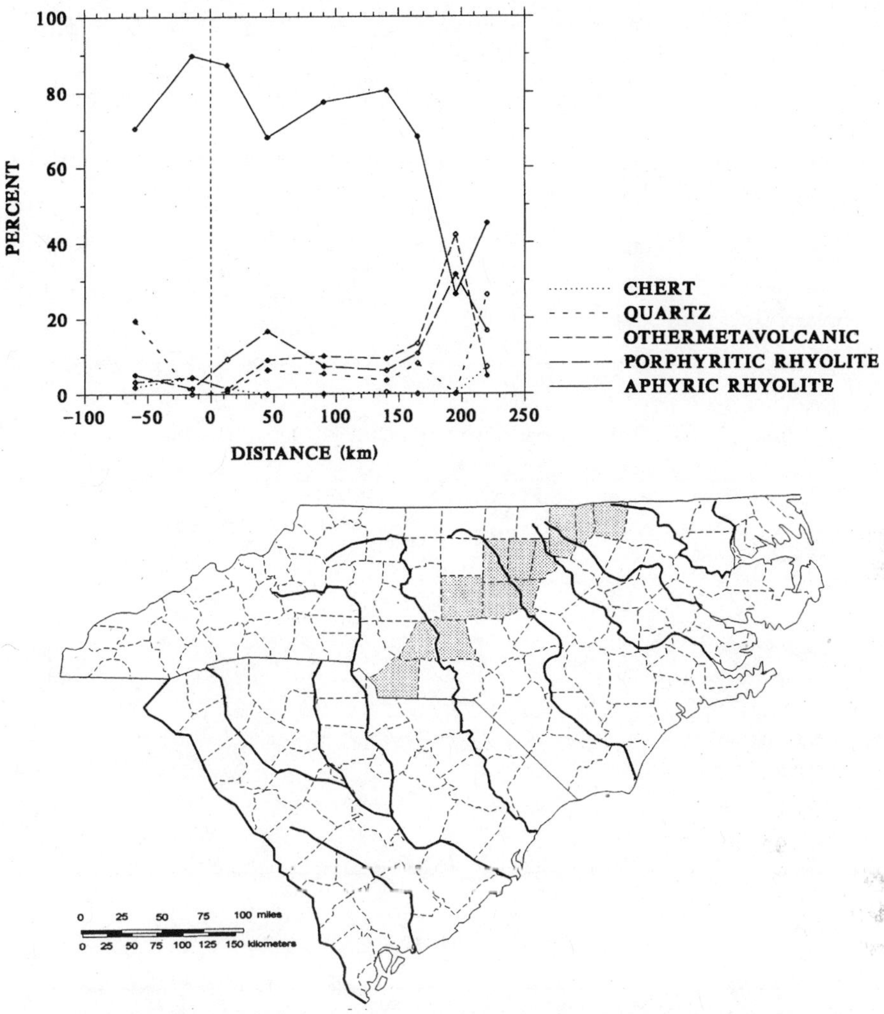

Figure 7.4. Raw material frequencies for Palmer and Kirk Corner-Notched points across the eastern Piedmont. Morrow Mountain is at distance 0. Distances are west (negative) and east (positive) of Morrow Mountain. Shaded areas on the map represent the counties composing the transect.

specimens, because the weathering process often increased the contrast between the groundmass and phenocrysts. The three types of porphyritic rhyolites identified in Chapter 3 have all been combined in a single category called "porphyritic rhyolite."

The category "other metavolcanic" includes a variety of raw materials—primarily rhyolitic tuffs but also a few examples of rhyolitic breccia, green metasiltstone, and some specimens that Charles called argillite, basalt, and

Table 7.1. Frequencies of Hardaway Points by Raw Material Across the Eastern Piedmont

State/ County	Aphyric Rhyolite	Porphyritic Rhyolite	Other Metavolcanic	Quartz	Chert	Total
North Carolina						
Union/Mecklenburg	4	-	-	6	-	10
Stanly	31	-	6	-	1	38
Montgomery	11	1	1	-	-	13
Randolph/Moore	58	1	4	2	1	66
Chatham/Alamance	20	7	1	-	-	28
Durham/Orange	32	3	-	-	-	35
Granville/Vance/Warren	4	-	-	3	-	7
Total	160	12	12	11	2	197

Table 7.2. Frequencies of Hardaway Points by Raw Material Along the Yadkin-Pee Dee River

State/ County	Aphyric Rhyolite	Porphyritic Rhyolite	Other Metavolcanic	Quartz	Chert	Total
North Carolina						
Forsythe	8	-	2	-	-	10
Davie/Davidson	9	2	3	-	-	14
Stanly/Montgomery	42	1	7	-	1	51
Anson/Richmond	48	4	2	8	1	63
South Carolina						
Chesterfield/Marlboro	80	4	2	4	1	91
Dillon/Marion/Florence	13	3	2	6	2	26
Williamsburg/Georgetown/ Horry	6	-	-	1	1	8
Total	206	14	18	19	6	263

Table 7.3. Frequencies of Palmer and Kirk Corner-Notched Points by Raw Material Across the Eastern Piedmont

State/ County	Aphyric Rhyolite	Porphyritic Rhyolite	Other Metavolcanic	Quartz	Chert	Total
North Carolina						
Union	152	11	7	42	4	216
Stanly	61	1	3	-	3	68
Montgomery	123	13	2	1	2	141
Randolph	53	13	7	5	-	78
Chatham/Alamance	116	11	15	8	-	150
Durham/Orange	182	14	21	8	1	226
Granville	51	8	10	6	-	75
Vance	5	6	8	-	-	19
Warren	19	7	2	11	3	42
Total	762	84	75	81	13	1,015

Table 7.4. Frequencies of Palmer and Kirk Corner-Notched Points by Raw Material Along the Yadkin-Pee Dee River

State/ County	Aphyric Rhyolite	Porphyritic Rhyolite	Other Metavolcanic	Quartz	Chert	Total
North Carolina						
Forsythe	160	11	27	4	5	207
Rowan/Davie/Davidson	242	25	29	1	9	306
Stanly/Montgomery	184	14	5	1	5	209
Anson/Richmond	95	18	6	10	1	130
South Carolina						
Chesterfield/Marlboro	379	15	8	212	19	633
Dillon/Marion/Florence	225	33	12	84	21	375
Williamsburg/Georgetown/ Horry	17	11	-	17	20	65
Total	1,302	127	87	329	80	1,925

"unidentified metavolcanics." Even though the green metasiltstone and argillite are more correctly identified as a metasedimentary rock, I have grouped all of these materials together because of their presumed Piedmont origin.

Similarly, I have included quartz, quartzite, orthoquartzite, and crystal quartz under the category "quartz." The exact sources of these raw materials are also unknown, but they would have been available in either the Piedmont or in Coastal Plain (see Chapter 3). The milky white quartz dominates this category and presumably originated in the Piedmont.

Finally, all the cryptocrystalline rocks have been included under the label "chert." Most of them probably originated outside the Piedmont (Chapter 3). Virtually all of the cherts present in the Coastal Plain counties (Appendix C) are made from Coastal Plain chert, presumably from the Allendale sources. The chert points found in the Piedmont (Appendix C), however, are made of Ridge and Valley chert or of chert from some other unknown location. Finally, I have also included isolated examples of jasper and chalcedony under "chert."

The results of the collections survey are discussed below. I first examine the raw material graphs generated for the Hardaway point group and then discuss similar graphs for the Palmer and Kirk Corner-Notched point group.

RAW MATERIAL DISTRIBUTIONS FOR HARDAWAY-DALTON AND HARDAWAY SIDE-NOTCHED POINTS

The eastern Piedmont transect is dominated by aphyric rhyolite with frequencies between 70 percent and 90 percent (figure 7.1). The highest rhyolite frequencies extend from Morrow Mountain in Stanly County (represented in the figures by a vertical line at distance 0) to the northeast, covering a distance of about 150 km. Beyond this distance the occurrence of rhyolite drops rapidly to about 50 percent near 200 km. Southwest of the Uwharrie sources, the frequency of rhyolite decreases much more rapidly than it does to the northeast, falling to 40 percent just 60 km from the source.

Although the aphyric rhyolite curve exhibits a slight bimodality, this trend may not be particularly significant, since frequencies drop below 70 percent only at either end of the transect. This transect, then, crosses at least five major watersheds (i.e., the Catawba, Yadkin, Cape Fear, Neuse, and to a lesser extent the Tar).

The remaining raw materials (porphyritic rhyolite, other metavolcanics, quartz, and chert) make up relatively minor proportions of all points along the transect. Excluding quartz, these minor raw materials constitute less than 10 percent of the assemblage over most of the transect and only exceed that frequency about 20 km west and 60–130 km east of the Yadkin. Quartz, on the other hand, is virtually absent along the transect except for marked increases at either end of the Piedmont.

If we turn to the Yadkin–Pee Dee Transect, aphyric rhyolite dominates the raw materials in roughly the same frequencies as in the eastern Piedmont transect; these frequencies generally range between 70 percent and 90 percent at distances of about 100 km both up and down the river from Morrow Mountain (figure 7.2). This distance is probably even greater upriver, but no collections north of Forsythe County, near the headwaters of the Yadkin, were examined. Another, lesser peak is present near the coast, but this may be spurious, since the sample of points is very small there ($n = 8$) (table 7.1).

The remaining raw materials all constitute less than 20 percent of the points along the river with the exception of other metavolcanics (ca. 21 percent) at the north end of the transect and quartz (ca. 23 percent) near the coast. Finally, cherts represent the least frequently used raw material along the Yadkin–Pee Dee transect, although they are more frequent along the Yadkin–Pee Dee than across the eastern Piedmont. In fact, this group consists virtually entirely of Coastal Plain chert below the Fall Line, with isolated examples of jasper in the Piedmont (Appendix C).

How, then, are these patterns to be interpreted? Presumably, the marked decrease in rhyolite at either end of the eastern Piedmont transect and the southern end of the Yadkin–Pee Dee transect reflects an abrupt drop in use. Moreover, the relatively constant rhyolite frequencies across both transects probably reflect the direct acquisition of stone at its source by a group or groups and their subsequent use of rhyolite as they move through the presumed territory. Thus, keeping in mind the overwhelming dominance of rhyolite along both transects, I believe that the rhyolite curve outlines the territorial range of one or more bands focused on the exploitation of Uwharrie rhyolite.

This range probably included much of the Carolina Piedmont, extending about 300 km between the Broad and Roanoke Rivers. How far this range might have extended north into Virginia or south into the Coastal Plain is unknown. Presumably, however, it did not extend beyond the headwaters of the Yadkin. There the Yadkin is bordered by the Blue Ridge Mountains to the west and the Dan River to the east. The Dan River is part of the Roanoke drainage, which conforms to the proposed eastern boundary.

At the southern end of the Yadkin–Pee Dee transect, the range appears to have extended all the way to the coast: a linear distance of about 350 km along the length of the Yadkin–Pee Dee. Given lower sea levels during the early Holocene, band range may have extended even farther beyond the present coastline. How far band range extended into the Coastal Plain of the other major Piedmont drainages cannot be determined from the present data. The southern extent of the territory is a minimal border, extrapolated by circumscribing the two ends of the eastern Piedmont transect and the southern end of the Yadkin-Pee Dee transect (figures 7.1–7.2).

An alternative interpretation of the above data is admittedly also possible. Since frequencies alone do not in themselves constitute conclusive evidence on the *mechanism* of stone movement (Meltzer 1989), a similar rhyolite curve could result if rhyolite were traded from one band in the Yadkin to two or more contemporaneous bands occupying separate drainages.

A similar falloff pattern, for example, was used by Colin Renfrew (1972, 1975, 1977) to explain the distribution of obsidian on sites in the Near East via "down-the-line" exchange. That is, such a pattern may be produced if stone was initially supplied by one settlement and was exchanged with neighboring groups; these villages, in turn, used a portion of the material and passed on the remainder to other neighboring groups, which repeated the process "down the line." Thus, in this interpretation, the relatively high rhyolite frequencies in the preceding figures would represent "supply zones" from which stone was initially exchanged to neighboring groups, which subsequently supplied their neighbors.

Nevertheless, I view such an interpretation here as extremely unlikely, since it would be a highly disadvantageous adaptive strategy for a group to rely on exchange for a critical resource like stone—in quantities totaling about 70 percent of their tool assemblages (see Meltzer 1989:24). Moreover, an exchange interpretation would also, improbably, mean that a group at the socioeconomic level of a band society would be able to supply such a resource in bulk to another group. In short, direct acquisition of Uwharrie rhyolite by a band or bands within a territorial range encompassing the area depicted in figure 7.3 stands as a more plausible explanation.

I interpret the remaining raw materials, then, as representing stone that supplemented the use of rhyolite across the Piedmont. With the exception of some chert, these minority materials were presumably acquired incidentally through group movement across the region. Furthermore, the frequency curves of these other stone types suggests some interesting possibilities as to how these raw materials were used to supplement rhyolite.

The quartz and other metavolcanic curves along the Yadkin–Pee Dee, for example, complement each other and suggest that when more than one alternative stone was available, quartz was the least likely to be selected. This inference reflects the fact that quartz, which was present throughout the Piedmont in surface veins or river cobbles, is virtually absent except at either end of the eastern Piedmont transect. Similarly, quartz does not appear in large frequencies along the Yadkin–Pee Dee transect until the Fall Line, and then it appears regularly along the Coastal Plain. As mentioned in Chapter 3, quartz was probably obtained from secondary sources in the form of river cobbles along the Pee Dee.

But quartz was not the only stone exploited in cobble form. Charles (1981:14) has noted the presence of porphyritic rhyolite cobbles in the Pee Dee, and I have seen at least one such cobble (a plagioclase-porphyritic rhyolite) used as a core (this cobble is in a private collection in southern Marion County). This cobble presumably originated in the Uwharrie Mountains some 200 km upriver. Geologic mapping (Conley 1962) and the quarry survey undertaken as part of this project (Daniel and Butler 1991, 1996) indicate that plagioclase-porphyritic rhyolite is present at water's edge along the Yadkin. Some Uwharrie rhyolite (i.e., porphyritic rhyolite) thus appears to have been obtained from secondary sources along the Pee Dee.

Two other locations exhibit slight peaks in the frequencies of porphyritic rhyolite that are more difficult to explain. The first is about 60 km up river from the Uwharries along the Yadkin–Pee Dee transect, while the second is about 90 km east of Morrow Mountain across the eastern Piedmont transect. While this material was macroscopically similar to the porphyritic rocks from the Uwharries, its relatively high occurrence some distance from the Yadkin raises the possibility of another source outside the Uwharries.

Finally, the limited number and variety of cherts whose sources are known to lie outside the Piedmont may also have some significance with respect to the settlement range proposed here. If these "exotic" cherts do provide tantalizing glimpses of mobility or exchange beyond the Piedmont, then the absence of any Ridge and Valley chert suggests that the geographic range of Early Archaic Piedmont groups did not extend into the mountain region.

The presence of limited frequencies of Coastal Plain chert, on the other hand, does suggest some form of interaction with the South Carolina Coastal Plain. Although the presence of this chert along the Pee Dee is probably related to the river's proximity to the Allendale sources, the exact mechanism by which the chert arrived in the Pee Dee is unclear.

Nevertheless, the chert's occurrence also coincides with a marked decrease in rhyolite frequencies southwest of the Yadkin (i.e., Morrow Mountain), unlike the more gradual decline in rhyolite frequencies east of the river. I speculate that this asymmetrical falloff pattern may indicate an Early Archaic social boundary separating a group that used primarily Allendale chert from a group that used primarily Uwharrie rhyolite. I discuss this possibility in greater detail below.

In sum, I believe that the frequency of rhyolite use for Hardaway points reflects a territorial range focused on stone procurement from the Uwharrie Mountains. This range extended across the North Carolina Piedmont and encompassed most of the major watersheds within the region. Furthermore, this range minimally included much of the Pee Dee and probably the upper Coastal Plain portions of the Cape Fear and Wateree as well. Last, it is possible to see in these graphs the antecedents of a band range that is also reflected in the raw material frequencies for the Palmer and Kirk Corner-Notched points that I discuss next.

RAW MATERIAL DISTRIBUTIONS FOR PALMER AND KIRK CORNER-NOTCHED POINTS

As with the Hardaway points, the corner-notched point group is dominated by rhyolite. With aphyric rhyolite frequencies between about 70 percent and 90 percent, the eastern Piedmont transect curve is very similar to that of the Hardaway group, although exhibiting less bimodality (figure 7.4). The high rhyolite frequencies also cover the same distance across the eastern Piedmont as the Hardaway group and then exhibit a steep decline. If this curve represents the limits of the geographic range for a rhyolite-using group, as previously suggested, then there was apparently little change in this range during the latter part of the Early Archaic.

A somewhat different pattern exists for the rhyolite frequencies along the Yadkin–Pee Dee transect (figure 7.5). While rhyolite is moving at least

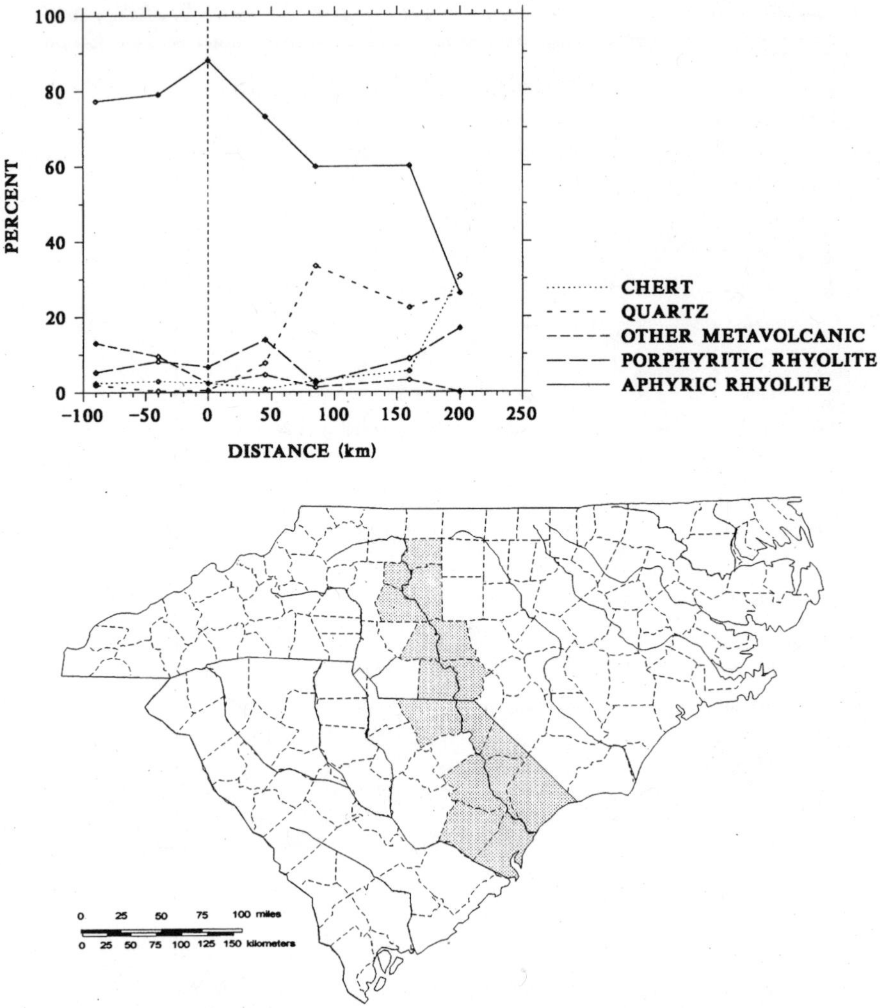

Figure 7.5. Raw material frequencies for Palmer and Kirk Corner-Notched points along the Yadkin–Pee Dee drainage. Morrow Mountain is at distance 0. Distances are north (negative) and south (positive) of Morrow Mountain. Shaded areas on the map represent the counties composing the transect.

as far along the watershed as it is across the eastern Piedmont, it exhibits a clinal decrease in frequencies rather than the relatively high (albeit slightly fluctuating) occurrence that we see across the Piedmont. Frequencies of about 90 percent begin in the Piedmont near the source and gradually decrease to about 25 percent near the coast; this curve is punctuated by a steplike interruption occurring across the Fall Line and upper Coastal Plain.

Given this pattern, the southern boundary of the postulated band range appears more vague than the proposed Piedmont boundaries. For two reasons, however, this ambiguity may be more apparent than real. First, a steplike decline in rhyolite takes place about 160 km downstream from the Uwharries, the same distance that rhyolite moves prior to its sharp decline across the eastern Piedmont. Second, both the eastern Piedmont and the Yadkin–Pee Dee transects display virtually the same frequency (ca. 25 percent) of rhyolite about 200 km from the source. This distance, it was proposed, represents the northeastern Piedmont boundary, and I suggest that it represents the boundary along the Pee Dee as well. In addition, 200 km was the proposed boundary along the Yadkin–Pee Dee transect for the Hardaway point group.

But if a band was exploiting rhyolite directly and was moving both downriver and across the Piedmont in a similar manner, why are the patterns so different? There is no straightforward answer, but I will propose two possibilities. First, the different patterns of stone use between the two transects may be related to the interpretation of exchange that I discussed above. That is, while the eastern Piedmont curve may indicate direct acquisition and movement of rhyolite via group mobility, the Yadkin–Pee Dee curve may reflect the indirect movement of rhyolite by exchange. This interpretation, then, suggests that there were two distinct bands: one band occupying the Piedmont and a second in the Coastal Plain. Such an interpretation, however, is subject to the same objection noted earlier: it is unlikely that one band supplied another with the bulk of a critical resource. Although the frequency of quartz is greater in the Coastal Plain than in the Piedmont, rhyolite still dominates the raw materials. Thus, while acknowledging that the interpretation of exchange is worthy of further investigation, it does not appear to present a very satisfying answer.

The higher frequencies of quartz in the Coastal Plain, however, suggest a second possibility: the increased availability of quartz. That is, the higher frequencies of quartz may reflect its increased availability in the form of river cobbles along the Pee Dee. Simply, rhyolite was conserved at the expense of quartz, which was readily obtainable along the length of the river. Thus, band range is not as clearly delineated along the Yadkin–Pee Dee transect as it is across the eastern Piedmont transect. The reason is that there was a greater emphasis on exploiting secondary stone sources along the Pee Dee than across the Piedmont.

In any event, the remaining minority stone types may be interpreted in the same manner as was the Hardaway group: they largely reflect the incidental use of stone acquired in the region intended to supplement the use of rhyolite. There appear to be no dramatic differences among frequencies of quartz, other metavolcanics, and porphyritic rhyolite used within most of the Piedmont. Frequencies for these stone types rarely exceed 20 percent and are usually at or below 10 percent. Quartz, for example, varies from 0 to 8 percent along the eastern Piedmont transect until it increases to 19 percent near the Broad River and 26 percent near the Roanoke. Similarly, the incidence of porphyritic rhyolite (31 percent) is greater near the Roanoke than elsewhere along the transect. Although this material looked very similar to the porphyritic rhyolites along the Yadkin, its peak here may reflect some as yet unknown porphyritic sources in northeast North Carolina or southern Virginia. I also interpret the relatively high frequencies of other metavolcanics (42 percent) here as reflecting stone sources local to the Roanoke. In fact, much of stone in this category consists of breccias that are unlike any I have seen elsewhere in the Piedmont (Daniel and Butler 1996).

It is also interesting to note that cherts, although extremely uncommon, were clustered at both ends of the eastern Piedmont transect: the first group clustered around the Yadkin River including Montgomery, Stanly, and Union Counties, while the second group occurred in Warren County (Appendix C). At least three of these cherts appear to be from the Ridge and Valley province, while isolated examples of jasper and chalcedony probably have more local sources (see Chapter 3). Of the remaining eight examples, three occurred in Warren County near the Roanoke River, and I speculate that they represent Virginia sources, used by another group in that region.

Turning to the Yadkin–Pee Dee Transect, the distribution of the minority raw materials probably reflects their availability in either the Piedmont or Coastal Plain. Except for the abundance of quartz in the lower portion of the transect and the occurrence of chert near the coast, the other stone types represent less than 20 percent of the raw material along the drainage and more often less than 10 percent. The relative increase in the frequencies of quartz in the Coastal Plain (about 30 percent) as compared to the Piedmont (near 0 percent) similarly reflects a pattern found in the Hardaway group. As I suggested above, this pattern probably reflects a preference for raw materials other than quartz. Nevertheless, while it appears that quartz was not a primary raw material if other stone sources were available, there is some evidence to suggest that its use did increase through the Early Archaic. In the Hardaway group, for instance, approximately 7 percent of the points were made of quartz, while in the Palmer/Kirk group the abundance of quartz increased to about 15 percent.

Similarly, the frequencies of porphyritic rhyolite probably reflects its availability from both primary and secondary sources along the drainage. The slight bimodality of the porphyritic rhyolite curve probably represents its exploitation in the Uwharrie Mountains and then some 200 km downriver in cobble form. It is interesting to note that the peak near the coast is slightly higher than in the Uwharries.

Finally, as in the Hardaway case, chert points were found along the Pee Dee but in greater frequencies than for the Hardaway group. In contrast to the Hardaway case, however, isolated examples of Ridge and Valley chert occur in the Piedmont sample. What the presence of Ridge and Valley chert suggests about interaction with the Mountain region is unclear, but the presence of Coastal Plain chert again corresponds with the asymmetrical falloff in rhyolite frequencies to the southwest of the Yadkin. As suggested previously, I interpret this decline in rhyolite use southwest of the Yadkin–Pee Dee to represent a social boundary separating two different settlement ranges for groups focused on the use of Uwharrie rhyolite and Allendale chert, respectively.

DISCUSSION

These results have important implications for the Anderson-Hanson model. At issue is whether band settlement was largely isomorphic with the Yadkin-Pee Dee drainage (Anderson and Hanson 1988). The absence of any significant difference in the occurrence of Uwharrie rhyolite along the Yadkin–Pee Dee versus its occurrence across the eastern Piedmont does not support such a notion. In fact, group settlement probably included some regular cross-drainage movement and appears to have been established very early in the Holocene (i.e., by Dalton times). This region would have covered much of the North Carolina Piedmont and upper Coastal Plain—an area approximating 80,000 km^2 (figure 7.3). While this area does exceed the annual ranges of most known hunter-gatherers, it needs to be examined from the diachronic perspective of hunter-gatherer land use. That is, the area encompassed by the high frequencies of rhyolite points represents a composite range, the product of several smaller territories exploited by groups that were probably "tethered" to the rhyolite outcrops of the Uwharrie Mountains throughout the Early Archaic. And while an Early Archaic band need not have traveled from the Broad to the Roanoke River within a seasonal cycle, a linear distance of 200–300 km is within the upper limits of annual ranges for some ethnographic groups (Kelly 1983:table 1). Thus, when viewed diachronically, hunter-gatherer adaptation on the order of tens of thousands of square kilometers is not unrealistic (Binford 1983:114–117). The following description of hunter-gatherer land use illustrates this point nicely. "Rather surprisingly, many hunters and gatherers do not reside exclusively in one territory, but—contrary to the assumptions of most archaeologists—exploit a series of discrete areas, occupying each one until the environment becomes degraded.

Often after a period of years, the firewood or animal resources become depleted and, at the point of diminishing returns, the group simply moves to a completely different territory, where the resources have been allowed to regenerate" (Binford 1983:114).

Finally, one additional inference can be made concerning the possibility of a former social boundary near the Broad River. An asymmetrical pattern of decline in rhyolite is clearly present along the eastern Piedmont transect for both the Hardaway and Palmer/Kirk groups. Although no data on raw material frequencies have been reported on Hardaway points in South Carolina, such data on Palmer and Kirk Corner-Notched points indicate that rhyolite (i.e., metavolcanic) frequencies continue to decline into South Carolina (Sassaman 1996). Data from South Carolina indicates that the highest occurrence of any metavolcanic material occurs along the Pee Dee—suggesting the influence of Uwharrie rhyolite. Metavolcanic Early Archaic points, for example, constitute about 40 percent of the sample in Lancaster County, South Carolina, which borders North Carolina and is about 100 km from the Uwharries (Sassaman 1996:figure 4.4). Moreover, the South Carolina data indicate that metavolcanic points are also present across the South Carolina Piedmont in roughly decreasing frequencies all the way to the Savannah River, where they constitute about 10 percent of the sample anywhere along the drainage. This decrease in metavolcanic points correlates with an increase in Coastal Plain as one approaches the Savannah River.

In sum, the Uwharrie Mountains—and Morrow Mountain in particular—served as the principal source of stone used for making points in the Carolina Piedmont during the Early Archaic. That such access to high quality knappable stone was a significant factor influencing Early Archaic settlement is also supported by a functional study of the Hardaway site. Hardaway played a unique role in Early Archaic settlement, serving as a quarry-related base camp where the refurbishment of tool kits was a primary activity. This activity was largely accomplished by the procurement of nearby Uwharrie rhyolite. Accordingly, approximately 70 percent of Hardaway's tool assemblage was made from rhyolite obtained at Morrow Mountain just 8 km away. The refurbishment of tool kits, including the manufacture of large quantities of bifacial cores and other tools at Hardaway, suggests an organizational strategy (Binford 1979) that focused on the procurement of rhyolite to be carried and used some distance from its source—a distance well documented here. Allendale chert probably represented an economic resource comparable to Uwharrie rhyolite. The possibility that settlement mobility was not restricted to drainage basins but was linked to stone outcrops forms the basis of a new Early Archaic settlement model that I outline in Chapter 8.

8

Rethinking Early Archaic Settlement

In this chapter, I reexamine current thinking regarding Early Archaic settlement. I begin by critically assessing certain assumptions underlying the band-macroband model. The results of this discussion, when combined with the preceding analyses, permit Hardaway to be placed in a regional context. Finally, the implications of this work make possible the construction of an alternative model of Early Archaic settlement.

THE BAND-MACROBAND MODEL REVISITED

The band-macroband model of Early Archaic settlement is characterized by a drainage-based band adaptation featuring seasonal residential shifts between the Piedmont and the Coastal Plain. As the name implies, two levels of settlement organization are represented in the model. At a local level, individual bands are postulated to have occupied eight major river basins along the South Atlantic Slope, from the Ocmulgee River in Georgia to the Neuse River in North Carolina (figure 8.1). These drainages are believed to have had band populations between 50 and 150 people. Furthermore, these bands were integrated at a regional level by periodic side trips to other drainages. These intermittent meetings, referred to as "macroband aggregations," formed the second level of settlement organization (Anderson and Hanson 1988).

Base camps were proposed for the winter, since it was "a time of low plant availability and high deer aggregation, when resources were most patchy and unpredictable" (Anderson and Hanson 1988:266). Winter base camps were the most intensively occupied sites (e.g., two to three months) during the settlement round and were provisioned by small task groups sent out on special forays. Band adaptation is thus characterized as reflecting a *collector* settlement adaptation during the winter. In the Savannah

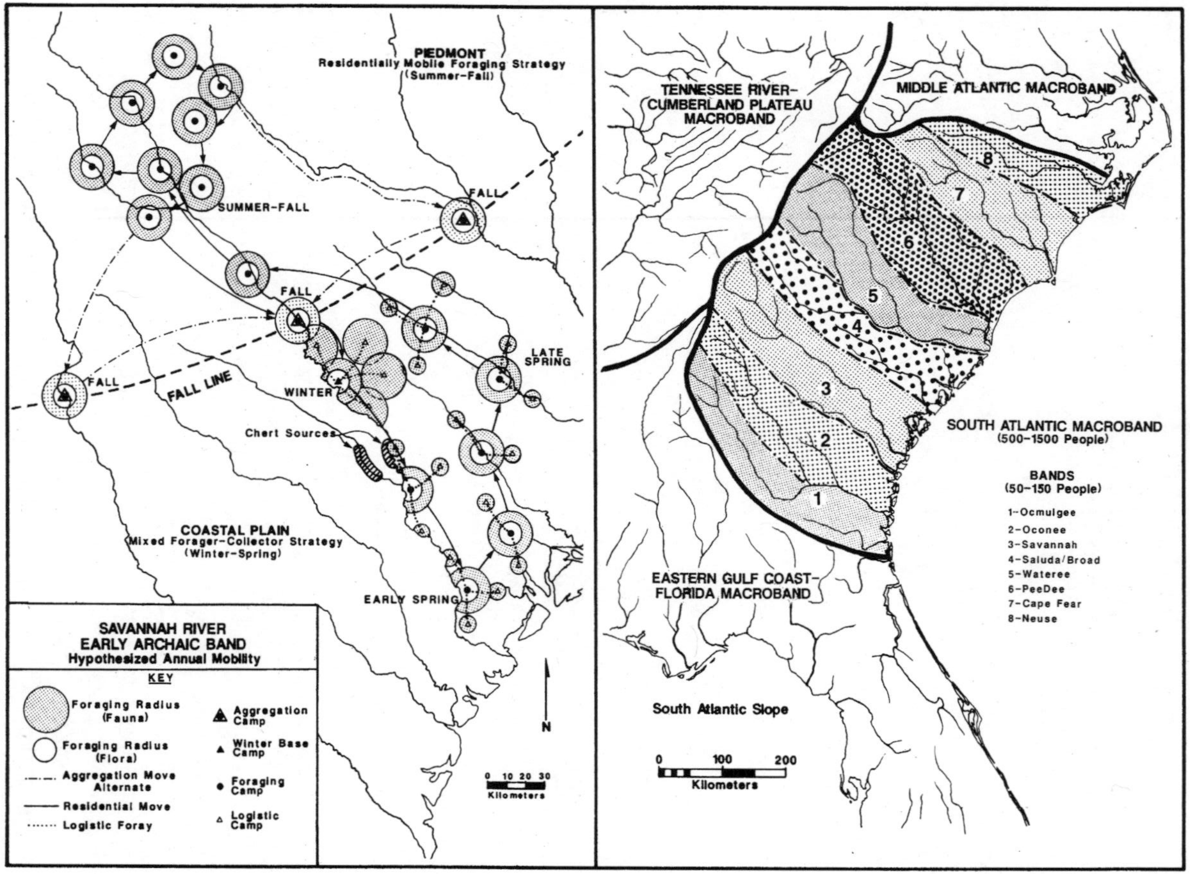

Figure 8.1. The band-macroband settlement model (reproduced by permission of the Society of American Archaeology, from *American Antiquity* 53[2], 1988)

River basin, winter base camps are believed to have been located in the middle and upper Coastal Plain, near the Allendale chert outcrops.

During the spring, with greater plant and animal availability, bands moved toward the coast. Movement by the entire group is posited, although Anderson and Hanson (1988:270) acknowledge that groups may also have dispersed into smaller family units. In any case, settlements moved more frequently, and less emphasis was placed on provisioning by logistical task groups. Moreover, these *forager* camps are postulated to have been occupied for a much shorter time period than winter base camps. As weather warmed, groups moved back into the upper Coastal Plain and eventually into the Piedmont by summer. Relatively short-term settlements continued to characterize the Piedmont during the summer and early fall, with a return to winter base camps by late fall (Anderson and Hanson 1988:270).

Although groups moved extensively along drainages, bands are thought to have moved across drainages only rarely. When cross-drainage movement did occur, it was undertaken as part of multiband aggregation events. Such events are believed to have promoted regular contact among several bands from nearby drainages in order to exchange information and maintain mating networks (Anderson and Hanson 1988:271).

Attractive as this model may be, it does not hold up under close scrutiny. In particular, two aspects of the model can be questioned: the proposed mixed forager-collector settlement strategy and the drainage-based settlement range. I address each of these issues below.

Technological Organization and Settlement Adaptation

In the absence of any subsistence data, the only evidence Anderson and Hanson presented to support a mixed forager-collector settlement strategy is an interassemblage comparison in the form of a "curated-to-expedient tool index" calculated for each of the seven Savannah River sites. This comparison indicated that most of the sites had a low index (i.e., were dominated by expedient tools), which is asserted to provide "a measure of site use and group mobility strategy" (Anderson and Hanson 1988:278). This index was used previously on the Haw River sites, where the degree of tool curation in an assemblage was purported to provide a measure of settlement adaptation (Claggett and Cable 1982:671–688). Simply put, a high frequency of curated tools is correlated with collector settlement systems, while predominantly expedient assemblages are associated with forager settlement systems. This link between curation level and subsistence-settlement organization is based on arguments by Binford (1977, 1979, 1980), who describes both tool curation and collector settlement organization as "efficient" behavioral strategies: "It should be clear that a logistic strategy in which foods are moved to consumers should be correlated with increases in curation and maintenance of tools, since both are organizational responses to conditions in which improving efficiency would pay off" (Binford 1977:35).

The assumption underlying this notion (and hence the curated:expedient index) is that assemblage composition (i.e., the level of tool curation) is determined at a settlement-subsistence level without regard to the local availability of stone as a raw material. Such an assumption, however, can seriously be questioned (Andrefsky 1994a, 1994b; Bamforth 1986, 1990). As I argue below, the relative level of tool curation among Savannah River sites is telling us less about logistical or residential mobility than about the differential use of raw material during the Early Archaic. A brief discussion of the Rucker's Bottom assemblage illustrates this point (figure 8.2). Rucker's Bottom was one of the Savannah River Piedmont sites that was characterized as having a low curated:expedient index and was interpreted as a *forager* camp (Anderson and Hanson 1988:table 1). "The stone assemblage included projectile points, well-flaked bifacial core/tools, and a range of less well-executed, presumably expedient bifacial and unifacial tools. Formal unifaces, characterized by evidence for hafting and carefully retouched margins, were rare. . . . Taken together, the evidence suggests short-duration site use, by groups using a predominantly expedient technology, and characterized (given the incidence of extralocal materials) by a mobile, wide ranging adaptation" (Anderson and Hanson 1988:274).

Significantly, most of the assemblage comprised local quartz (76.4 percent), with nonlocal Allendale chert (from some 175 km downstream) representing the dominant minority type (7.0 percent) (Anderson and Schuldenrein 1983:table 1). Rather than representing a *forager* technology, I believe the high frequencies of expedient tools in the assemblage reflect the more regular use and discarding of local quartz while tools made from nonlocal chert were being conserved. Such an interpretation, in fact, is implied with regard to bifaces in the Rucker's Bottom assemblage. "The formal biface assemblage, furthermore, was dominated by fine-grained extralocal materials, while the crude biface assemblage was dominated by quartz. The formal biface category appears to be part of a carefully maintained and curated assemblage, while the crude bifaces appear to reflect the expedient reduction and (probably) short-term use of local materials" (Anderson and Schuldenrein 1983:188).

In essence, the assemblage at Rucker's Bottom is exactly the sort of lithic refuse one might expect from a group focused on the exploitation of Allendale chert supplemented by material procured while exploiting subsistence resources within a region. What this strategy of raw material use tells us about settlement-subsistence organization, however, is unclear. "The search for a 'forager technology' or for any other technology defined

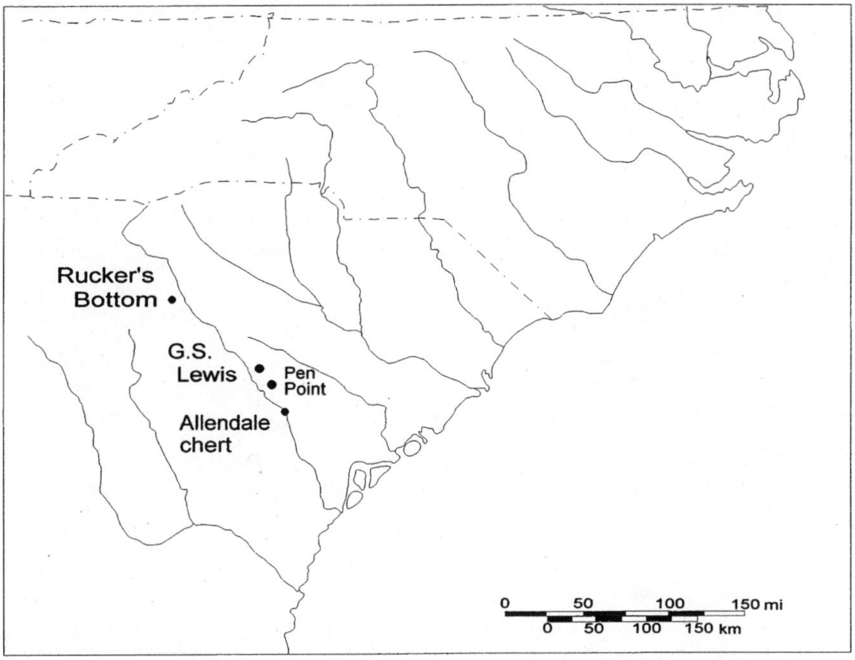

Figure 8.2. Early Archaic sites along the Savannah River

only by a society's food-getting habits, is unlikely to be fruitful, because material for tool manufacture is a resource in the same sense as plants and animals: its nature and distribution fundamentally condition the ways in which it can be exploited" (Bamforth 1986:40).

Thus in the absence of any explicit reason why the "expedient" technology at Rucker's Bottom actually reflects a forager settlement adaptation, a far simpler explanation seems warranted. That is, the technology at Rucker's Bottom (and presumably the other sites in the region) informs us less about settlement configuration than about how an Early Archaic technology was organized with respect to the availability of stone. In particular, the abundance and quality of knappable stone conditioned the production, use, and discarding of stone tools as strongly as or more strongly than the availability of food resources (Andrefsky 1994a, 1994b; Bamforth 1986, 1990).

Band Range and Raw Material Distribution

A second aspect of the band-macroband model is the proposed watershed-based settlement range. Anderson and Hanson (1988) have presented two arguments in support of this assertion.

The first argument was based on the relative frequencies of points made from chert and quartz, materials with mutually exclusive sources in the Coastal Plain and Piedmont, respectively. Frequencies of tools made from these stone types along the drainage exhibited "a gradual, rather than a dramatic or step-like fall off" as a function of the distance from their respective geologic sources (Anderson and Hanson 1988:280). This pattern was presented as evidence of "minimal social boundaries," implying direct access to stone sources via group mobility (Anderson and Hanson 1988:280).

Second, Anderson and Hanson suggested that "extralocal [chert] raw material use appears greatest along rather than across drainages, suggesting that most group activities (except for possibly seasonal or annual aggregation events) occurred within individual drainages" (1988:280). Although no similar graphs for adjacent drainages were presented to support this statement, Anderson and Hanson did cite an earlier study (Anderson and Schuldenrein 1983:201) comparing projectile point raw materials from portions of the Santee River with those from the Savannah River. As implied in the above statement and noted elsewhere in their discussion (Anderson and Hanson 1988:280), the relatively smaller flow of raw materials between drainages was largely explained by indirect acquisition such as exchange during periods of macroband aggregation.

Anderson and Hanson's argument notwithstanding, there exists no reason why lesser chert frequencies across drainages must be the result of exchange. Such would be the case, for example, if, after visiting the Allendale sources and moving along a portion of the Savannah River, a group incorporated some cross-drainage movement in its settlement round. In this case chert frequencies would reflect the temporal more than the spatial distance of stone transport.

Indeed, recent data from South Carolina belie Anderson and Hanson's statements concerning the differences in frequencies of Allendale chert across drainages. Sassaman (1996:figure 4.6) depicts two transects originating from the Allendale sources: one transect travels up the Savannah River, while the other crosses the middle Coastal Plain, traversing the state's major watersheds. Both transects depict a similar clinal decline in the frequencies of chert from its source, which, given Anderson and Hanson's argument, should not be present. Rather, the Savannah River curve should be gradual, while the cross-drainage curve should be dramatic or steplike. If anything, the along-drainage decline in chert is more dramatic than the cross-drainage pattern. Moreover, a comparison of the two transects indicates that at distances of 25–175 km from the Allendale sources, chert frequencies are as much as 30 percent greater across the middle Coastal Plain than up the Savannah River. In fact, chert frequencies along the Savannah River exceed chert frequencies only across drainages at distances between about 175 km and 200 km from the Allendale sources, and even then the differences are insignificant (ca. 1–2 percent). In short, Allendale chert appears to be moving the same distance and with the same (if not slightly greater) frequencies across the Coastal Plain as it is along the Savannah River.

These results, of course, mirror the rhyolite distributions discussed earlier. In fact, given Allendale chert's localized abundance and high flaking quality, together with its predominant and widespread use in the Coastal Plain, the Allendale sources probably represent the Coastal Plain equivalent of Uwharrie rhyolite. As also in the Yadkin–Pee Dee case, it is unlikely that band range was confined to the Savannah River. Rather, Early Archaic settlement range probably encompassed at least portions of several drainages adjacent to the Savannah.

Also, like Uwharrie rhyolite, Allendale chert was supplemented by other raw materials such as quartz, Ridge and Valley chert, and metavolcanic stone (Anderson and Hanson 1988:figure 8; Sassaman et al. 1988:85; Sassaman 1996). Moreover, it appears that many, if not most, of the Early Archaic metavolcanic points in South Carolina were probably made from Uwharrie rhyolite. While some metavolcanic stone may have been quarried in South Carolina (see Goodyear et al. 1989:32), it is unlikely that any major metavolcanic sources were ever exploited to the same extent as those in the Uwharries. Although no systematic attempt has been made to locate metavolcanic stone quarries in the state, collections data indicate that metavolcanic stone was used in much lesser frequencies than Allendale chert (Anderson and Hanson 1988:280–281; Sassaman 1996; Sassaman et al. 1988). What is more, data on Palmer and Kirk Corner Notched point raw material frequencies from South Carolina show clinal declines in metavolcanic stone use both across the middle Coastal Plain and Fall Line from the Pee Dee river (Sassaman 1996). Although it is difficult to know how much Uwharrie rhyolite is included in this category, the clinal decreases strongly suggest that much of the tool stone has its origins in the North Carolina Piedmont. Indeed, this pattern in the South Carolina data matches well the decreasing frequencies in Uwharrie rhyolite for Palmer and Kirk Corner Notched points from Morrow Mountain depicted in figure 7.4. In sum, data from both the Carolinas indicate that only two stone sources provided the vast majority of the raw materials used during the Early Archaic: Uwharrie rhyolite and Allendale chert.

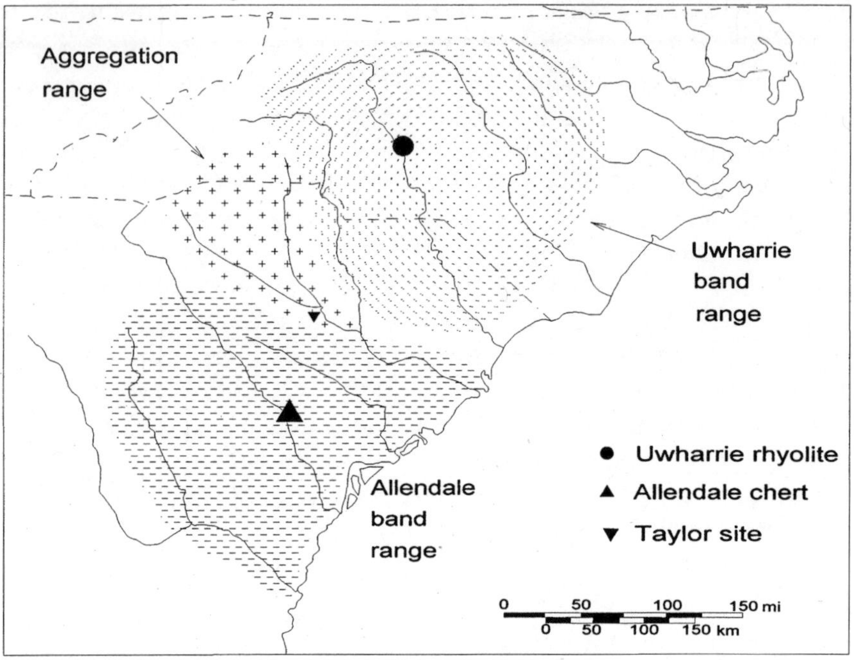

Figure 8.3. The Uwharrie-Allendale settlement model

THE UWHARRIE-ALLENDALE MODEL

As should be clear by now, my analysis suggests a different view of Early Archaic settlement from that proposed by Anderson and Hanson. In brief, present evidence suggests that sources of knappable stone (i.e., Uwharrie rhyolite and Allendale chert) rather than watersheds formed the geographical focus of Early Archaic adaptation; in fact, band ranges cross-cut several drainages. At some point during the early Holocene, hunter-gatherer groups coalesced around the Uwharrie and Allendale sources forming at least two regions (figure 8.3). While band mobility was restricted by and included scheduled visits to primary quarry sources, movement was otherwise quite variable across the Piedmont and Coastal Plain.

We may only speculate about the population size of the bands that inhabited these regions. But given that this period closely follows the initial human colonization of the New World, population densities must have been fairly low. Anderson and Hanson (1988:267), for example, propose individual bands of 50 to 150 people. This range seems reasonable.

For the sake of simplicity, I postulate that single bands occupied the Uwharrie and Allendale regions, although as noted in Chapter 7 the Uwharrie area is large enough to have accommodated several contemporary bands. Presumably this was also true for the Allendale territory. If it can eventually be demonstrated that more than one band simultaneously occupied these ranges, then each could represent a "macroband" region in the sense used by Anderson and Hanson (1988:271).

In any event, these two regions are defined on the basis of the distributions of rhyolite points (discussed in Chapter 7) and chert points (discussed earlier in this chapter). The proposed southern boundary of the Allendale region, it should be noted, is an exception. No studies of Early Archaic point frequencies by raw material exist for Georgia, but Coastal Plain chert points are known from the Oconee River Valley (O'Steen 1992; Goad 1979). This drainage also provides a boundary roughly equivalent in distance from Allendale chert as the northern boundary is in figure 8.3. Collections surveys are needed for Georgia in order to provide data for an accurate assessment of this boundary.

Not coincidentally, I believe, these two regions also mirror the geographic distributions of two local artifact types of the Early Archaic horizon: Taylor and Hardaway Side-Notched points. Taylor points—about 80 percent of which are made of Allendale chert—are concentrated in the southern part of South Carolina in an area south and west of the Santee River. Occurrence of Taylor points north of the Santee River are rare (Michie 1966; Sassaman 1996). This boundary also coincides with the northern limit of the Allendale band range proposed here.

Hardaway Side-Notched points, in contrast, occur with much less frequency than Taylor points in South Carolina (Sassaman 1996). Also in contrast to Taylor points, Hardaway Side-Notched points are found in South Carolina north of the Santee River in the area bordering North Carolina. In addition, over half of the Hardaway Side-Notched points found in South Carolina are made of metavolcanic stone, while quartz constitutes most of the remaining specimens (Sassaman 1996). The proximity of the metavolcanic point distribution to the Uwharrie Mountains suggests that these artifacts originated from the Uwharrie region. Furthermore, this artifact distribution nicely reflects the southwestern edge of the proposed Uwharrie band range. In short, the existence of two different but presumably coeval side-notched point types, with mutually exclusive geographic distributions predominantly associated with either Allendale chert or Uwharrie rhyolite, lends credence to the two settlement ranges proposed here.

The presence of relatively long-term base camps associated with the raw material sources in both regions provides additional support for these two ranges. Hardaway, of course, is an example in the Uwharrie region, while G. S. Lewis and Pen Point (figure 8.2) are examples from the Allendale region (Anderson and Hanson 1988:274–278). Both G. S. Lewis and

Pen Point are located within 30 km of the Allendale quarries, while Hardaway is located only 8 km from Morrow Mountain. In the band-macroband model, it is proposed that the former two sites functioned as winter base camps occupied for a period of two to three months. Among other activities, the quarrying of nearby Allendale chert is hypothesized to have taken place during their occupation. While the seasonal occupation is conjectural, the functional interpretation accords with the model proposed here.

Although most lithic demands were satisfied at the Uwharrie and Allendale sources, stone supplies were also supplemented while moving within each region by exploiting secondary cobble sources and lesser quality outlying bedrock outcrops. Since these "expedient quarries" were dispersed across the region, they served to extend the time spent or distance moved prior to scheduling a return visit to either the Uwharrie or Allendale sources. Procurement of these minor raw materials was probably "embedded" (Binford 1980:259) in basic subsistence schedules as groups moved across the landscape, and it is likely that no extra effort was expended in acquiring them. Moreover, since these minor sources were not systematically revisited, they will probably be less visible archaeologically than the Uwharrie and Allendale quarries.

The location of base camps relatively close to exploited outcrops also indicates that the mining of tool stone was probably integrated with other resource procurement activities. That is, these sites were not just specialized lithic procurement stations but rather habitations occupied by entire Early Archaic social units positioned within foraging distance of quarries. In other words, these Early Archaic groups most closely resembled *forager* hunter-gatherer adaptations, where social groups travel as a unit to the resources they intend to exploit (Binford 1980).

While not conclusive, a forager adaptation is also consistent with our limited understanding of both subsistence practices and environmental conditions during the Early Archaic. Although subsistence data are lacking from sites along the South Atlantic Slope, limited data from other Early Archaic sites suggests that a broadly similar "species-rich" foraging strategy probably existed elsewhere in the Southeast (Meltzer and Smith 1986). This subsistence strategy is characterized by "a broad-based utilization of both closed-canopy climax forest resources (e.g., gray squirrel and nuts), as well as early successional species more commonly associated with edge areas and relatively open and more disturbed situations (e.g., cottontail rabbits, pioneering seed bearing plants, and white-tailed deer)" (Meltzer and Smith 1986:17). Exactly how group mobility related to subsistence resources in the Uwharrie and Allendale regions, however, we can only guess; still, palynological reconstructions of early Holocene vegetational history in the Eastern Woodlands indicates that similar resources (including the above-mentioned plants and animals) should have been equally abundant in both the Piedmont and Coastal Plain.

Two major vegetational communities encompassed the South Atlantic region during the early Holocene (ca. 12,500–9,000 B.P.): a mixed hardwood forest and an oak-hickory-southern pine forest (Delcourt and Delcourt 1981:147–149). During this period biotic adjustments were in progress as a result of postglacial climatic warming.

By 10,000 years ago a mixed hardwood forest had replaced a late glacial boreal forest across the midlatitudes of the Southeast (i.e., 33–37 degrees). Along the South Atlantic Slope, this area included all of North Carolina, the northern half of Georgia, and all but the southern tip of South Carolina. This mixed hardwood forest included oak, maple, beech, basswood, elm, walnut, hemlock, and gum (Delcourt and Delcourt 1981:126) and was characterized by a "cool-temperate climate and abundant moisture during the growing season" (Delcourt and Delcourt 1984:276). The climate of this region at 10,000 B.P. was affected by two different weather systems, the Pacific Airmass, influencing the winter, and the Maritime Tropical Airmass, influencing the summer (Delcourt 1985:figure 1; Delcourt and Delcourt 1984:276–277), so that there was "increased seasonality of temperatures" (Delcourt and Delcourt 1984:280).

Just to the south (29–33 degrees latitude), a oak-hickory-southern pine forest remained stable from at least the last late glacial cycle and covered the southern tip of South Carolina and the southern half of Georgia (Delcourt and Delcourt 1981:figure 7). This region was dominated by oak, hickory, sweetgum, and southern pine; the climate was warm and temperate, as it is today (Delcourt and Delcourt 1981:147; 1983:269).

With an essentially deciduous forest covering most of the Piedmont and Coastal Plain during the Early Archaic, there were probably more similarities than differences in resource availability along river valleys. In fact, river valleys to the north of the Savannah—including the Yadkin–Pee Dee—would have been contained entirely within the mixed hardwood forest. River valleys south of and including the Savannah River would have encompassed portions of both the mixed hardwood and the oak-hickory-southern pine forests. This latter group of river valleys would have exhibited the greatest environmental variation in terms of seasonality and biota.

But in actuality, how different would the adaptational responses in the two vegetational regimes have been? Given the presumed "species rich" nature of both environmental zones, a generalized strategy of exploiting a variety of resources, including nuts, seeds, small mammals, and deer, would not have required a strict seasonal transhumance between the Piedmont and the Coastal Plain (cf. Ward 1983; Steponaitis 1986). Rather, it seems to me more reasonable to suppose that there was a forager settlement adaptation in which these early hunter-gatherers "mapped onto" available resources in either the Piedmont or the Coastal Plain through "residential moves and adjustments in group size" that were not restricted by watersheds (Binford 1980:10).

The seven Early Archaic components described by Anderson and Hanson (1988:272–280) from along the Savannah River can also be interpreted as *forager* sites. Two site types are predominantly produced by foragers: *residential bases* of varying sizes and locales, and *locations* where extractive tasks were carried out (Binford 1980:9). G. S. Lewis, for example, has already been mentioned as a residential base camp. Pen Point may also have been one. The remaining sites (e.g., Rucker's Bottom, Cal Smoak, and Theriault) probably represent somewhat smaller and shorter-term residential sites or extractive locations. *Locations,* on the other hand, may produce little in the way of archaeological residue, unless the activity involves repeated and/or high-bulk extraction (Binford 1980:9). Examples of the former are isolated point finds or small lithic scatters often noted across the landscape; the Allendale or Uwharrie quarries are examples of the latter.

Forager settlement also exhibits considerable variability in both residential size and the number of residential moves during an annual cycle (Binford 1980:5). The variability in residential size relates to another characteristic of hunter-gatherer adaptation: cycles of group dispersal (e.g., into family units) and aggregation. Dispersal and aggregation, of course, are usually associated with ecological variables, but the influence of cultural factors (such as social or ritual needs) on band aggregation is also well documented (Conkey 1980:609–611; Jochim 1976:19; Wilmsen 1970:80; Williams 1974:26–29). The stated purpose and apparent functions of these aggregations are varied: provision of mates, exchange, performance of ritual and curing, and information sharing.

Similarly, I believe aggregation sites were present during the Early Archaic and can be identified on the basis of the diversity of stone raw materials within assemblages. The emphasis on "diversity" as a criterion for identifying hunter-gatherer aggregation sites follows Conkey (1980), who argues that aggregation sites should exhibit products of greater diversity than dispersed sites as a result of group concentration. Conkey tested this expectation by analyzing the diversity of design elements on engraved bone artifacts from several upper Paleolithic sites in Spain. Her results were provocative and have clear implications for identifying other hunter-gatherer aggregation sites as well.

Accordingly, I suggest that the diversity of raw materials from the Taylor site (Michie 1996), which exhibits frequencies of raw material types from both the Piedmont and the Coastal Plain that are unique among known assemblages in the Carolinas, reflect aggregation events held between groups from the Uwharrie and Allendale regions. And while band aggregation (incorporating Taylor and other upper Congaree River sites) is also an issue raised in the band-macroband model, I suggest that the Uwharrie-Allendale model better explains the location of such sites along the Congaree than does the band-macroband model.

According to Anderson and Hanson, the Fall Line is a strategically favored ecological location for aggregations because of its position relative to the resources of the Piedmont and the Coastal Plain. Several sites, including Manning, Thom's Creek, and Taylor located in the upper Congaree River Valley near the Fall Line, have been identified as possible aggregation sites (Anderson and Hanson 1988:271). These sites are often cited as having diverse assemblages with respect to both stone and tool types (Anderson et al. 1974:11; Sassaman 1996: 80–81; Wogaman et al. 1976:20–22). High diversity in raw materials and diversity of tool types are two assemblage criteria that Anderson and Hanson (1988:280) associate with aggregation.

Unfortunately, with the recent exception of Taylor (Michie 1996), none of these sites has been reported in detail. The Taylor site, which covers some 14 ha, is one of the largest Paleo-Indian and Early Archaic sites known in South Carolina. The site lies near present day Columbia, about 400 m from the Congaree River. Surface collections from Taylor have yielded an impressive number of Clovis, Suwannee, Dalton, and Palmer points, while excavations have revealed a remarkably pure Early Archaic assemblage represented primarily by Dalton and Palmer points.

Several tool categories were identified from Taylor, including points, bifaces, adzes, end scrapers, side scrapers, and pièces esquillées. On the basis of the wide variety of tool types in the assemblage, Michie (1996) interprets Taylor as a macroband aggregation site consistent with the band-macroband model. While a wide range of activities is apparently reflected in the Taylor assemblage, Michie (1996) does not explicitly consider why Taylor should necessarily represent an aggregation site as opposed to, say, a residential base camp—since the latter also produces assemblages with a wide variety of tool types. Rather, following Anderson and Hanson, Michie implicitly relies on the site's Fall Line *location* in interpreting Taylor as an aggregations site. "The attractiveness of the Anderson and Hanson (1988) model is that it explains why there are large Early Archaic sites in Fall Line locations. Not only are these areas suitable for band aggregation, but provide environmental diversity with access to floral and faunal resources of the Piedmont and the Coastal Plain, while providing a natural ford for unrestricted river crossings. The latter consideration would have extended their kinetic range allowing for greater environmental exploitation on the opposite side of three major river systems, i.e., the Saluda, Broad, Congaree Rivers" (Michie 1996:266).

Regardless of the functional interpretation of Taylor, Michie (1996:264–267) departs from the Anderson and Hanson (1988) model by questioning whether band movement was primarily within specific river systems. Moreover, taking a view similar to mine, he interprets the presence of Coastal Plain chert across drainages as evidence of regular band mobility. "Therefore, when Coastal Plain chert or other non-local lithic raw materials are found along major drainages in central South Carolina it suggests that groups have crossed several river systems, and that procurement of raw materials must have been incidental to some broad scale annual range involving several hundred miles" (Michie 1996:266).

This interpretation, however, leaves an interesting contradiction. While Michie's functional interpretation of Taylor is consistent with the band-macroband model, he rejects the model's watershed-based band territories. The question then becomes: if Taylor was a macroband aggregation site but doesn't represent occupations by bands based in adjacent drainages, what were the territories of the groups involved? If my argument has been convincing thus far, the answer should be obvious: the Uwharrie and Allendale regions.

Taylor's Fall Line location along the Congaree thus reflects its proximity to both the Uwharrie and the Allendale sources rather than any presumed logistical advantage that this locale might have had with respect to subsistence resources in the Piedmont and Coastal Plain. In fact, I earlier questioned the notion that the environmental structure between the two physiographic zones was significant enough to have warranted such a seasonal transhumance during the early Holocene.

An examination of the two band ranges outlined in figure 8.3 indicates that Taylor (as well as all of Anderson and Hanson's other proposed aggregation sites) are located exactly where expected—in places readily accessible to both regions, roughly equidistant from the Allendale and Uwharries sources (ca. 150–160 km). The equal frequencies of chert and metavolcanic points from Taylor support the notion of group movement from both the Coastal Plain and the Piedmont. In a total of fifty-six excavated Palmer Corner-Notched points, for example, approximately equal percentages of Coastal Plain chert and metavolcanic stone are present (ca. 20 percent). Quartz occurs in the highest frequencies (44 percent), while orthoquartzite (13 percent), quartz crystal (2 percent), and black chert (2 percent) constitute the minority groups (Michie 1996:251).

Although Michie did not specifically identify any of the metavolcanic artifacts as Uwharrie rhyolite, stone from the Uwharrie Mountains is present in the Taylor assemblage. As a part of this study Michie graciously allowed me to examine a portion of the Taylor assemblage, in which I identified several aphyric rhyolite specimens from Morrow Mountain.

If aggregation events did take place midway between the Uwharrie and Allendale regions, this settlement characteristic has an important implication for Early Archaic site distributions: no other sites exhibiting the raw material diversity of Taylor should be found far from the Congaree. Such a pattern does, in fact, seem to hold true, and indicates another weakness of the band-macroband model. Anderson and Hanson (1988:271) posit that sites similar in size as well as assemblage and raw material diversity should exist at the Fall Line of each of the major watersheds along the South Atlantic Slope, yet no such sites have been identified outside the Congaree. In short, the Uwharrie-Allendale model better explains both the concentration of sites such as Taylor along the Congaree *and* their marked absence elsewhere in the Carolinas.

In light of the above argument, I have designated an "aggregation range" separate from the Uwharrie and Allendale band ranges (figure 8.3). I propose that the Congaree, Broad, and Saluda River Valleys were part of a territorial range exploited by groups aggregated along the Congaree. Collections data from these areas reveal relatively equal frequencies of chert and metavolcanic Early Archaic points (ca. 10–20 percent), albeit in lower proportions than quartz (ca. 50–80 percent) (Sassaman 1996:figures 4.3–4.4). Some group movement also took place downriver as evidenced by the presence of points in the assemblage made from orthoquartzite (13 percent), which outcrops south of Taylor along the Santee (Michie 1996:251) (see Chapter 3). Although the presence of orthoquartzite points suggests that the Santee was exploited by groups at Taylor, the relatively high frequencies (ca. 50 percent) of Coastal Plain chert points from the Santee suggest that this drainage was exploited more regularly by an Allendale band.

This aggregation range, however, does not preclude the possibility that portions of the Saluda and Broad could have been exploited by the Allendale or Uwharrie bands as well. Still, if the Congaree was used primarily for aggregation events, there is a practical reason why the Saluda and Broad Rivers may not have been a regular part of the Allendale or Uwharrie ranges. Presumably, these events resulted in a greater-than-usual drain on local resources relative to other regions. Assuming then, that these aggregations were regularly scheduled occurrences, it may have been beneficial to avoid this area between events to allow resources to regenerate.

The question of contact outside the Piedmont and Coastal Plain has already been addressed with respect to the collections survey. Given the general absence of raw materials from outside the Piedmont or Coastal

Plain (e.g., Ridge and Valley chert), it would appear that group interaction took place primarily between the Uwharrie and Allendale ranges rather than with other regions.

CONCLUSION

By now, many readers may have noticed similarities between the Uwharrie-Allendale model and the Flint Run settlement model advocated by William Gardner since the 1970s. On the basis of his work in the Shenandoah Valley of northern Virginia, Gardner (1974, 1977, 1983, 1989) has proposed that Paleo-Indian and Early Archaic settlement in this region was directly linked to the primary use of Flint Run jasper outcrops. Moreover, he has geographically expanded this model to account for other areas of the Southeast where cryptocrystalline quarry sources were located, including the Allendale sources as well as Williamson chert in Virginia and "Ocala" chert in Florida (Gardner 1983:57–58).

While both the Uwharrie-Allendale and Flint Run models feature the limited availability of high quality knappable stone as a significant factor influencing settlement, there are some differences between the two models. First, Gardner (1983:50–51; 1989:12–18) emphasizes the near exclusive preference of cryptocrystalline stone (such as jasper, chert, and chalcedony) during the Paleo-Indian and Early Archaic periods and only occasional use of "less desirable" materials as rhyolite. Thus in the absence of various cherts, high quality knappable rhyolite permitted the extensive settlement of the Piedmont, which contains cryptocrystalline to microcrystalline stone such as rhyolite. Second, rather limited settlement ranges are proposed in the Flint Run model covering a maximum extent of 50–130 km that are primarily riverine focused (Gardner 1983:58). As outlined above, the maximum Early Archaic range in the Piedmont was probably twice as great. Finally, while the settlement complexes of both models are similar, aggregation site locations in the Uwharrie-Allendale model, unlike the Flint Run model, are based less on proximity to quarry sources than on proximity to neighboring social groups. Thus while the "lithic determinist" underpinnings of the two models cannot be denied, the Uwharrie-Allendale settlement model is distinguished from Flint Run by an emphasis on rhyolite rather than chert, a band range that is not geographically bound by watersheds, and a settlement distribution including one site type whose location is influenced more by social than economic needs.

Unlike the two models discussed above, which treat the distribution of knappable stone as a significant resource influencing settlement, the band-macroband model places little emphasis on stone resources as a factor shaping settlement. Replenishment of the tool kit "is not thought to have been an overly critical factor influencing settlement. In the Piedmont, where lithic raw materials are widespread, this was not a factor" (Anderson and Hanson 1988:270). The notion that chippable stone was widely available in the Piedmont, however, is simply untrue. While metavolcanic outcrops occur throughout the Piedmont, not all such outcrops contained usable stone. The fact that Early Archaic peoples relied extensively on Uwharrie rhyolite and Allendale chert belies Anderson and Hanson's comments concerning the widespread availability of potential raw materials. The band-macroband model simply understates the importance of local conditions with respect to raw material availability in shaping settlement.

The band-macroband model, however, is not the first to understate the significance of stone resources in Early Archaic settlement. Following Binford (1979:259–261), virtually all southeastern settlement models have largely assumed that stone acquisition was "embedded" in (i.e., largely incidental to) subsistence practices (e.g., Goodyear et al. 1979:199; see Chapter 1).

Although some lithic procurement probably took place under such conditions, I would argue that this behavior accounted for only the minor amounts of raw material that supplemented assemblages predominantly made of chert and rhyolite. Rather, as I have suggested above, scheduled trips were probably made to the Uwharrie and Allendale quarries specifically to acquire stone. This scheduling did not necessarily involve any extra effort in settlement mobility, since (turning the notion of embeddedness around) subsistence procurement would then have been incidental to stone procurement. Once groups had refurbished their tool kits and left the quarry settlements, the stone that they did obtain was probably acquired incidentally in the region they were exploiting for food.

Finally, this discussion brings me to the question of why the role of lithic procurement has been overlooked as a significant factor in Early Archaic settlement. Previous settlement models have either implicitly or explicitly relied heavily on ethnographic or ethnoarchaeological data in which to frame their interpretations. Since none of the groups in these accounts relies extensively upon stone resources, it is not surprising that discussions have stressed subsistence practices rather than stone procurement. House and Wogaman (1978:12–26), for example, used the seasonal round of the historic Creek "as a useful baseline" to construct their model of Archaic settlement. Similarly, Anderson and Hanson have relied heavily upon the forager-collector continuum that is derived from the ethnoarchaeological studies of hunter-gatherers.

By uncritically borrowing ethnographic frameworks for Early Archaic settlement models, archaeologists in the Southeast have fallen into the trap of doing "ethnography with a shovel" and thereby giving too much weight to the ethnographic record in interpreting archaeological evidence (Wobst 1978). In essence, we have been blinded to the potential existence of a settlement pattern unlike any known ethnographically—a settlement pattern largely conditioned by the limited distribution of knappable stone.

There is, of course, no a priori reason why Early Archaic settlement should have been conditioned more greatly by the presence of plant or animal resources than by stone resources. (This misplaced priority is all the more ironic, given the absence of subsistence data.) There is also no reason why, given the vast cultural and environmental changes that the Southeast has undergone since the early Holocene, any ethnographic accounts of southeastern Indians—or any other ethnographically known group—should provide an appropriate analog for Early Archaic settlement. In fact, given these circumstances, one might be suspicious of such attempts. If archaeologists are successful in reevaluating the relationship between stone and subsistence resources as they affect hunter-gatherer settlement, we will be in a position to contribute uniquely to an anthropological understanding of hunter-gatherers: archaeologists can then provide insights into hunter-gatherer settlement strategies that are unknown ethnographically. Moreover, since hunter-gatherers are the "quintessential anthropological topic" (Bettinger 1991:v), such insights should ensure that the southeastern archaeology of prehistoric hunter-gatherers will remain a topic of wider anthropological interest for some time to come.

Appendix A
Variables Recorded in the Analysis

The variables used in the analysis of the chipped-stone tools in the Hardaway assemblage are listed below. All bifacial and unifacial tools were initially classified according to tool class (see Chapter 4) and raw material type (see Chapter 3). Additional variables were recoded for specific tool classes as indicated below. All metric variables were recorded to the nearest millimeter. Chapters 4 and 5 present summaries of the metric and nonmetric variables.

POINTS

The following variables were recorded on all Early Archaic points in the Hardaway assemblage.

Condition

"Condition" indicates whether the artifact was intact or broken. If the specimen was broken but was still identifiable as a point type, the tool portion was recorded: base, body, ear, or barb. If the point was essentially complete but some tool portion was missing (i.e., tip, ear, barb, or some combination), it was recorded as such.

Total Length

Total length was measured from base to tip on Palmer and Kirk points. On Hardaway points this dimension was measured from a line drawn perpendicular to both ears and the point tip. Only values for intact specimens were used in calculating this dimension.

Axial Length

Axial length was measured on Hardaway points along the tool midline from the top of the basal concavity to the point tip. In corner-notched points, this measurement is the same as total length.

Tang Length

This dimension records the maximum tang length from the point base to the top of the tang; in the case of notched points, the latter was defined as a line drawn perpendicular to tang length tangent to the top of both notches.

Basal Width

"Basal width" records the maximum width of the base or the maximum distance between ears in the case of Hardaway points.

Tang Width

On all notched points, tang width was taken as the minimum distance between notches; on Hardaway-Dalton points, tang width was measured as the minimum width of the base.

Shoulder Width

Shoulder width was taken parallel to tang width. On notched points, this dimension records the maximum distance between blade barbs, which usually corresponds to maximum blade width. On Hardaway-Dalton points, however, shoulder width was often greater than blade width. In this case, shoulder width was recorded as the maximum distance along the top of the base.

Midblade Width

Midblade width was measured parallel to shoulder width midway up the blade.

Maximum Thickness

This dimension was recorded as the maximum distance perpendicular to total length and basal width.

Basal Grinding

The presence/absence of basal grinding was monitored by a series of the following categories: complete, partial, absent, or indeterminate. "Complete" refers to the presence of continuous grinding along the point base. "Partial" refers to incomplete or discontinuous basal grinding. "Absent" and "indeterminate" refer to the absence or indeterminacy of basal grinding, respectively.

Degree of Basal Grinding

The amount of basal grinding was indicated by three categories: distinct, light, and indeterminate.

Blade Beveling

The presence/absence of blade beveling was recorded.

Blade Serrations

Four values recorded the presence or absence of blade serrations: distinct, light, absent, and indeterminate.

BIFACES

The following variables were recorded on bifaces.

Biface Condition

"Condition" indicates whether the specimen was intact or broken. If it was broken, the tool portion was recorded: tip, body, base/end, or unidentified fragment. If the specimen was essentially whole but was missing a small portion of the tip, body, or base, it was classified as complete.

Maximum Length

Maximum length was recorded as the total length of the specimen from base to tip.

Maximum Width

The maximum width was recorded perpendicular to maximum length.

Maximum Thickness

Maximum thickness was measured perpendicular to both maximum length and maximum width.

Fractures

If the specimen was broken, the type of fracture was recorded: hinge/step, reverse, perverse, lateral snap, and material flow. These determinations largely follow Crabtree (1972) and Johnson (1981:43–52).

UNIFACIAL TOOL BLANKS

The following variables were recorded on unifacial tools. Variables relating to tool blanks are defined first.

Blank Type

All tools were classified according to whether they derived from a block, a biface, or an indeterminate core (see Chapter 5).

Transverse Cross-Section Shape

A cross-section shape was attributed to each tool: triangular, offset triangular, flat trapezoidal, convex trapezoidal, concave trapezoidal, plano-convex, other, or indeterminate. Cross-section determination was made from the proximal end of the specimen with the dorsal surface up.

Maximum Length

Maximum length, like the other dimensions, was recorded to the nearest 0.1 mm. Length was recorded on the longest dimension of the artifact, which usually corresponded to the flaking or bulbar axis (cf. Movius et al. 1968:33). In a few cases, however, maximum length was taken at perpendicular or oblique angles to the flaking axis (see platform orientation). Types I and IV side scrapers, for example, usually had their maximum dimension oriented perpendicular to the flaking angle.

Maximum Width

Maximum width was measured at right angles to maximum length.

Maximum Thickness

Maximum thickness was measured at the maximum point of tool thickness other than the bulb of percussion.

Platform Orientation

Four types of platform orientations were identified: parallel, perpendicular, oblique, and indeterminate. A parallel striking platform is oriented so that the axis of percussion and the long axis of the tool are parallel. A perpendicular striking platform is oriented so that the axis of percussion of the flake intersects the tool long axis at 90 degrees. An oblique striking platform is oriented so that the axis of percussion of the tool intersects the tool long axis at an oblique angle (cf. Claggett and Cable 1982:appendix 2).

Exterior Platform Angle

Exterior platform angle was measured to the nearest 5 degrees with a contact goniometer at the intersection of the striking platform and dorsal surface of the artifact (cf. Dibble and Whittaker 1981:286).

Striking Platform Thickness

Striking platform thickness is the distance from the dorsal surface of the striking platform drawn perpendicular to the point of percussion (i.e., the thickness of the platform at the point of percussion) (cf. Dibble and Whittaker 1981:286).

Striking Platform Width

Striking platform width is recorded perpendicular to the striking platform thickness.

END SCRAPERS

The following variables were recorded only on end scrapers. Side determination was made by placing end scrapers with dorsal surface up and striking platform facing toward the observer.

Lateral Retouch Location

The following observations were made on the location of lateral retouch: right lateral, left lateral, bilateral, absent, and indeterminate.

Proximal Thinning Location

Proximal thinning was defined as flaking occurring at the proximal end of the tool in order to thin that tool segment to facilitate hafting (see Chapter 4). The following occurrences of this retouch were observed: ventral surface, dorsal surface, ventral and dorsal surface, absent, and indeterminate.

Spur Location

The presence/absence of spurs was determined for each tool. If present, its location (i.e., lateral edge) was recorded (see lateral notch location).

Bit Width

Bit width was measured as the maximum distance between the lateral margins of the tool bit.

Bit Thickness

Bit thickness was measured as the maximum dimension between the distal termination of retouch scars on the bit dorsal surface and the opposing ventral surface of the tool.

Bit Depth

Bit depth was measured as the maximum distance between the convex end of the bit, usually near its center, and an imaginary line drawn between the opposite corners of the bit.

Bit Edge Angle

Bit edge angles were measured with a contact goniometer to the nearest 5 degrees at the juncture of the ventral surface and the retouched bit edge on the dorsal surface. Both maximum and minimum values were recorded.

Bit Edge Retouch Scar Length

Bit edge retouch scar length was measured from the origin of the retouch flake scar at the bit edge (i.e., the intersection of the dorsal and ventral surface) to a point where the distal termination of the flake scar invaded the dorsal surface of the tool blank. Both maximum and minimum values were recorded.

OTHER UNIFACIAL SCRAPERS

The following values were recorded on all side scrapers, pointed scrapers, oval scrapers, and miscellaneous scrapers. Tool orientation for side determination was as follows. Tools that had parallel platform orientations were placed with the dorsal surface up and striking platform facing toward the observer. Side scrapers with perpendicular or oblique platform orientations were placed with the dorsal surface up and striking platform to the right in order to preserve the consistency of measurement within the type (i.e., all Type I and Type IV side scrapers were classified as having left retouched edges). All side scrapers that were classified as indeterminate with regard to platform orientation or number of retouched edges (see below) were arbitrarily classified as having left edges.

Number of Bits

The number of bits on each tool were recorded. Only pointed scrapers and miscellaneous scrapers had any tools exhibiting more than two bit edges.

Bit Shape Combination

A series of bit shape categories were used: single convex, single concave, single straight, single irregular, double convex, double concave, double straight, convex straight, concave straight, and other.

Bit Shape

Individual shape categories were recorded for each bit location (i.e., left, right, or other): straight, concave, convex, irregular, or indeterminate.

Bit Retouch Surface Location

Bit retouch was recorded as occurring on the dorsal surface, ventral surface, or a combination of the two.

Bit Thickness

Measurements were taken as the thickness of the bit edge between the distal termination of flake scars on the dorsal surface of the tool and a point on the opposing ventral surface. Both maximum and minimum values were recorded.

Bit Edge Angle

Bit edge angles were measured in the same manner as for end scrapers.

Bit Flake Scar Length

Flake scar length was measured for bits as it was for end scrapers.

Bit Thickness

Thickness was measured for bits as it was for end scrapers.

Appendix B
Artifact Counts

Table B.1 shows total artifact counts by square from the undisturbed portions of CBM, Zone 3, and Zone 4. Table B.2 lists the proportion of each square that was undisturbed. Dividing the artifact count in Table B.1 by the proportion in Table B.2 yielded the "corrected" artifact count used for the spatial analysis in Chapter 6.

Table B.1. Artifact Counts by Provenance Unit

Type	Provenance					
	-45L10	-45L15	-50L05	-50R05	-55L00	-55L05
Hardaway-Dalton	-	-	-	-	-	-
Hardaway Side-Notched	-	-	-	-	1	-
Small Dalton	1	-	-	1	-	-
Palmer Corner-Notched	-	-	-	-	-	-
Kirk Corner-Notched	-	-	-	-	-	-
Indeterminate corner-notched	-	-	-	-	-	-
Indeterminate side-notched	-	-	-	-	-	-
Indeterminate point	-	-	4	-	1	-
Biface I	-	1	4	-	-	-
Biface II	2	-	9	-	-	-
Biface III	-	-	3	-	-	-
Indeterminate biface	1	-	-	-	1	1
End scraper Ia	-	-	3	-	-	-
End scraper Ib	-	1	2	-	1	1
End scraper IIa	-	-	1	1	-	-
End scraper IIb	-	1	-	-	-	-
End scraper III	-	-	-	-	-	-
End scraper IV	-	-	-	-	-	-
End scraper V	-	-	1	-	-	-
Side scraper I	1	-	1	-	-	-
Side scraper IIa	3	-	7	-	1	1
Side scraper I I b	-	-	-	-	-	-
Side scraper III	-	-	4	-	1	-
Side scraper IV	-	-	1	-	-	-
Pointed scraper	-	-	-	-	-	-
Oval scraper	-	-	-	-	-	-
Miscellaneous scraper	-	-	-	-	-	-
Indeterminate scraper	3	-	8	3	1	-
Perforator/drill/graver	-	-	-	-	-	-
Denticulate	-	-	-	-	-	-
Hafted spokeshave	-	-	-	-	-	-
Waller knife	-	-	-	-	-	-
Core/scraper	-	-	-	-	-	-
Chopper	-	-	-	-	-	-
Adze	-	-	-	-	-	-
Hammerstone	-	-	-	-	-	-
Hammerstone/abrader	-	-	-	-	-	-
Hammerstone/anvil	-	-	-	-	-	-
Grinding stone/anvil	1	-	1	-	-	-
Anvil	-	-	-	-	-	-
Core	-	-	-	-	1	-
Pièces esquillées	-	-	-	-	-	-
Engraved Stone	-	-	-	-	-	-
Indeterminate ground stone	-	-	-	-	-	-
Other worked stone	-	-	-	-	-	-
Unmodified cobble/stone	-	-	1	-	-	-

(continued)

Table B.1 (continued). Artifact Counts by Provenance Unit

Type	Provenance					
	-55L10	-55L15	-55L20	-55L25	-55R05	-60L00
Hardaway-Dalton	-	-	-	-	-	-
Hardaway Side-Notched	-	-	1	-	-	-
Small Dalton	1	1	-	-	-	-
Palmer Corner-Notched	1	1	1	-	-	-
Kirk Corner-Notched	-	1	-	-	-	-
Indeterminate corner-notched	-	1	-	-	-	-
Indeterminate side-notched	1	1	-	-	-	-
Indeterminate point	3	7	-	-	1	-
Biface I	3	12	3	-	-	1
Biface II	11	13	1	2	-	1
Biface III	3	13	1	2	-	-
Indeterminate biface	9	12	1	1	1	-
End scraper Ia	1	7	2	-	-	1
End scraper Ib	2	1	-	-	-	-
End scraper IIa	-	2	-	-	-	-
End scraper IIb	2	-	-	-	-	-
End scraper III	-	1	-	-	-	-
End scraper IV	1	1	1	-	-	-
End scraper V	3	3	1	-	-	-
Side scraper I	1	1	-	-	-	-
Side scraper IIa	7	16	3	1	-	2
Side scraper IIb	5	1	-	-	-	-
Side scraper III	5	12	2	-	-	-
Side scraper IV	-	-	1	-	-	-
Pointed scraper	-	1	1	-	-	-
Oval scraper	-	-	-	-	-	-
Miscellaneous scraper	1	1	1	-	-	-
Indeterminate scraper	10	16	1	1	-	2
Perforator/drill/graver	-	1	-	-	-	-
Denticulate	-	-	-	-	-	-
Hafted spokeshave	-	-	-	-	-	-
Waller knife	-	-	-	-	-	-
Core/scraper	-	-	-	-	-	-
Chopper	1	1	-	-	-	-
Adze	-	-	-	-	-	-
Hammerstone	2	3	1	-	-	-
Hammerstone/abrader	-	-	-	-	-	-
Hammerstone/anvil	1	2	1	-	-	-
Grinding stone/anvil	-	1	-	-	-	-
Anvil	1	-	-	-	-	-
Core	3	5	1	-	1	1
Pièces esquillées	-	-	-	-	-	-
Engraved Stone	-	-	-	-	-	-
Indeterminate ground stone	-	-	-	-	-	-
Other worked stone	-	-	-	-	-	-
Unmodified cobble/stone	1	7	1	-	1	-

(continued)

Table B.1 (continued). Artifact Counts by Provenance Unit

	Provenance					
Type	-60R10	-60R15	-60R20	-60R25	-60R30	-60R35
Hardaway-Dalton	-	-	-	1	-	-
Hardaway Side-Notched	-	1[a]	-	-	-	-
Small Dalton	-	-	-	-	-	-
Palmer Corner-Notched	-	1	1	-	-	-
Kirk Corner-Notched	-	1	-	-	-	-
Indeterminate corner-notched	1	-	-	-	-	1
Indeterminate side-notched	-	-	-	-	-	-
Indeterminate point	-	1	1	-	-	3
Biface I	-	-	1	-	-	-
Biface II	-	3	5	2	1	-
Biface III	1	-	1	1	-	-
Indeterminate biface	1	3	1	1	2	1
End scraper Ia	1	1	2	-	1	-
End scraper Ib	-	-	-	1	-	1
End scraper IIa	-	4	-	-	-	-
End scraper IIb	-	-	-	-	-	-
End scraper III	-	-	-	-	-	-
End scraper IV	-	-	-	-	-	-
End scraper V	-	2	1	-	-	-
Side scraper I	-	-	-	-	-	-
Side scraper IIa	-	-	-	2	-	2
Side scraper IIb	-	-	1	-	-	-
Side scraper III	-	3	-	1	-	-
Side scraper IV	-	-	-	-	-	-
Pointed scraper	-	-	-	-	-	-
Oval scraper	-	-	-	-	-	-
Miscellaneous scraper	-	-	-	-	-	-
Indeterminate scraper	1	-	-	3	1	-
Perforator/drill/graver	-	-	1	1	-	1
Denticulate	-	-	-	-	-	-
Hafted spokeshave	-	-	-	-	-	-
Waller knife	-	-	-	1	-	-
Core/scraper	-	-	-	-	-	-
Chopper	-	-	-	-	1	-
Adze	-	-	-	-	-	-
Hammerstone	-	-	1	-	-	1
Hammerstone/abrader	-	-	-	-	-	-
Hammerstone/anvil	-	-	-	-	-	-
Grinding stone/anvil	-	-	-	-	-	-
Anvil	-	-	-	-	-	-
Core	-	2	1	-	-	-
Pièces esquillées	-	-	-	-	-	-
Engraved Stone	-	-	-	-	-	-
Indeterminate ground stone	-	-	-	-	-	-
Other worked stone	-	-	-	-	-	-
Unmodified cobble/stone	-	-	-	-	-	-

(continued)

Table B.1 (continued). Artifact Counts by Provenance Unit

	Provenance					
Type	-60L05	-60L10	-60L15	-60L20	-60L25	-60R05
Hardaway-Dalton	1	-	-	-	-	1
Hardaway Side-Notched	-	1	-	-	-	-
Small Dalton	-	-	-	-	-	-
Palmer Corner-Notched	-	-	-	-	-	-
Kirk Corner-Notched	-	1	-	-	-	1
Indeterminate corner-notched	-	2	-	-	2	-
Indeterminate side-notched	-	-	-	-	-	-
Indeterminate point	-	2	-	-	2	-
Biface I	1	1	1	2	-	1
Biface II	2	11	2	3	-	1
Biface III	3	2	3	1	1	-
Indeterminate biface	-	10	-	3	2	-
End scraper Ia	-	3	1	-	-	-
End scraper Ib	1	1	2	-	-	-
End scraper IIa	1	1	-	-	-	-
End scraper IIb	-	-	-	1	-	-
End scraper III	-	-	-	-	-	1
End scraper IV	-	-	-	2	-	-
End scraper V	-	2	-	-	-	-
Side scraper I	-	-	1	-	-	-
Side scraper IIa	2	10	3	1	1	-
Side scraper IIb	-	2	-	-	-	-
Side scraper III	1	3	1	-	1	-
Side scraper IV	1	3	-	-	-	-
Pointed scraper	-	-	-	-	-	-
Oval scraper	-	-	-	1	-	-
Miscellaneous scraper	-	-	-	-	-	-
Indeterminate scraper	1	9	-	-	1	1
Perforator/drill/graver	-	2	-	-	-	-
Denticulate	-	-	-	-	-	-
Hafted spokeshave	-	-	-	-	-	-
Waller knife	-	-	-	-	-	-
Core/scraper	-	-	-	-	-	-
Chopper	-	-	-	1	-	-
Adze	-	-	-	-	-	-
Hammerstone	-	-	-	2	-	-
Hammerstone/abrader	-	-	1	-	-	-
Hammerstone/anvil	1	1	1	-	-	-
Grinding stone/anvil	1	-	-	-	-	-
Anvil	-	-	-	-	-	-
Core	1	5	3	-	-	-
Pièces esquillées	-	-	-	-	-	-
Engraved Stone	-	-	-	-	-	-
Indeterminate ground stone	-	-	-	-	-	-
Other worked stone	-	-	-	-	-	-
Unmodified cobble/stone	1	3	-	1	-	-

(continued)

Table B.1 (continued). Artifact Counts by Provenance Unit

	Provenance					
Type	-60R40	-60R45	-65L00	-65L05	-60L10	-65L25
Hardaway-Dalton	-	-	-	2[a]	1[a]	-
Hardaway Side-Notched	-	-	-	1	1	-
Small Dalton	-	-	-	1	-	-
Palmer Corner-Notched	-	-	-	1	-	-
Kirk Corner-Notched	-	-	-	-	-	-
Indeterminate corner-notched	-	-	-	-	-	-
Indeterminate side-notched	-	-	-	-	-	-
Indeterminate point	2	4	1	3	1	-
Biface I	2	1	-	-	-	-
Biface II	7	6	-	8	1	1
Biface III	2	1	-	7	1	-
Indeterminate biface	-	-	-	10	3	-
End scraper Ia	-	-	-	3	-	-
End scraper Ib	-	-	-	-	1	-
End scraper IIa	2	1	-	2	-	-
End scraper IIb	-	-	-	-	-	-
End scraper III	-	-	-	-	-	-
End scraper IV	-	-	-	-	-	-
End scraper V	-	-	-	1	-	2
Side scraper I	-	-	-	-	-	-
Side scraper IIa	1	2	-	4	5	-
Side scraper IIb	-	-	-	2	2	-
Side scraper III	-	1	1	-	2	-
Side scraper IV	-	-	-	1	1	-
Pointed scraper	-	-	-	-	-	-
Oval scraper	-	-	-	-	-	-
Miscellaneous scraper	-	-	-	1	-	-
Indeterminate scraper	-	1	-	7	4	2
Perforator/drill/graver	-	-	-	5	-	-
Denticulate	-	-	-	-	-	-
Hafted spokeshave	-	-	-	1	-	-
Waller knife	-	-	-	-	-	-
Core/scraper	-	-	-	-	-	-
Chopper	-	-	-	-	-	-
Adze	-	-	-	-	-	-
Hammerstone	1	-	-	1	-	1
Hammerstone/abrader	-	-	-	-	-	-
Hammerstone/anvil	-	-	-	-	-	-
Grinding stone/anvil	-	-	-	-	1	-
Anvil	-	-	-	-	-	-
Core	1	1	-	-	2	-
Pièces esquillées	-	-	-	-	-	-
Engraved Stone	-	-	-	-	-	-
Indeterminate ground stone	-	-	1	-	-	-
Other worked stone	-	-	1	-	-	-
Unmodified cobble/stone	1	-	1	-	2	-

[a]Preforms

(continued)

Table B.1 (continued). Artifact Counts by Provenance Unit

Type	Provenance					
	-65R05	-65R10	-70L00	-75L00	-70L05	-70L10
Hardaway-Dalton	-	1	4[b]	2	-	-
Hardaway Side-Notched	-	1[a]	1	-	-	-
Small Dalton	-	-	1	-	-	-
Palmer Corner-Notched	-	1	3	1	-	1
Kirk Corner-Notched	-	-	2	2	1	-
Indeterminate corner-notched	-	-	-	-	-	-
Indeterminate side-notched	-	-	-	1	-	-
Indeterminate point	-	2	4	2	3	-
Biface I	3	-	4	2	3	1
Biface II	2	1	18	6	4	2
Biface III	1	-	1	5	4	1
Indeterminate biface	1	4	2	-	4	-
End scraper Ia	-	-	6	5	4	3
End scraper Ib	-	-	1	1	1	1
End scraper IIa	-	-	-	-	-	-
End scraper IIb	-	-	1	-	-	-
End scraper III	-	-	-	-	-	-
End scraper IV	-	1	1	-	-	2
End scraper V	-	1	5	4	1	-
Side scraper I	-	-	-	1	1	-
Side scraper IIa	-	-	10	3	3	3
Side scraper IIb	-	1	-	-	3	-
Side scraper III	2	-	-	-	4	1
Side scraper IV	-	-	1	2	-	-
Pointed scraper	-	-	-	-	5	-
Oval scraper	-	-	-	-	-	-
Miscellaneous scraper	-	-	2	-	-	-
Indeterminate scraper	1	1	5	6	5	1
Perforator/drill/graver	-	-	1	-	-	-
Denticulate	-	-	-	-	-	-
Hafted spokeshave	1	-	-	-	-	-
Waller knife	-	-	-	-	-	-
Core/scraper	-	-	-	-	-	-
Chopper	-	-	-	-	-	-
Adze	-	1	-	-	-	-
Hammerstone	-	-	-	1	1	1
Hammerstone/abrader	-	-	-	-	-	-
Hammerstone/anvil	-	-	1	-	1	-
Grinding stone/anvil	-	-	-	-	-	-
Anvil	-	-	-	-	-	-
Core	-	1	1	-	-	-
Pièces esquillées	-	-	-	-	-	-
Engraved Stone	-	-	-	-	-	-
Indeterminate ground stone	-	-	-	-	-	-
Other worked stone	-	-	1	-	-	-
Unmodified cobble/stone	-	-	1	-	-	-

[a]Preform.

[b]Includes one preform.

(continued)

Table B.1 (continued). Artifact Counts by Provenance Unit

Type	Provenance					
	-70L15	-70L20	-70R05	-70R10	-75L05	-75L10
Hardaway-Dalton	-	-	1[a]	1[a]	-	-
Hardaway Side-Notched	-	-	-	-	-	-
Small Dalton	-	-	-	-	-	-
Palmer Corner-Notched	-	-	2	-	-	-
Kirk Corner-Notched	-	-	2	-	-	-
Indeterminate corner-notched	-	-	-	-	-	-
Indeterminate side-notched	-	-	1	-	-	-
Indeterminate point	-	-	3	1	1	-
Biface I	1	-	3	-	3	2
Biface II	1	-	7	1	5	1
Biface III	-	-	1	-	6	-
Indeterminate biface	3	-	5	4	5	1
End scraper Ia	-	-	-	1	4	4
End scraper Ib	-	-	1	-	2	2
End scraper IIa	-	-	1	-	-	-
End scraper IIb	-	-	2	1	1	-
End scraper III	-	-	-	-	-	-
End scraper IV	-	-	-	-	1	-
End scraper V	-	-	5	-	2	-
Side scraper I	-	-	2	-	-	-
Side scraper IIa	2	-	8	1	5	-
Side scraper IIb	1	-	-	-	5	-
Side scraper III	2	-	2	1	5	2
Side scraper IV	-	-	1	1	-	-
Pointed scraper	-	-	-	-	-	-
Oval scraper	-	-	1	-	-	-
Miscellaneous scraper	-	-	-	-	2	1
Indeterminate scraper	1	2	7	2	4	6
Perforator/drill/graver	-	-	-	-	2	-
Denticulate	-	-	-	-	-	-
Hafted spokeshave	-	-	-	-	-	-
Waller knife	-	-	-	-	-	-
Core/scraper	-	-	-	-	-	-
Chopper	-	-	-	-	-	-
Adze	-	-	-	-	-	-
Hammerstone	-	-	-	-	-	-
Hammerstone/abrader	-	-	-	-	-	-
Hammerstone/anvil	-	-	-	1	-	-
Grinding stone/anvil	-	-	-	-	1	-
Anvil	-	-	-	-	-	-
Core	-	-	-	-	1	1
Pièces esquillées	-	-	-	-	-	-
Engraved Stone	-	-	-	-	-	-
Indeterminate ground stone	-	-	-	-	-	-
Other worked stone	-	-	-	1	-	-
Unmodified cobble/stone	2	3	1	1	3	1

[a]Preform.

(continued)

Table B.1 (continued). Artifact Counts by Provenance Unit

	Provenance					
Type	-75L20	-75R05	-75R10	-80L00	-80L20	-80R05
Hardaway-Dalton	-	-	-	-	-	1
Hardaway Side-Notched	-	-	-	-	-	-
Small Dalton	-	1	1	-	-	-
Palmer Corner-Notched	-	2	1	-	-	-
Kirk Corner-Notched	-	-	-	-	-	1
Indeterminate corner-notched	-	-	-	-	-	-
Indeterminate side-notched	-	-	-	-	-	-
Indeterminate point	-	1	-	-	2	1
Biface I	-	1	-	-	-	1
Biface II	-	2	-	-	1	1
Biface III	1	-	-	-	-	-
Indeterminate biface	-	1	4	-	1	-
End scraper Ia	-	1	2	-	-	-
End scraper Ib	-	-	1	-	-	1
End scraper IIa	1	-	1	-	-	-
End scraper IIb	1	1	-	-	-	-
End scraper III	-	3	-	-	-	-
End scraper IV	-	-	-	-	-	-
End scraper V	1	2	1	-	-	-
Side scraper I	-	-	-	-	-	-
Side scraper IIa	1	3	1	-	1	1
Side scraper IIb	-	-	-	-	-	-
Side scraper III	-	3	-	-	-	1
Side scraper IV	-	-	-	-	-	-
Pointed scraper	-	-	-	-	-	-
Oval scraper	-	-	-	-	-	-
Miscellaneous scraper	-	-	-	-	-	-
Indeterminate scraper	-	3	-	-	-	-
Perforator/drill/graver	-	-	-	-	-	-
Denticulate	-	-	-	-	-	-
Hafted spokeshave	-	-	-	-	-	-
Waller knife	-	-	-	-	-	-
Core/scraper	-	-	-	-	-	-
Chopper	-	-	1	-	-	-
Adze	-	-	-	-	-	-
Hammerstone	-	-	1	1	-	-
Hammerstone/abrader	-	-	-	-	-	-
Hammerstone/anvil	-	-	-	-	-	-
Grinding stone/anvil	-	1	-	-	-	-
Anvil	-	-	-	-	-	-
Core	1	1	-	1	-	-
Pièces esquillées	-	-	-	1	-	-
Engraved Stone	-	-	-	-	-	-
Indeterminate ground stone	-	-	-	-	-	-
Other worked stone	-	-	-	-	-	-
Unmodified cobble/stone	3	1	2	-	-	-

(continued)

Table B.1 (continued). Artifact Counts by Provenance Unit

Type	Provenance					
	-80R10	-85L00	-85R05	-85R10	-05L05	-05L40
Hardaway-Dalton	-	-	-	-	-	2[a]
Hardaway Side-Notched	-	-	-	-	-	-
Small Dalton	-	-	-	-	-	-
Palmer Corner-Notched	-	-	-	-	-	-
Kirk Corner-Notched	-	-	-	-	-	1
Indeterminate corner-notched	-	-	-	-	-	-
Indeterminate side-notched	-	-	-	-	-	-
Indeterminate point	1	1	1	-	-	3
Biface I	-	-	-	-	6	8
Biface II	1	-	2	3	19	8
Biface III	-	-	-	-	4	6
Indeterminate biface	-	2	-	-	2	3
End scraper Ia	-	-	2	2	1	6
End scraper Ib	-	-	-	-	1	2
End scraper IIa	-	-	-	-	1	3
End scraper IIb	-	-	-	-	1	3
End scraper III	-	-	-	-	-	-
End scraper IV	-	-	-	-	-	1
End scraper V	-	-	-	-	2	5
Side scraper I	-	-	-	-	-	1
Side scraper IIa	1	-	2	-	5	9
Side scraper IIb	-	-	-	-	-	-
Side scraper III	-	-	-	1	1	4
Side scraper IV	-	-	-	-	-	2
Pointed scraper	-	-	-	-	-	-
Oval scraper	-	-	-	-	-	-
Miscellaneous scraper	-	-	-	1	-	-
Indeterminate scraper	1	-	1	1	5	4
Perforator/drill/graver	-	-	-	-	-	1
Denticulate	-	-	-	-	-	-
Hafted spokeshave	-	-	-	-	-	-
Waller knife	-	-	-	-	-	-
Core/scraper	-	-	-	-	-	-
Chopper	-	-	-	-	-	2
Adze	-	-	-	-	-	-
Hammerstone	-	-	-	-	2	1
Hammerstone/abrader	-	-	-	-	-	-
Hammerstone/anvil	-	-	-	-	-	-
Grinding stone/anvil	-	-	-	-	-	-
Anvil	-	-	-	-	-	-
Core	-	-	1	-	2	-
Pièces esquillées	-	-	-	-	-	-
Engraved Stone	-	-	-	-	-	-
Indeterminate ground stone	-	-	-	-	-	-
Other worked stone	-	-	-	-	-	-
Unmodified cobble/stone	-	-	-	-	-	-

[a]Preforms

(continued)

Table B.1 (continued). Artifact Counts by Provenance Unit

Type	Provenance					
	-10L05	-15L05	-20L00	-20L05	-25L05	-25L30
Hardaway-Dalton	2[a]	1[b]	1[b]	1	-	2
Hardaway Side-Notched	-	-	-	-	-	-
Small Dalton	-	-	-	-	-	-
Palmer Corner-Notched	-	-	-	-	1	1
Kirk Corner-Notched	4	1	1	-	-	1
Indeterminate corner-notched	-	-	1	-	-	-
Indeterminate side-notched	-	-	-	-	-	-
Indeterminate point	-	3	-	2	3	4
Biface I	4	6	-	9	2	4
Biface II	3	15	6	19	12	10
Biface III	4	7	-	8	3	5
Indeterminate biface	5	1	1	7	1	2
End scraper Ia	4	7	2	2	2	-
End scraper Ib	3	-	-	-	-	2
End scraper IIa	3	-	1	5	1	3
End scraper IIb	-	-	2	2	1	1
End scraper III	-	-	-	-	-	1
End scraper IV	1	-	-	1	-	1
End scraper V	2	3	-	1	-	2
Side scraper I	1	-	2	-	1	1
Side scraper IIa	3	7	2	11	2	5
Side scraper IIb	-	-	-	-	-	-
Side scraper III	2	1	3	3	4	4
Side scraper IV	-	-	2	-	-	1
Pointed scraper	-	-	-	-	-	-
Oval scraper	-	-	-	-	-	-
Miscellaneous scraper	-	1	-	1	-	-
Indeterminate scraper	8	4	6	6	7	2
Perforator/drill/graver	1	-	-	-	1	1
Denticulate	-	-	-	1		
Hafted spokeshave	-	-	-	-	-	-
Waller knife	-	-	-	-	-	-
Core/scraper	1	1	-	-	-	1
Chopper	1	-	-	-	-	-
Adze	-	-	-	-	-	-
Hammerstone	2	2	-	-	-	-
Hammerstone/abrader	-	-	-	-	-	-
Hammerstone/anvil	-	1	-	2	-	-
Grinding stone/anvil	-	1	-	-	-	2
Anvil	-	1	-	-	-	-
Core	-	2	2	3	5	1
Pièces esquillées	-	-	-	-	1	-
Engraved Stone	-	-	-	-	-	-
Indeterminate ground stone	-	-	-	-	-	-
Other worked stone	-	1	-	2	-	-
Unmodified cobble/stone	-	-	-	-	-	-

[a]Includes one preform.

[b]Preform.

(continued)

Table B.1 (continued). Artifact Counts by Provenance Unit

	Provenance					
Type	-30L05	-30L30	-35L00	-35L05	-35L30	-40L00
Hardaway-Dalton	1	1	-	-	-	2
Hardaway Side-Notched	-	-	-	-	-	1
Small Dalton	-	-	-	-	-	-
Palmer Corner-Notched	-	-	-	-	-	2
Kirk Corner-Notched	-	1	1	2	-	-
Indeterminate corner-notched	-	-	1	-	-	-
Indeterminate side-notched	-	-	-	-	-	-
Indeterminate point	6	2	1	1	1	2
Biface I	9	5	7	2	4	5
Biface II	19	11	16	5	13	17
Biface III	3	8	6	1	4	8
Indeterminate biface	2	1	2	7	4	3
End scraper Ia	3	2	1	3	3	5
End scraper Ib	-	4	1	1	-	1
End scraper IIa	6	4	9	-	-	9
End scraper IIb	3	-	1	-	1	-
End scraper III	-	1	-	-	-	1
End scraper IV	1	1	-	-	1	1
End scraper V	1	3	2	2	-	2
Side scraper I	-	1	-	-	-	-
Side scraper IIa	6	6	4	2	4	3
Side scraper IIb	-	-	-	-	-	-
Side scraper III	2	-	-	5	2	5
Side scraper IV	-	-	1	-	1	2
Pointed scraper	1	-	-	-	-	-
Oval scraper	-	-	-	1	-	-
Miscellaneous scraper	-	-	-	-	1	-
Indeterminate scraper	1	-	1	-	2	11
Perforator/drill/graver	1	-	1	-	3	-
Denticulate	-	-	-	-	-	1
Hafted spokeshave	-	-	-	-	-	-
Waller knife	-	-	-	-	-	-
Core/scraper	-	-	-	-	-	-
Chopper	1	1	-	-	-	1
Adze	-	-	-	-	-	-
Hammerstone	1	-	1	2	-	5
Hammerstone/abrader	-	-	-	2	-	-
Hammerstone/anvil	-	-	-	-	-	1
Grinding stone/anvil	1	-	-	-	-	-
Anvil	-	-	-	-	-	-
Core	5	1	2	1	3	3
Pièces esquillées	1	-	-	-	-	-
Engraved Stone	-	-	-	-	-	-
Indeterminate ground stone	-	-	-	-	-	-
Other worked stone	-	-	-	-	1	2
Unmodified cobble/stone	-	-	-	-	-	-

(continued)

Table B.1 (continued). Artifact Counts by Provenance Unit

Type	Provenance					
	-40L05	-40L25	-45L00	-45L05	-45L25	-50L00
Hardaway-Dalton	2	-	1[a]	3[a]	-	-
Hardaway Side-Notched	-	-	-	-	-	-
Small Dalton	-	-	-	-	-	-
Palmer Corner-Notched	-	-	-	-	-	-
Kirk Corner-Notched	-	-	-	2	1	-
Indeterminate corner-notched	-	-	-	-	-	-
Indeterminate side-notched	-	-	-	-	-	-
Indeterminate point	2	1	-	-	1	-
Biface I	4	2	-	3	1	-
Biface II	8	7	4	6	5	1
Biface III	2	2	-	5	6	-
Indeterminate biface	6	4	2	3	4	-
End scraper Ia	1	2	1	8	2	3
End scraper Ib	1	-	-	1	-	-
End scraper IIa	1	1	2	5	-	-
End scraper IIb	1	2	-	2	3	-
End scraper III	-	-	-	-	1	-
End scraper IV	2	-	1	-	-	-
End scraper V	-	1	-	1	-	1
Side scraper I	-	-	-	1	-	1
Side scraper IIa	2	-	4	3	3	-
Side scraper IIb	-	1	-	-	-	-
Side scraper III	8	1	-	1	1	-
Side scraper IV	-	-	1	-	-	-
Pointed scraper	-	-	-	-	-	-
Oval scraper	-	-	-	-	-	-
Miscellaneous scraper	-	-	-	-	1	-
Indeterminate scraper	2	1	4	6	3	7
Perforator/drill/graver	-	-	-	-	-	1
Denticulate	-	-	-	-	-	-
Hafted spokeshave	-	-	-	-	-	-
Waller knife	-	-	-	-	-	-
Core/scraper	-	-	-	1	-	-
Chopper	-	-	1	-	-	-
Adze	-	-	-	1	-	-
Hammerstone	1	3	1	1	2	1
Hammerstone/abrader	-	-	-	-	-	-
Hammerstone/anvil	-	-	-	-	1	-
Grinding stone/anvil	-	-	-	-	1	-
Anvil	-	-	-	-	-	-
Core	3	3	-	1	2	1
Pièces esquillées	-	1	-	-	-	-
Engraved Stone	-	-	-	-	-	-
Indeterminate ground stone	-	-	-	-	-	-
Other worked stone	1	2	-	-	-	-
Unmodified cobble/stone	-	-	1	-	1	-

[a]Preforms.

(continued)

Table B.1 (continued). Artifact Counts by Provenance Unit

Type	Provenance					
	-50L10	-50L15	-50L20	-50L25	-25L00	-30L00
Hardaway-Dalton	-	3[a]	-	-	1	-
Hardaway Side-Notched	-	-	-	-	-	-
Small Dalton	-	-	-	-	-	-
Palmer Corner-Notched	2	2	2	-	-	-
Kirk Corner-Notched	3	1	5	-	-	-
Indeterminate corner-notched	1	-	-	-	-	-
Indeterminate side-notched	-	1	-	-	-	-
Indeterminate point	3	1	5	-	-	-
Biface I	1	7	5	-	4	1
Biface II	3	19	13	-	13	2
Biface III	2	11	5	1	2	-
Indeterminate biface	2	4	4	-	1	-
End scraper Ia	3	10	2	-	2	-
End scraper Ib	2	2	-	-	-	-
End scraper IIa	1	2	1	-	3	3
End scraper IIb	-	2	2	-	-	1
End scraper III	-	-	-	-	-	-
End scraper IV	1	1	2	-	1	-
End scraper V	2	1	8	-	2	-
Side scraper I	-	1	-	-	1	-
Side scraper IIa	-	6	5	-	1	1
Side scraper IIb	-	-	-	-	-	-
Side scraper III	1	7	5	1	1	-
Side scraper IV	-	-	-	-	-	-
Pointed scraper	1	-	-	-	-	-
Oval scraper	-	1	1	-	-	-
Miscellaneous scraper	1	-	-	-	-	-
Indeterminate scraper	1	3	3	-	1	1
Perforator/drill/graver	2	1	-	-	1	-
Denticulate	-	-	-	-	-	-
Hafted spokeshave	-	-	-	-	-	-
Waller knife	-	-	-	-	-	-
Core/scraper	-	1	-	-	-	-
Chopper	-	-	-	-	-	-
Adze	-	-	-	-	-	-
Hammerstone	2	1	3	-	2	1
Hammerstone/abrader	-	-	-	-	-	-
Hammerstone/anvil	-	1	1	-	-	-
Grinding stone/anvil	-	-	-	-	-	-
Anvil	-	-	-	-	-	-
Core	3	1	1	-	5	-
Pièces esquillées	-	-	-	-	-	-
Engraved Stone	-	-	-	-	-	-
Indeterminate ground stone	-	-	-	-	-	-
Other worked stone	-	-	1	-	1	-
Unmodified cobble/stone	-	-	-	-	-	-

[a]Includes 2 Preforms.

Table B.2. Estimated Proportion of Undisturbed Deposits by Square

Unit	%
-05L05	100.0
-05L40	100.0
-10L05	100.0
-15L05	100.0
-20L00	100.0
-20L05	100.0
-25L00	100.0
-25L05	100.0
-25L30	100.0
-30L00	100.0
-30L05	100.0
-30L30	100.0
-35L00	100.0
-35L05	100.0
-35L30	100.0
-40L00	100.0
-40L05	100.0
-40L25	100.0
-45L00	100.0
-45L05	100.0
-45L10	72.0
-45L15	58.0
-45L25	100.0
-50L00	100.0
-50L05	100.0
-50L10	100.0
-50L15	100.0
-50L20	100.0
-50L25	100.0
-50R05	76.0
-55L00	38.0
-55L05	30.0
-55L10	93.0
-55L15	100.0
-55L20	67.0
-55L25	69.0
-55R05	77.0
-60L00	39.0
-60L05	96.0

(continued)

Table B.2. (continued) Estimated Proportion of Undisturbed Deposits by Square

Unit	%
-60L10	64.0
-60L15	100.0
-60L20	40.0
-60L25	86.0
-60R05	82.0
-60R10	72.0
-60R15	100.0
-60R20	100.0
-60R25	100.0
-60R30	100.0
-60R35	100.0
-60R40	100.0
-60R45	100.0
-65L00	100.0
-65L05	88.0
-65L10	82.0
-65L25	100.0
-65R05	71.0
-65R10	100.0
-70L00	100.0
-70L05	100.0
-70L10	61.0
-70L15	44.0
-70L20	77.0
-70R05	97.0
-70R10	85.0
-70L00	100.0
-75L05	79.0
-75L10	74.0
-75L20	100.0
-75R05	86.0
-75R10	50.0
-80L00	52.0
-80L20	100.0
-80R05	57.0
-80R10	12.0
-85L00	23.0
-85R05	46.0
-85R10	44.0

Appendix C
Data from the Collections Survey

Table C.1 lists the Hardaway-Dalton and Hardaway Side-Notched points by county and raw material recorded in the collections survey. Table C.2 lists the Palmer and Kirk Corner-Notched points that were similarly recorded in the collections survey. These data were used in the point distribution analysis in Chapter 7.

Appendix C.1. Hardaway-Dalton and Hardaway Side-Notched Point Frequencies from Collections Survey, Cross-Tabulated by Raw Material and County

State/ County	Aphyric Rhyolite	Weathered Rhyolite	Porphyritic Rhyolite: Plagioclase	Porphyritic Rhyolite: Quartz	Porphyritic Rhyolite: Plagioclase-Quartz	Porphyritic Rhyolite: Rhyolitic Tuff
North Carolina						
Alamance	7	1	3	-	1	-
Anson	4	3	-	-	-	3
Chatham	7	5	1	1	-	1
Davidson	4	2	2	-	-	3
Davie	2	1	-	-	-	-
Durham	10	19	3	-	-	-
Forsyth	4	4	-	-	-	2
Granville	1	3	-	-	-	-
Mecklenburg	-	-	-	-	-	-
Montgomery	7	4	-	-	1	1
Moore	2	8	-	-	-	-
Orange	1	2	-	-	-	-
Randolph	34	14	1	-	-	4
Richmond	28	13	2	-	2	2
Stanly	21	10	-	-	-	4
Union	1	3	-	-	-	-
Vance	-	-	-	-	-	-
Warren	-	-	-	-	-	-
South Carolina						
Chesterfield	40	27	2	-	2	-
Dillon	2	-	-	-	-	-
Florence	8	-	3	-	-	-
Georgetown	1	1	-	-	-	-
Horry	2	-	-	-	-	-
Marion	-	3	-	-	-	-
Marlboro	11	2	-	-	-	1
Williamsburg	1	1	-	-	-	-

(continued)

Appendix C.1 (continued). Hardaway-Dalton and Hardaway Side-Notched Point frequencies from Collections Survey, Cross-Tabulated by Raw Material and County

State/ County	Quartz	Orthoquartzite	Chert: Coastal Plain	Chert: Jasper	Chert: Unidentified	Quartz Crystal
North Carolina						
Alamance	-	-	-	-	-	-
Anson	1	-	-	-	-	-
Chatham	-	-	-	-	-	-
Davidson	-	-	-	-	-	-
Davie	-	-	-	-	-	-
Durham	-	-	-	-	-	-
Forsyth	-	-	-	-	-	-
Granville	1	-	-	-	-	-
Mecklenburg	3	-	-	-	-	-
Montgomery	-	-	-	-	-	-
Moore	2	-	-	-	-	-
Orange	-	-	-	-	-	-
Randolph	-	-	-	1	-	-
Richmond	6	1	1	-	-	-
Stanly	-	-	-	1	-	-
Union	2	-	-	-	-	1
Vance	1	-	-	-	-	-
Warren	1	-	-	-	-	-
South Carolina						
Chesterfield	4	-	-	-	-	-
Dillon	5	-	1	-	-	-
Florence	1	-	-	-	-	-
Georgetown	-	-	-	-	-	-
Horry	-	-	-	-	-	-
Marion	-	-	1	-	-	-
Marlboro	-	-	-	-	-	-
Williamsburg	1	-	1	-	-	-

(continued)

Appendix C.1 (continued). Hardaway-Dalton and Hardaway Side-Notched Point frequencies from Collections Survey, Cross-Tabulated by Raw Material and County

State/ County	Green Metasiltstone	Argillite
North Carolina		
Alamance	-	-
Anson	-	-
Chatham	-	-
Davidson	-	-
Davie	-	-
Durham	-	-
Forsyth	-	-
Granville	-	-
Mecklenburg	-	-
Montgomery	-	-
Moore	-	-
Orange	-	-
Randolph	-	-
Richmond	-	-
Stanly	2	-
Union	-	-
Vance	-	-
Warren	-	-
South Carolina		
Chesterfield	1	-
Dillon	-	-
Florence	-	2
Georgetown	-	-
Horry	-	-
Marion	-	-
Marlboro	-	-
Williamsburg	-	-

Appendix C.2. Palmer and Kirk Corner-Notched Point Frequencies from Collections Survey, Cross-Tabulated by Raw Material and County

			Porphyrtitic Rhyolite			
State/ County	Aphyric Rhyolite	Weathered Rhyolite	Plagioclase	Quartz	Plagioclase-Quartz	Rhyolitic Tuff
North Carolina						
Alamance	9	-	1	-	1	-
Anson	2	1	2	1	-	1
Chatham	25	82	7	-	2	15
Davidson	57	19	7	-	2	17
Davie	56	65	12	-	1	11
Durham	70	80	8	1	1	10
Forsyth	99	61	6	1	4	25
Granville	30	21	8	-	-	8
Montgomery	90	33	13	-	-	2
Orange	14	18	3	-	1	2
Randolph	32	21	10	-	3	4
Richmond	72	20	5	-	10	2
Rowan	30	15	1	-	2	1
Stanly	38	23	1	-	-	3
Union	55	97	5	1	5	7
Vance	2	3	6	-	-	4
Warren	10	9	7	-	-	1
South Carolina						
Chesterfield	241	15	13	-	-	-
Dillon	91	11	25	-	-	4
Florence	101	1	6	-	-	-
Georgetown	1	1	-	-	-	-
Horry	13	-	10	-	-	-
Marion	12	9	2	-	-	-
Marlboro	123	-	2	-	-	-
Williamsburg	2	-	1	-	-	-

(continued)

Appendix C.2 (continued). Palmer and Kirk Corner-Notched Point Frequencies from Collections Survey, Cross-Tabulated by Raw Material and County

State/ County	Quartz	Quartz Crystal	Ortho-quartzite	Quartzite	Green Metasiltstone	Argillite
North Carolina						
Alamance	-	-	-	-	1	-
Anson	-	-	-	1	-	-
Chatham	7	1	-	-	-	-
Davidson	1	-	-	-	-	-
Davie	-	-	-	-	-	-
Durham	5	2	-	1	-	-
Forsyth	4	-	-	-	2	-
Granville	5	1	-	-	-	-
Montgomery	1	-	-	-	-	-
Orange	-	-	-	-	-	-
Randolph	5	-	-	-	2	-
Richmond	9	-	-	-	2	-
Rowan	-	-	-	-	1	-
Stanly	-	-	-	-	-	-
Union	41	1	-	-	-	-
Vance	-	-	-	-	-	-
Warren	9	-	1	1	-	-
South Carolina						
Chesterfield	181	-	2	-	-	2
Dillon	33	-	3	-	-	-
Florence	40	-	5	-	-	1
Georgetown	-	-	-	-	-	-
Horry	12	-	-	-	-	-
Marion	3	-	-	-	1	-
Marlboro	28	-	1	-	-	1
Williamsburg	5	-	-	-	-	-

(continued)

Appendix C.2. (continued). Palmer and Kirk Corner-Notched Point Frequencies from Collections Survey, Cross-Tabulated by Raw Material and County

			Chert			
State/ County	Rhyolitic Breccia	Other Metavolcanic	Coastal Plain	Ridge and Valley	Jasper	Unidentified Chert
North Carolina						
Alamance	-	-	-	-	-	-
Anson	-	-	-	-	-	-
Chatham	7	-	-	-	-	-
Davidson	-	-	-	2	-	-
Davie	-	-	-	-	-	-
Durham	8	-	-	-	-	-
Forsyth	-	-	-	-	-	-
Granville	2?	-	-	-	-	-
Mecklenburg	-	-	-	-	-	-
Montgomery	-	-	-	1	-	-
Moore	-	-	-	-	-	-
Orange	1	-	-	-	-	-
Randolph	1	-	-	-	-	-
Richmond	1	-	-	-	2	-
Stanly	-	-	-	-	-	-
Union	-	-	-	2	1	1[b]
Vance	4?	-	-	-	-	-
Warren	1?	-	-	-	-	-
South Carolina						
Chesterfield	-	4[a]	14	3	-	-
Dillon	-	2	6	-	-	-
Florence	-	3[a]	11	-	-	-
Georgetown	-	-	2	-	-	-
Horry	-	-	9	-	-	2
Marion	-	-	3	-	-	-
Marlboro	-	1[a]	1	-	-	-
Williamsburg	-	-	5	-	-	2

[a]basalt

[b]chalcedony

References

Anderson, D. G. (1979). Prehistoric selection for thermal alteration: Tests of a model employing southeastern archaeological materials. *Midcontinental Journal of Archaeology* 4:221–254.

Anderson, D. G., C. E. Cantley, and A. L. Novick. (1982). *The Matassee Lake sites: Archeological investigations along the lower Santee River in the Coastal Plain of South Carolina.* Special Publication. Atlanta: Interagency Archeological Services Division, National Park Service.

Anderson, D. G., and G. T. Hanson. (1985). Early Archaic occupation of the Savannah River basin. Paper presented at the forty-second annual meeting of the Southeastern Archaeological Conference, Birmingham, Alabama.

———. (1988). Early Archaic settlement in the southeastern United States: A case study from the Savannah River. *American Antiquity* 53:262–286.

Anderson, D. G., J. L. Michie, and M. B. Trinkley. (1974). *An Archaeological survey of the proposed Southwestern Beltway extension and Twelfth Street extension highway route in the vicinity of Congaree Creek.* Research Manuscript Series 60. Columbia: South Carolina Institute of Archaeology and Anthropology, University of South Carolina.

Anderson, D. G., and K. E. Sassaman. (1996). *The Paleoindian and Archaic Southeast.* Tuscaloosa: University of Alabama Press.

Anderson, D. G., and J. Schuldenrein. (1983). Early Archaic settlement on the southeastern Atlantic Slope: A view from the Rucker's Bottom site, Elbert County, Georgia. *North American Archaeologist* 4:117–210.

———. (1985). *Prehistoric human ecology along the upper Savannah River: Excavations at the Rucker's Bottom, Abbeville, and Bullard site groups.* Russell Papers. Atlanta: Interagency Archeological Services Division, National Park Service.

Andrefsky, W., Jr. (1994a). Raw-material availability and the organization of technology. *American Antiquity* 59:21–34.

———. (1994b). The geological occurrence of lithic material and stone tool production strategies. *Geoarchaeology: An International Journal* 9:375–391.

Ascher, R. (1968). Time's arrow and the archaeology of a contemporary community. In *Settlement Archaeology,* edited by K. C. Chang, pp. 43–52. Palo Alto: National Press Books.

Baker, C. M. (1978). The size effect: An explanation of variability in surface artifact assemblage content. *American Antiquity* 43:228–293.

Bamforth, D. B. (1986). Technological efficiency and tool curation. *American Antiquity* 51:38–50.

———. (1990). Settlement, raw material, and lithic procurement in the central Mojave Desert. *Journal of Anthropological Archaeology* 9:70–104.

Bettinger, R. L. (1991). *Hunter-gatherers: Archaeological and evolutionary theory.* New York: Plenum Press.

Binford, L. R. (1973). Interassemblage variability: The Mousterian and the "functional" argument. In *Explanation of culture change: Models in prehistory,* edited by C. Renfrew, pp. 227–254. London: Duckworth.

———. (1977). Forty-seven trips: A case study in the character of archaeological formation processes. In *Stone tools as cultural markers: Change, evolution, and complexity,* edited by R. V. S. Wright, pp. 24–36. Canberra: Australian Institute of Aboriginal Studies.

———. (1978). Dimensional analysis of behavior and site structure: Learning from an Eskimo hunting stand. *American Antiquity* 43:330–361.

———. (1979). Organization and formation processes: Looking at curated technologies. *Journal of Anthropological Research* 35:255–273.

———. (1980). Willow smoak and dogs' tails: Hunter-gatherer settlement systems and archaeological site formation. *American Antiquity* 45:4–20.

———. (1982). The archaeology of place. *Journal of Anthropological Archaeology* 1:5–31.

———. (1983). *In pursuit of the past.* New York: Thames and Hudson.

Binford, L. R., and S. R. Binford. (1966). A preliminary analysis of functional variability in the Mousterian of Levallois facies. *American Anthropologist* 68 (2):238–295.

Binford, L., and J. F. O'Connell. (1984). An Alywara day: The stone quarry. *Journal of Anthropological Research* 40:406–432.

Binford, L., and G. Quimby. (1963). Indian sites and chipped stone materials in the northern Lake Michigan area. *Fieldiana-Anthropology* 36:277–307.

Broyles, B. J. (1971). *Second preliminary report: The St. Albans site, Kanawha Valley.* Report of Archaeological Investigations 3. Charleston: West Virginia Geological and Economic Survey.

Bullen, R. P. (1975). *A guide to the identification of Florida projectile points.* Rev. ed. Gainesville, Fla.: Kendall Books.

Bullen, R. P., and L. E. Bielman. (1973). The Nalcrest site, Lake Weohyakapa, Florida. *Florida Anthropologist* 26:1–22.

Butler, J. R. (1986). Carolina Slate Belt near Albemarle, North Carolina. In *Southeastern section of the Geological Society of America, continental field guide,* vol. 6, edited by T. L. Neathery, pp. 235–237. Boulder: Geological Society of America.

Butler, J. R., and D. T. Secor, Jr. (1991). The central Piedmont. In *The geology of the Carolinas: Carolina Geological Society, fiftieth anniversary volume,* edited by J. W. Horton, Jr., and V. A. Zullo, pp. 59–78. Knoxville: University of Tennessee Press.

Cable, J. S. (1982). Description and analysis of lithic assemblages. In *The Haw River sites: Archaeological investigations at two stratified sites in the North Carolina Piedmont.* Report No. 23386. Jackson: Wilmington District Corps of Engineers.

———. (1996). The Haw River sites revisited: Implications for modeling terminal late Glacial and early Holocene hunter-gatherer settlement systems in South Carolina. In *The Paleoindian and Early Archaic Southeast,* edited by D. G. Anderson and K. E. Sassaman, pp. 107–148. Tuscaloosa: University of Alabama Press.

Cahen, D., L. Keeley, and F. Van Noten. (1979). Stone tools, tool kits, and human behavior in prehistory. *Current Anthropology* 20:661–683.

Caldwell, J. R. (1958). *Trend and tradition in the prehistory of the Eastern United States.* Memoir No. 88. Washington, D.C.: American Anthropological Association.

Carr, P. J. (1995). Hunter-gatherers, mobility, and technological organization: The Early Archaic of East Tennessee. Ph.D. diss., University of Tennessee, Knoxville.

Chapman, J. (1973). *The Icehouse Bottom site (40MR23).* Report of Investigations No. 13. Knoxville: Department of Anthropology, University of Tennessee.

——. (1975). *The Rose Island site and the bifurcate point tradition.* Report of Investigations 14. Knoxville: Department of Anthropology, University of Tennessee.

——. (1976). The Archaic Period in the lower Little Tennessee River Valley: The radiocarbon dates. *Tennessee Anthropologist* 1:1–12.

——. (1977). *Archaic Period research in the lower Little Tennessee River Valley, 1975: Icehouse Bottom, Thirty Acre Island, Calloway Island.* Report of Investigations 18. Knoxville: Department of Anthropology, University of Tennessee.

——. (1978). *The Bacon Farm site and a burial site reconnaissance.* Report of Investigations 23. Knoxville: Department of Anthropology, University of Tennessee.

Charles, T. (1981). *Dwindling resources: An overture to the future of South Carolina's archaeological resources.* Notebook 13. Columbia: Institute of Archaeology and Anthropology, University of South Carolina.

——. (1983). *Thoughts and records from the survey of private collections of prehistoric artifacts throughout South Carolina: A second report.* Notebook 15. Columbia: Institute of Archaeology and Anthropology, University of South Carolina.

——. (1986). *The fifth phase of the collectors survey.* Notebook 18. Columbia: Institute of Archaeology and Anthropology, University of South Carolina.

Claggett, S. R., and J. S. Cable. (1982). *The Haw River sites: Archaeological investigations at two stratified sites in the North Carolina Piedmont.* Report No. 23386. Jackson: Wilmington District Corp of Engineers.

Cleland, C. E. (1976). The Focal-Diffuse Model: An evolutionary perspective on the prehistoric cultural adaptations of the Eastern United States. *Midcontinental Journal of Archaeology* 1:59–76.

Coe, J. L. (1964). *The formative cultures of the Carolina Piedmont.* Transactions 54. Philadelphia: American Philosophical Society.

Conkey, M. W. (1980). The identification of prehistoric hunter-gatherer aggregation sites: The case of Altamira. *Current Anthropology* 21:609–630.

Conley, J. F. (1962). *Geology of the Albemarle quadrangle, North Carolina.* Bulletin 75. Raleigh: Division of Mineral Resources, North Carolina Department of Conservation and Development.

Crabtree, D. E. (1972). *An introduction to flintworking.* Occasional Paper No. 28. Pocatello: Idaho State Museum.

Daniel, I. R., Jr. (1986). An analysis of unifacial stone tools from the Hardaway Site, North Carolina. *Southern Indian Studies* 35:3–53.

Daniel, I. R., Jr., and J. R. Butler. (1991). Rhyolite sources in the Carolina Slate Belt, Central North Carolina. *Current Research in the Pleistocene* 8:64–66.

——. (1996). An archaeological survey and petrographic description of rhyolite sources in the Uwharrie Mountains, North Carolina. *Southern Indian Studies* 45:1–37.

Daniel, I. R., Jr., and M. Wisenbaker. (1987). *Harney Flats: A Florida Paleo-Indian site.* New York: Baywood.

Davis, R. P., Jr., and I. R. Daniel, Jr. (1990). The classification of projectile points in collections from North Carolina. Unpublished report. Chapel Hill: Research Laboratories of Anthropology, University of North Carolina.

Delcourt, P. A. (1985). The influence of late-Quaternary climate and vegetational change on paleohydrology in unglaciated Eastern North America. *Ecologia Mediterranea* 11 (1):17–26.

Delcourt, P. A., and H. R. Delcourt. (1981). Vegetation maps for Eastern North America: 40,000 years B.P. to present. In *Geobotany,* edited by R. Romans, pp. 123–166. New York: Plenum.

———. (1983). Late-Quaternary vegetational dynamics and community stability reconsidered. *Quaternary Research* 19:265–271.

———. (1984). Late Quaternary paleoclimates and biotic responses in Eastern North America and the western North Atlantic Ocean. In *Palaeogeography, Palaeoclimatology, Palaeoecology* 48:263–284.

Dibble, H. L. (1984). Interpreting typological variation of middle Paleolithic scrapers: Function, style, or sequence of reduction? *Journal of Field Archaeology* 11:431–436.

———. (1985). Technological aspects of flake variation. *American Archaeology* 5:236–240.

———. (1987a). Reduction sequences in the manufacture of Mousterian implements of France. In *The Pleistocene Old World: Regional perspectives,* edited by O. Soffer, pp. 33–45. New York: Academic Press.

———. (1987b). The interpretation of middle Paleolithic scraper morphology. *American Antiquity* 52:109–117.

Dibble, H. L., and J. Whittaker. (1981). New experimental evidence on the relation between percussion flaking flake variation. *Journal of Archaeological Science* 6:283–296.

Dragoo, D. (1976). Some aspects of Eastern North America prehistory: A review, 1975. *American Antiquity* 41:3–27.

Driskell, B. (1996). Stratigraphy and chronology at Dust Cave. *Journal of Alabama Archaeology* 40:17–34.

Ellis, C. J., and D. B. Deller. (1988). Some distinctive Paleo-Indian tool types from the lower Great Lakes Region. *Midcontinental Journal of Archaeology* 13:111–158.

Ensor, H. B. (1985). The Joe Powell site (1Pi38): A Dalton manifestation on the Alabama Gulf Coastal Plain. *Journal of Alabama Archaeology* 31(1):1–47.

———. (1986). San Patrice and Dalton affinities on the central and western Gulf Coastal Plain. *Bulletin of the Texas Archeological Society* 57:69–81.

Flenniken, J. J., and A. W. Raymond. (1986). Morphological projectile point typology: Replication experimentation and technological analysis. *American Antiquity* 51:603–614.

Gaertner, L. M. (1994). Determining the function of Dalton adzes from Northeast Arkansas. *Lithic Technology* 19:97–109.

Gardner, W. M. (1974). *The Flint Run Paleo-Indian complex: A preliminary report, 1971 through 1973 seasons.* Occasional Paper No. 1, Archaeology. Washington, D.C.: Catholic University of America.

———. (1977). Flint Run Paleo-Indian complex and its implications for Eastern North America prehistory. *Annals of the New York Academy of Sciences* 288:251–263.

——. (1983). Stop me if you've heard this one before: The Flint Run PaleoIndian complex revisited. *Archaeology of Eastern North America* 11:49–59.

——. (1989). An examination of cultural change in the late Pleistocene. In *Paleoindian research in Virginia: A synthesis,* edited by J. M. Wittkofski and T. R. Reinhart, pp. 5–51. Special Publication No. 19. Richmond: Archaeological Society of Virginia.

Geiger, C. L., and T. Brown. (1983). Waller hafted scraper knives from Southeast Mississippi. *Mississippi Archaeology* 18:3–14.

Goad, S. I. (1979). *Chert resources in Georgia: Archaeological and geological perspectives.* Report 21. City: Laboratory of Archaeology, University of Georgia.

Goldman-Finn, N., and B. Driskell. (1994). Introduction to archaeological research at Dust Cave. *Journal of Alabama Archaeology* 40:1–16.

Goodyear, A. C. (1973). Archaic hafted spokeshaves with graver spurs from the Southeast. *Florida Anthropologist* 26:39–44.

——. (1974). *The Brand site: A techno-functional study of a Dalton site in Northeast Arkansas.* Research Series No. 7. Fayetteville: Arkansas Archaeological Survey.

——. (1979). *A hypothesis for the use of cryptocrystalline raw materials among Paleo-Indian groups of North America.* Research Manuscript Series No. 156. Columbia: Institute of Archaeology and Anthropology, University of South Carolina.

——. (1982). The chronological position of the Dalton horizon in the southeastern United States. *American Antiquity* 47:382–395.

——. (1993). Tool kit entropy and bipolar reduction: A study of interassemblage lithic variability among Paleo-Indian sites in the Northeastern United States. *North American Archaeologist* 14:1–23.

——. (in press). The early Holocene occupation of the southeastern United States: A geoarchaeological summary. In *Ice Age peoples of North America,* edited by R. Bonnichsen, G. C. Frison, and K. Turnmire. Orono, Maine: Center for the Study of the First Americans. MS 1991.

Goodyear, A. C., and T. Charles. (1984). *An archeological survey of chert quarries in western Allendale County, South Carolina.* Research Manuscript Series No. 195. Columbia: Institute of Archaeology and Anthropology, University of South Carolina.

Goodyear, A. C., J. H. House, and N. W. Ackerly. (1979). *Laurens-Anderson: An archaeological study of the interriverine Piedmont.* Anthropological Papers 4. Columbia: Institute of Archaeology and Anthropology, University of South Carolina.

Goodyear, A. C., J. L. Michie, and T. Charles. (1989). The earliest South Carolinians. In *Studies in South Carolina archaeology: Essays in honor of Robert L. Stephenson,* edited by A. C. Goodyear and G. T. Hanson, pp. 19–52. Anthropological Studies 9. Columbia: Institute of Archaeology and Anthropology, University of South Carolina.

Goodyear, A. C., S. B. Upchurch, M. J. Brooks, and N. N. Goodyear. (1983). Paleo-Indian manifestations in the Tampa Bay Region, Florida. *Florida Anthropologist* 36:40–66.

Gould, R. A. (1980). *Living archaeology.* New York: Cambridge University Press.

Gramly, R. M. (1982). *The Vail site: A Palaeo-Indian encampment in Maine.* Bulletin 30. Buffalo, N.Y.: Buffalo Society of Natural Sciences.

Gregg, S. A., K. W. Kintigh, and R. Whallon. (1991). Linking ethnoarchaeological interpretation and archaeological data: The sensitivity of spatial analytical methods to postdepositional disturbance. In *The interpretation of archaeological spatial patterning,* edited by E. M. Kroll and T. D. Price, pp. 149–196. New York: Plenum Press.

Griffin, J. F. (1974). *Investigations in Russell Cave.* Publications in Archaeology No. 13. Washington, D.C.: National Park Service.

Grimes, J., W. Eldridge, B. Grimes, A. Vaccaro, F. Vaccaro, J. Vaccaro, N. Vaccaro, and N. Orsini. (1984). Bull Brook II. *Archaeology of Eastern North America* 12:159–183.

Hall, Linda G. (1983). Variability among unifacial tools from the Hardaway Site. Master's thesis, Department of Anthropology, University of North Carolina, Chapel Hill.

Hanson, G. T., and K. E. Sassaman. (1984). Recent investigations of Archaic period typology and technology in the Upper Coastal Plain of South Carolina. Paper presented at the forty-first annual meeting of the southeastern Archaeological Conference, Pensacola, Florida.

Hargrove, T. (1989). *An archaeological survey in Morrow Mountain State Park, Stanly County, North Carolina.* Raleigh: North Carolina Division of Parks and Recreation.

Harris C. W., and L. Glover III. (1988). The regional extent of the ca. 600 Ma Virgilina deformation: Implications for stratigraphic correlation in the Carolina terrane. *Geologic Society of America Bulletin* 100:200–217.

Hayden, B. G. (1979). Snap, shatter, and superfractures: Use-wear of stone skin scrapers. In *Lithic use-wear analysis,* edited by B. Hayden, pp. 207–229. New York: Academic Press.

——. (1980). Confusion in the bipolar world: Bashed pebbles and splintered pieces. *Lithic Technology* 9:2–7.

Hietala, H., ed. (1984). *Intrasite spatial analysis in archaeology.* New York: Cambridge University Press.

House, J. H., and D. L. Ballenger. (1976). *An archaeological survey of the Interstate 77 route in the South Carolina Piedmont.* Research Manuscript Series 104. Columbia: Institute of Archaeology and Anthropology, University of South Carolina.

House, J. H., and R. W. Wogaman. (1978). *Windy Ridge, A prehistoric site in the inter-riverine Piedmont in South Carolina.* Anthropological Studies, Series 3. Columbia: Institute of Archaeology and Anthropology, University of South Carolina.

Jochim, M. A. (1976). *Hunter-gatherer subsistence and settlement: A predictive model.* New York: Academic Press.

Johnson, J. K. (1981). *Yellow Creek archaeological project.* Vol. 2. Archaeological Papers of the Center for Archaeological Research No. 1. Jackson: University of Mississippi.

Keeley, L. E. (1980). *Experimental determination of stone tool uses.* Chicago: University of Chicago Press.

——. (1982). Hafting and retooling: Effects on the archaeological record. *American Antiquity* 47:798–809.

Kelly, R. L. (1983). Hunter-gatherer mobility strategies. *Journal of Anthropological Research* 39:277–306.

——. (1988). The three sides of a biface. *American Antiquity* 53:717–734.

Kent, S., ed. (1987). *Method and theory for activity area research: An ethnoarchaeological approach.* New York: Columbia University Press.

Kesel, R. H. (1974). Inselbergs on the Piedmont of Virginia, North Carolina, and South Carolina: Types and characteristics. *Southeastern Geology* 16:1–30.

Kimball, L. (1982). Lithic artifact analysis. In *An archaeological survey of aboriginal settlement within the lower Little Tennessee River Valley,* edited by R. P. S. Davis, Jr., L. R. Kimball, and W. W. Baden, pp. 120–252. Technical report submitted to the Tennessee Valley Authority, Norris, Tenn. (Copies available from the Department of Anthropology, University of Tennessee, Knoxville.)

———. (1985). *The archaeological reconnaissance: An overall assessment of the archaeological resources of Tellico Reservoir.* Report of Investigations No. 40. Knoxville: Department of Anthropology, University of Tennessee.

———. (1993). Island revisited: The detection of Early Archaic site structure using grid count data. *Southeastern Archaeologist* 12:93–116.

———. (1996). Early Archaic settlement technology: Lessons from Tellico. In *The Paleoindian and Early Archaic Southeast,* edited by D. G. Anderson and K. E. Sassaman, pp. 149–186. Tuscaloosa: University of Alabama Press.

Kimball, L. R., and J. Chapman. (1977). Other Chipped Stone Tools. In *Archaic period research in the Little Tennessee River Valley,* edited by J. Chapman, pp. 54–90. Publications in Anthropology No. 13. Knoxville: Tennessee Valley Authority.

Kintigh, K. (1991). *Tools for quantitative archaeology.* Tempe, Ariz.: Author.

Kintigh, K. W., and A. Ammerman. (1982). Heuristic approaches to spatial analysis in archaeology. *American Antiquity* 47:31–63.

Kroll, E. M., and T. D. Price, eds. (1991). *The interpretation of archaeological spatial patterning.* New York: Plenum Press.

Kuhn, S. L. (1990). A geometric index of reduction for unifacial stone tools. *Journal of Archaeological Science* 17:583–593.

———. (1991). "Unpacking" reduction: Lithic raw material economy in the Mousterian of west-central Italy. *Journal of Anthropological Archaeology* 10:76–106.

———. (1992). Blank form and reduction as determinants of Mousterian scraper morphology. *American Antiquity* 57:115–128.

Lothrop, J. C. (1988). The organization of Paleoindian lithic technology at the Potts Site. Ph.D. dissertation, State University of New York, Binghamton, New York. Ann Arbor: University Microfilms.

Lothrop, J. C., and R. M. Gramly. (1982). Pièces esquillées from the Vail site. *Archaeology of Eastern North America* 10:1–22.

MacDonald, G. F. (1968). *Debert: A Palaeo-Indian site in central Nova Scotia.* Anthropology Papers No. 16. Ottawa, Ontario: National Museum of Man.

McDevitt, K. B. (1994). Results of replicative hide-working experiments: The roles of raw material, hide condition, and use-wear patterns in the determination of rhyolite end scraper function. *Lithic Technology* 19:93–97.

McGill, R., J. W. Tukey, and W. A. Larsen. (1978). Variation of box plots. *American Statistician* 32:12–16.

Meltzer, D. J. (1989). Was stone exchanged among Eastern North American Paleoindians? In *Eastern Paleoindian lithic resource use,* edited by C. J. Ellis and J. C. Lothrop, pp. 11–39. Boulder, Colo.: Westview Press.

Meltzer, D. J., and B. D. Smith. (1986). Paleo-Indian and Early Archaic subsistence strategies in Eastern North America. In *Foraging, collecting, and harvesting: Archaic period subsistence and settlement in the Eastern Woodlands,* edited by S. Neusius, pp. 1–30. Carbondale: Center for Archaeological Investigations, Southern Illinois University.

Michie, J. L. (1966). The Taylor point. *Chesopiean* 6:30–31.

———. (1996). The Taylor site: An early occupation in central South Carolina. In

The Paleoindian and Early Archaic Southeast, edited by D. G. Anderson and K. E. Sassaman, pp. 238–269. Columbia: Council of South Carolina Professional Archaeologists.

Milton, D. J. (1984). Revision of the Albemarle group, North Carolina. *U.S. Geological Survey Bulletin* 1537:A69–A72.

Moore, D. G. (1977). Field notes from the Hardaway site excavations. Research Laboratories of Anthropology, University of North Carolina, Chapel Hill.

Morse, D. F., Jr. (1971). Recent indications of Dalton settlement patterns in Northeast Arkansas. *Southeastern Archaeological Conference Bulletin* 13:5–10.

———. (1973). Dalton culture in Northeast Arkansas. *Florida Anthropologist* 26:23–28.

———. (1975a). Reply to Schiffer. In *The Cache River Archaeological Project: An experiment in contract archaeology,* assembled by M. B. Schiffer and J. M. House, pp. 113–119. Arkansas Archaeological Survey Research Series, vol. 8. Fayetteville: Arkansas Archaeological Survey.

———. (1975b). Paleo Indian in the land of opportunity: Preliminary report on the excavations at the Sloan site (3GE94). In *The Cache River Archaeological Project: An experiment in contract archaeology,* assembled by M. B. Schiffer and J. M. House, pp. 93–113. Arkansas Archaeological Survey Research Series, vol. 8. Fayetteville: Arkansas Archaeological Survey.

———. (1977). Dalton settlement systems: Reply to Schiffer (2). *Plains Anthropologist* 22:149–158.

Morse, D. F., Jr., and A. C. Goodyear. (1973). The significance of the Dalton adze in Northeast Arkansas. *Plains Anthropologist* 18:316–322.

Morse, D. F., Jr., and P. A. Morse. (1983). *Archaeology of the central Mississippi Valley.* New York: Academic Press.

Movius, H. L., D. C. Nicholas, H. M. Bricker, and R. B. Clay. (1968). *The analysis of certain major classes of Upper Paleolithic tools.* American School of Prehistoric Research, Bulletin No. 26. Cambridge, Mass.: Peabody Museum, Harvard University.

Muto, G. (1971). A stage analysis of the manufacture of stone tools. In *Great Basin Anthropology Conference, 1970: Selected Papers,* pp. 109–118. Eugene: Department of Anthropology, University of Oregon.

Novick, L. A. (1978). Prehistoric lithic material sources and types in South Carolina: A preliminary statement. *South Carolina Antiquities* 10:23–38.

O'Connell, J. F. (1987). Alyawara site structure and its archaeological implications. *American Antiquity* 52:74–108.

O'Connell, J. F., K. Hawkes, and N. B. Jones. (1991). Distribution of refuse-producing activities at Hadza residential base camps: Implications for analyses of archaeological site structure. In *The interpretation of archaeological spatial patterning,* edited by E. M. Kroll and T. D. Price, pp. 61–76. New York: Plenum Press.

O'Dell, G. H. (1981). The morphological express at Function Junction: Searching for meaning in lithic tool types. *Journal of Anthropological Research* 37:319–343.

Oliver, B. L. (1985). Tradition and typology: Basic elements of the Carolina projectile point sequence. In *Structure and process in southeastern archaeology,* edited by R. S. Dickens and H. T. Ward, pp. 195–211. Tuscaloosa: University of Alabama Press.

O'Steen, L. D. (1983). Early Archaic settlement patterns in the Wallace Reservoir: An inner Piedmont perspective. Master's thesis, Department of Anthropology, University of Georgia, Athens.

———. (1992). Paleoindian and Early Archaic settlement along the Oconee drainage. In *Paleoindian and Early Archaic research in the lower Southeast: A South Carolina perspective,* edited by D. G. Anderson, K. E. Sassaman, and C. Judge, pp. 78–95. Columbia: Council of South Carolina Professional Archaeologists.

Parry, W. J., and R. L. Kelly. (1986). Expedient core technology and sedentism. In *The organization of core technology,* edited by J. K. Johnson and C. A. Morrow, pp. 285–304. Boulder: Westview Press.

Perkinson, P. H. (1971). North Carolina fluted projectile points. Survey Report No. 1. *Southern Indian Studies* 23:3–40.

———. (1973). North Carolina fluted projectile points—Survey Report No. 2. *Southern Indian Studies* 25:3–60.

Phelps, D. (1958). Field notes from the Hardaway site excavations. Research Laboratories of Anthropology, University of North Carolina, Chapel Hill.

———. (1959). Field notes from the Hardaway site excavations. Research Laboratories of Anthropology, University of North Carolina, Chapel Hill.

Price, J. E., and J. J. Krakker. (1975). *Dalton occupations of the Ozark border.* Museum Briefs No. 20. Columbia: University of Missouri.

Purdy, B. A. (1981). *Florida's prehistoric stone technology.* Gainesville: University of Florida Press.

Renfrew, C. (1972). *The emergence of civilization.* London: Methuen.

———. (1975). Trade as action at a distance: Questions of interaction and communication. In *Ancient civilization and trade,* edited by C. C. Lamberg-Karlousky, pp. 3–60. Albuquerque: University of New Mexico Press.

———. (1977). Alternate models for exchange and spatial distribution. In *Exchange systems in prehistory,* edited by T. Earle and J. Ericson, pp. 71–90. New York: Academic Press.

Sassaman, K. E. (1996). Early Archaic settlement in the South Carolina Coastal Plain. In *The Paleoindian and Early Archaic Southeast,* edited by D. G. Anderson, K. E. Sassaman, pp. 58–83. Tuscaloosa: University of Alabama Press.

Sassaman, K. E., G. T. Hanson, and T. Charles. (1988). Raw material procurement and the reduction of hunter gatherer range in the Savannah River Valley. *Southeastern Archaeological Bulletin* 7:79–94.

Schiffer, M. B. (1975a). An alternative to Morse's Dalton settlement hypothesis. *Plains Anthropologist* 20:253–266.

———. (1975b). Some further comments on the Dalton settlement pattern hypothesis. In *The Cache River Archaeological Project: An experiment in contract archaeology,* assembled by M. B. Schiffer and J. M. House, pp. 103–111. Arkansas Archaeological Survey Research Series, vol. 8. Fayetteville: Arkansas Archaeological Survey.

Seiders, V. M. (1981). *Geologic map of the Asheboro, North Carolina, and adjacent areas.* Map I-1314. Washington, D.C.: U.S. Geological Survey.

Semenov, S. A. (1964). *Prehistoric technology.* Translated by M. W. Thompson. New York: Barnes and Noble.

Shafer, H. J. (1970). Notes on uniface retouch technology. *American Antiquity* 35:480–487.

Shott, M. J. (1989a). On tool-class use lives and the formation of archaeological assemblages. *American Antiquity* 54:9–30.

———. (1989b). Technological organization in Great Lakes Paleoindian assemblages. In *Eastern Paleoindian lithic resource use,* edited by C. J. Ellis and J. C. Lothrop, pp. 221–237. Boulder: Westview Press.

——. (1989c). Bipolar industries: Ethnographic evidence and archaeological implications. *North American Archaeologist* 10:1–24.

Smith, B. D. (1986). The archaeology of the southeastern United States, from Dalton to Desoto (10.500 B.P.–500 B.P.). In *Advances in world archaeology,* vol. 5, edited by Fred Wendorf and Angela E. Close, pp. 1–92. Orlando: Academic Press.

Speth, J. (1972). The mechanical basis of percussion flaking. *American Antiquity* 37:34–60.

——. (1975). Miscellaneous studies in hard-hammer percussion flaking: The effects of oblique impact. *American Antiquity* 40:203–207.

——. (1981). The role of platform angle and core size in hard-hammer percussion flaking. *Lithic Technology* 10:16–21.

Steponaitis, V. P. (1986). Prehistoric archaeology in the southeastern United States, 1970–1985. *Annual Review of Anthropology* 15:363–404.

Stoltman, J. B. (1978). Temporal models in prehistory: An example from Eastern North America. *Current Anthropology* 19:703–746.

SURFER. (1987). *Reference manual.* Golden, Colo.: Golden Software.

Tippitt, V. A., and I. R. Daniel, Jr. (1987). Lithic artifacts from the Fredricks, Wall, and Mitchum sites. In *The Siouan Project: Seasons I and II,* edited by R. S. Dickens, Jr., H. T. Ward, and R. P. S. Davis, Jr., pp. 217–236. Monograph Series No. 1. Chapel Hill: Research Laboratories, University of North Carolina.

Tippitt, V. A., and W. H. Marquardt. (1984). *The Gregg Shoals and Clyde Gulley sites: Archaeological and geological investigations at two Piedmont sites on the Savannah River.* Russell Papers. Atlanta: Archaeological Services Branch, National Park Service.

Tukey, J. (1977). *Exploratory data analysis.* Reading, Mass.: Addison-Wesley.

Upchurch, S. (1984). Petrology of selected lithic materials from the South Carolina Coastal Plain. In *An archeological survey of chert quarries in Western Allendale County, South Carolina.* Research Manuscript Series No. 195. Columbia: Institute of Archaeology and Anthropology, University of South Carolina.

Upchurch, S. B., R. N. Strom, and M. G. Nuckels. (1981). *Methods of provenance determination of Florida cherts.* Tallahassee: Florida Bureau of Historic Sites and Properties.

Velleman, P. F., and D. C. Hoaglin. (1981). *Applications, basics, and computing of exploratory data analysis.* Boston: Doxbury Press.

Waller, B. I. (1971). Hafted flake knives. *Florida Anthropologist* 24:173–174.

Ward, H. T. (1975). Field notes from the Hardaway site excavations. Research Laboratories of Anthropology, University of North Carolina, Chapel Hill.

——. (1976). Field notes from the Hardaway site excavations. Research Laboratories of Anthropology, University of North Carolina, Chapel Hill.

——. (1977). Field notes from the Hardaway site excavations. Research Laboratories of Anthropology, University of North Carolina, Chapel Hill.

——. (1979). Field notes from the Hardaway site excavations. Research Laboratories of Anthropology, University of North Carolina, Chapel Hill.

——. (1980). Field notes from the Hardaway site excavations. Research Laboratories of Anthropology, University of North Carolina, Chapel Hill.

——. (1983). A review of archaeology in the North Carolina Piedmont: A Study of Change. In *Prehistory of North Carolina: An archaeological symposium,* edited by M. A. Mathis and J. A. Crow, pp. 53–81. North Carolina Division of Archives and History, Department of Cultural Resources.

Ward, H. T., and R. P. S. Davis, Jr. (1993). *Indian communities on the North Carolina*

Piedmont, A.D. *1000–1700.* Research Laboratories of Anthropology Monograph No. 2. Chapel Hill: University of North Carolina.

Webb, C. H. (1946). Two unusual types of chipped stone artifacts from Northwest Louisiana. *Bulletin of the Texas Archeological and Paleontological Society* 17:9–17.

Webb, C. H., J. L. Shiner, and E. W. Roberts. (1971). The John Pearce site (16CD56): A San Patrice site in Caddo Parish, Louisiana. *Bulletin of the Texas Archaeological Society* 42:1–49.

Whallon, R. (1984). Unconstrained clustering for the analysis of spatial distributions in archaeology. In *Intrasite spatial analysis in archaeology,* edited by H. Hietala, pp. 242–277. Cambridge: Cambridge University Press.

Williams, B. J. (1974). *A model of Band society.* Memoirs No. 29. Washington, D.C.: Society for American Archaeology.

Wilmsen, E. (1970). *Lithic analysis and cultural inference: A Paleo-Indian case.* Anthropological Papers No. 16. Tucson: University of Arizona.

Wise, S., Jr., M. Ausburn, D. Textoris, W. Wheller, R. Daniels, and E. Gamble. (1981). Lithologic characteristics and diagenesis of some siliceous Coastal Plain rocks. *Scanning Electron Microscopy* 1:577–584.

Wobst, H. M. (1978). The archaeo-ethnology of hunter-gatherers; or, The tyranny of the ethnographic record in archaeology. *American Antiquity* 43:303–309.

Wogaman, R. W., J. H. House, and A. C. Goodyear. (1976). *An archaeological reconnaissance of the four proposed Twelfth Street extension routes, Lexington County, South Carolina.* Research Manuscript Series No. 106. Columbia: Institute of Archaeology and Anthropology, University of South Carolina.

Yellen, J. E. (1977). *Archaeological approaches to the present.* New York: Academic Press.

Index

About the Author

I. Randolph Daniel, Jr., is Assistant Professor in the Department of Anthropology at East Carolina University. He received his bachelor's and master's degrees from Florida State University and his doctorate from the University of North Carolina, Chapel Hill, where he earned the Manning Award for outstanding dissertation (1994). Among his other publications is *Harney Flats: A Florida Paleo-Indian Site* (1987).